D0240299

ROGER DALTREY

ROGER DALTREY

THANKS A LOT MR KIBBLEWHITE

MY STORY

BLINK

bringing you closer

Published by Blink Publishing
The Plaza,
535 Kings Road,
Chelsea Harbour,
London, SW10 0SZ

www.blinkpublishing.co.uk

facebook.com/blinkpublishing
twitter.com/blinkpublishing

Hardback – 978-1-788700-28-3
Trade Paperback – 978-1-788700-29-0
eBook – 978-1-788700-30-6

All rights reserved. No part of the publication may be reproduced, stored
in a retrieval system, transmitted or circulated in any form or by any
means, electronic, mechanical, photocopying, recording or otherwise,
without prior permission in writing of the publisher.

A CIP catalogue of this book is available from the British Library.

Designed by seagulls.net
Printed and bound by Clays Ltd, Elcograf S.p.A.

1 3 5 7 9 10 8 6 4 2

Copyright © RHD LLP 2018

Roger Daltrey has asserted his moral right to be identified as
the author of this Work in accordance with the Copyright,
Designs and Patents Act 1988.

Every reasonable effort has been made to trace copyright holders of
material reproduced in this book, but if any have been inadvertently
overlooked the publishers would be glad to hear from them.

Blink Publishing is an imprint of the Bonnier Books UK
www.bonnierbooks.co.uk

For Heather

ONE

THE
FLANNEL
SHIRT

On a muggy Florida night in March 2007, Pete and I walked out onto the stage at the Ford Amphitheatre in Tampa. For the ninth time that month, the seventy-ninth in the last nine months, the band started into 'I Can't Explain'. I swung my mic straight out towards the audience, ready to go like always. Ready to hit that first line ... '*Got a feeling inside.*' But the mic weighed a ton. Out it went like a ship's anchor. Whether or not it came back, I can't tell you. Everything went black.

The next thing I knew, I was backstage. The lights were swimming, concerned voices came and went. Pete was there, wanting to know what was wrong. And in the distance, I could hear the din of 20,000 disappointed fans.

For 50 years straight I'd always made it. I'd always turned up and performed. Hundreds of gigs. Thousands. Pubs, clubs, community centres, church halls, concert halls, stadiums, the Pyramid Stage, the Hollywood Bowl, the Super Bowl,

Woodstock. When the lights came up, I was there. Front of stage. Ready to drive. But not that night. For the first time since I'd picked up a microphone, aged twelve, and sang Elvis, I couldn't perform. As they bundled me into the back of an ambulance I was more disappointed than anyone that night. I listened to the sirens and – another new experience – I felt helpless.

In the days after, the doctors did a lot of poking and prodding, and eventually worked out that the salt levels in my body were way lower than they should have been. It seems obvious now, but I'd never worked it out. Every time we were on tour, two or three months in, I'd get sick. Really, really sick. And now, after all these years, I find out the reason was simple. It was salt or the lack thereof. All that running around, all that sweating, it drained me. We were athletes, but we'd never trained like athletes. Two, three hours, night in, night out, and we'd think nothing of it. No warm downs. No stretching. No vitamin supplements. Just a dressing room with alcohol in it. Because we're a rock band, not a football team.

That wasn't the only thing I learned that week. A few days later, one of the many doctors walked in clutching a chest X-ray.

'So, Mr Daltrey, when did you break your back?' he asked.

Politely, I pointed out that I hadn't.

Politely, he pointed out that I had. He had the evidence, right there on the X-ray – one previously broken back, one not very careful owner.

You'd think I'd have noticed when I did it, but I've been in enough scrapes in my time. There is an element of luck to any rock and roll story, but the luck only comes with hard graft.

When you fall down, you get up again. You just keep on going. That's how it was at the beginning and it's how it still is today.

I can think of three occasions when I might have broken my back. There was the time we were filming 'I'm Free' on *Tommy* in 1974. One minute 15 seconds in, you'll see me being thrown into a somersault by an army bloke. It was an easy enough stunt, but I fell badly. I can't remember if I heard anything snap but it bloody hurt. And for the rest of the day we were shooting the opening of the song, the part where my character Tommy Walker falls through the glass. We did it outside first and then we went into the studio to mimic it on the blue screen. All afternoon we did that. Me, falling four or five feet onto a mat. And cut.

'One more time, Roger.' That was one of Ken Russell's favourite catchphrases. He always liked to take his actors over the edge.

'Are you sure we haven't got it, Ken?' I replied with my possibly broken back.

'One more time, Roger.'

'Sure thing, Ken.'

Or I could have done it on 5 March 2000, on my way to the Ultimate Rock Symphony gig at the Sydney Entertainment Centre. Paul Rodgers of Bad Company had called in sick so I was going to cover his songs as well. They sent a van early, I jumped in and I was warming up my voice on the way to the arena. I've got this process where I hold my tongue with a towel in one hand and my chin with the other and I do these strange scales. It sounds mad and it looks mad, like I've been possessed by a demon. I'd like to think it's a relatively tuneful demon, but it's still not what you want to be doing when you have a car crash.

The woman joining the freeway had other ideas. She swerved into our lane with no warning. My driver managed to brake and we hit her side-on. It wasn't too bad. I still had my tongue wrapped in a towel and we were all still alive. I didn't hear anything snap but it hurt like hell. When we finally arrived at the gig, an osteopath turned up and clicked everything back before I went onstage. I got through it on pure adrenaline, I suppose, but for the next three years I was in constant pain.

I think the most likely time was when I was at band camp, aged about nine or ten. Let's say 1953. I was the Boys' Brigade company singer and I used to go up and down the beach on the sergeant's shoulders belting out uplifting American marching songs at unsuspecting holidaymakers. I sang like a little angel.

The only problem was a boy called Reggie Chaplin. Reggie was also in the Boys' Brigade. He was this big kid. I'm not kidding. He was a foot taller than me and two feet wider. He lived on Wendell Road in Shepherd's Bush, which was only five minutes from where I lived on Percy Road, but that made a world of difference. There were certain families you didn't get on the wrong side of. There still are. London's like that. And in Shepherd's Bush, it was the Chaplins of Wendell Road. They were a rough family from a rough street and, unfortunately, Reggie – big Reggie – had it in for me.

So there we were, at band camp, and because I was the little one I was being thrown up in the air in a blanket. It's the sort of thing kids used to do for entertainment before iPads were invented.

Reggie was the ringleader and, while I'm 15 foot up in the air, he shouts, 'Let's let go.' I can still hear the bugger saying it now. 'Let's let go.'

Of course, they all let go of the blanket. There was nothing I could do. I crashed to the ground and I was knocked out cold. There might have been a snap but I was away with the fairies. Now, on the one hand, it meant band camp was ruined. I had to spend the rest of the day down the bloody hospital and the rest of the week stuck in a Boys' Brigade tent in agony with what I now reckon was a broken back. On the other hand, I was sorted – my problems with Reggie had come to an end. As I lay there on the ground unconscious, he thought he'd killed me.

When I came round, Reggie was the first person I saw and he was crying. The meanest kid in Shepherd's Bush sobbing great, fat tears of guilt and fear. He felt terrible. Well, after that, he was like my guardian angel and I was in with a Chaplin. I was on the right side of the rough family from the rough street. Everyone treated me differently. I was untouchable. That lasted me all the way to grammar school, at which point everything went to shit. But I'm getting ahead of myself here. We should go back to a time before suspected broken backs, before good schools and bad ones. We should begin at the beginning.

• • •

My mum held on until the small hours of 1 March 1944 before giving birth to yours truly. Any earlier and I'd have been a leap-year baby and she didn't want that. Only one birthday every four years. That wouldn't do, would it? Even though I'd only be eighteen and a half today.

I was lucky to have been born at all. Grace Irene Daltrey – but you can call her Irene like everyone else did – had been diagnosed with a kidney disease in 1938. When they removed one of her kidneys, her health deteriorated further and she ended up contracting polio. She spent two months in one of Britain's first iron lungs in a hospital in Fulham, and for a long time it was touch and go. She survived, only just, but for the next few years she was stuck in a wheelchair.

More importantly, from my point of view, the doctors told her she would never be able to have children. If they'd been right, this would have been a short book, but Dad took up the challenge. When the war broke out, he went off to France with the Royal Artillery and that still didn't stop him. He was allowed back quite regularly to see Mum on compassionate leave. Nine months after one of these very compassionate visits, against all the odds, along I came: Roger Harry Daltrey.

It wasn't an easy time to bring a child into the world. People assume the Blitz was over in 1941. Fake news! March 1944 was the third and worst month of Operation Steinbock, a five-month Little Blitz which, to those living through it, wasn't very little at all. The Luftwaffe were dropping bombs all over London and then, when they got more desperate, they launched the doodle-bugs (V-1 flying bombs). The first one hit when I was eight weeks old. A month later, the Germans were sending over more than a hundred a day.

One of their targets was the munitions factory in Acton Green, a good two miles from Percy Road, but the V-1s always came up short. Eddie Chapman, the double agent, was responsible for reporting the accuracy of the bombing raids to the Germans and he lied so they never corrected their aim. Thank God he did what he did, but it meant that the streets of Shepherd's Bush bore the brunt. Every time you took refuge down on the Tube, you never knew if you'd come back to find a crater where your house once stood.

Mum, and me I suppose, spent a lot of nights sheltering down the Hammersmith Tube. About a week before I arrived, she thought she was going into labour during one difficult night camped out on platform four. It's hard now, all these years later, to imagine her handling all that alone while Dad was away at war. It must have been hard, too, when Mum and I were evacuated to a farmhouse in Stranraer in south-west Scotland for 13 months to escape the worst of the attacks. Mrs Jameson, our host, already shared her four-room cottage with another farming family, but she still made space for my mother and me, my Aunt Jessie and her two daughters. All five of us in one room. More than seven decades later, it's time to extend a belated thank you to Mrs Jameson and her family.

What an upheaval for a new mother, but Irene never complained. Even many years later I never heard either my mother or father say anything bad about their lives in wartime. They only spoke of the good times. Six years of death and destruction on an unprecedented scale, and everything was just fine and dandy.

I don't think any of us war children were fooled. Kids are perceptive. They know when things aren't just fine and dandy.

And in the space between the jolly stories, they see the truth. Even when I was very young, I knew it had been tough for Dad. He lost his brother in Burma. They said it was dysentery but he was in a Japanese prisoner-of-war camp so who knows what he died of? Dad never really talked about it, but there were signs.

One day, we were driving down to Lancing in Sussex to visit my youngest sister, Gillian. She'd been diagnosed with a heart murmur and they'd sent her to a convalescent home. Somehow, Dad had got hold of a grand old taxi – I don't know how he did it – but it was the only way we could see her every Sunday during her year away. That day was Remembrance Sunday. Just before 11, he pulled the taxi over and made us stand on the pavement in silence like he did every year. I noticed a tear coming down his cheek.

It was a shock for a young boy to see his dad like that. He was a gentle man, but kind of empty. That's what the war did to him. I remember he had the same look in his eyes the day before he died. It was nine months after the death of my youngest sister Carol from breast cancer. She was only 32. That day I understood that my dad had been crying on the inside – not only since her death but since he returned from the war.

That's what it did to a lot of people. It took something away.

Pete's dad, Cliff, was very similar to mine, although he talked a lot more. I'm sure the fact that he played saxophone in an RAF band must have helped him cope with the trauma. My dad just wanted quiet and that never changed. I'm sure he was shell-shocked for the rest of his life.

• • •

My very first memory is of my dad coming home from the war. He had been wounded on D-Day, but he went straight into an administrative role, so he wasn't demobbed until late in 1945. I would have been about 20 months old, so perhaps that first memory has been pieced together from fragments. But I remember the whole family being together for the first time in our front room with all the chairs round the sides. I remember the webbing on a man's boots, and his rucksack and tin hat, and then I remember being surprised that this man, this complete stranger, just arrived and shared a bed with my mum.

It all seems so far off now, that life, that childhood, growing up in the aftermath of war. If you didn't live it, it's almost impossible to imagine it. It's no coincidence that everyone born in my year was stunted. The first two years of my life were the worst years for food shortages. In 1945, the Americans decided to end their policy of Lend-Lease, which had allowed Britain to get food from the US on the never-never. At the same time, as soon as hostilities ended, we found ourselves having to share what food there was with the Germans.

I never heard anyone complain about that. The Germans were the enemy until the war was over, and then we shared without any objection. After all, they were in a worse state than we were. I thought about that the first time I went to Germany with The Who in 1966. I was just amazed. How did we end up fighting these people? They're so similar to us. They're great people. And we spent six years in all-out war with them. It's crazy.

The rationing went on for most of my childhood and our appetites shrunk with our stomachs. We had porridge for breakfast and sugar sandwiches for tea. The 'national loaf' came with 'added calcium' – it was half chalk – a ruse to make us think we were getting white bread. You had to queue for a weekly ration of one powdered egg.

Twice a year, as a treat, we'd have a roast chicken. It was a big event back then, but those chickens wouldn't have made it onto a supermarket shelf today. They were mangy, skinny, stringy little things, more bone and sinew than meat. In 1998, I played Ebenezer Scrooge in *A Christmas Carol* at Madison Square Garden, and Bob Cratchit, the poor, hard-done-by office clerk, had a chicken at least twice the size of the ones we had after the war. And we were supposed to feel sorry for him.

Nothing was ever thrown away – old rags, paper, tins, bits of string and empty bottles all had a value. There were no toys on the shelves. You couldn't pop down the shops for a new pram or even children's clothes and shoes. Everything was second-, third-, fourth-, sixth-hand. We wore our shoes till we had holes in them and then Dad showed us how to mend them. How many people today know how to mend their own shoes?

It was normal then but it's almost unimaginable now. It's three dramatic generations and thousands of miles from life today and it still blows my mind that we've gone from there to here. The thing is, though, I don't remember ever feeling like I was hard done by. Deep down, it must have had an effect, but on the surface, my childhood, not counting Reggie and his blanket, was a happy one.

The more I think about it, the more I realise our parents' generation was amazing. They never really wanted for much.

They wanted to live in peaceful times and they wanted, on occasion, to enjoy themselves.

A knees-up with a few bottles of brown ale felt like the party of the century. It was so simple but they knew how to have a good time with nothing. It's the opposite today. We've got so much and everything is instant. I find it very difficult to know where it's all heading. I'm sure if you're young and that's all you know, you just go with the flow. Maybe you can explain it to me some time.

Before my sister became so ill, Sundays were about family. All of us, the whole extended Daltrey brigade, would begin the day at the church on Ravenscourt Park Road. I was in the choir. I told you, a little angel. Then, after Sunday School, we'd drive over to Hanwell in convoy, Dad's taxi leading the way. It was an Austin 12/4 Low Loader with coachwork by Strachan of Acton. The roof at the back folded down, very much like a top-of-the-range Rolls-Royce. He was up front, our chauffeur. Mum was sitting next to him, behind a makeshift door, on a seat he'd screwed in where the luggage compartment had been. We were all in the back, giving the royal wave to one's subjects. It was fabulous.

There was a place called Bunny Park, right under the Wharncliffe Viaduct in Hanwell, and we'd spend all Sunday afternoon playing cricket there as the Great Western steam trains raced past. It went on for hours and hours on long summer's days, and all the cousins and aunts and uncles joined in.

Maybe I'm just remembering the good times. Maybe I'm making the best of it, just like they were. There must have been arguments, but I don't remember them. They used to say I was a terror. I was always up to mischief. I was always building something and making a mess. What I do remember is having to fight for everything I wanted. In those days nothing was handed to you on a plate. That was all right, though. I doubt my life would have turned out the way it has if I hadn't learned that particular lesson very early on.

• • •

We lived in rented rooms at number 16 Percy Road. My Aunt Jessie and my Uncle Ed were downstairs with my three cousins, Enid and Brenda, both older than me, and Margaret, the youngest. Me, Mum and this strange man in army boots who turned out to be my dad were upstairs. We had two bedrooms, a lounge and a kitchen, which became a little cramped when my two sisters came along. Behind the kitchen, down a little flight of stairs, was the communal bathroom. I was the only boy sharing a bathroom with two sisters and three cousins. Five girls versus one boy. I learned to cross my legs.

My aunt and uncle were staunch Labour – when I was older they used to take us away for Labour social weekends – all smoke-filled community centres and beer. I never spoke to Dad about his politics. He should have been Labour, too, but for reasons that never became clear he hated them. He just said they were full of shit.

My cousins, by the way, were very bright. They used to talk endlessly about the things they had learned that day at school, and I would listen in with fascination. Like most kids, I was up for learning. The system hadn't beaten it out of me yet. Enid was an early follower of fashion. She was into what she called the

Beatniks. To me, they all looked like old men with their knitted baggy pullovers and scruffy beards. The girls all dressed up like Doris Day. They listened to trad jazz, which was certainly more lively than the Billy Cotton band that played on the radio every Sunday lunchtime.

Enid and Brenda passed all their exams. They went to university. I don't know where they got their brains from. It's baffling. My mum's other sister Lorna married a bloke called Ernie, who was an electrician. They had two sons, one of whom got into Oxford when he was 14. Both of them became top nuclear physicists. You wouldn't have guessed that I have nuclear physicists in the family, would you? All these cousins got on because of the grammar school system. They were the clever working class – the grammar school generation which rebuilt Britain after the war – and they went up in the world. It shows that the system worked. It just didn't work for me. I think I struggled more with the conformity than the actual education. I was more rebellious than my cousins. I hated being told what to do.

No, that's not true. I was happy enough following orders in the Boys' Brigade, singing away on the sergeant's shoulders, promenading up and down the beach in formation. I was happy sticking to the rules at primary school. In fact, I loved it. I got on well with the teachers. I came top of my class. And my favourite part of the day was the walk to Victoria Junior Boys' School. How many kids can say that?

I had to wear short trousers, a vest and a pullover. The pullover was the only cloud in an otherwise clear-blue sky. It was made of wool. Not nice, soft, comfortable lambs' wool. This was the early

1950s. It was thick, scratchy, horrible wool. Mutton wool. Horse wool. Steel wool would have been less itchy. I was stuck with that pullover for years and years, and I hated it. Then, when I was eight, Mum bought me a grey flannel shirt, and it meant the world to me.

Mum used to tell me I could only wear it two days in a row, and then it had to be washed. Back to the itchy, scratchy, horrible, bloody pullover. So I used to get up at six in the morning and wash that shirt, dry it and iron it so I could wear it every day. I was a slave to fashion. Or comfort.

My form teacher for my last three years of primary school was called Mr Blake and I loved him almost as much as I loved that flannel shirt. He taught me about history and geography, and all the things I was interested in. He took us on school trips and we did interesting stuff with him; we learned naturally, which is the best way. And he thought I had potential. 'A boy of wide interests – practical, intellectual, musical and athletic,' he wrote in my end-of-year report in 1955. Maybe I could have been a nuclear physicist, too.

That summer I passed my 11-plus and 'won' a place to Acton County Grammar. At the same time, Dad got a promotion at Armitage Shanks, the 'sanitary pottery' manufacturer, and so the family moved up in the world, too. We moved two miles west to the leafy, semi-detached delights of 135 Fielding Road in Bedford Park. We had our own bathroom, our own gardens, front and back. It was an aspiring working-class family's dream. To me, I didn't care about any of that. I didn't want to go. I didn't want to move away from my friends. Two miles may as well have been a million. I felt like we'd moved to Mars.

TWO

SCHOOL'S OUT

T he first week of life at my new school and I already knew this was a terrible mistake. The kids were from places like Greenford and Ruislip, places with trees and grass and wide pavements. They spoke middle class, or 'posh', as me and my mates would have called it. It wasn't just a different accent, it was a different language. I didn't understand a word they were saying.

It didn't help that I was very skinny and quirky-looking. I'm not exaggerating. I looked … unusual. Because of the accident. Not that one, another one. It happened four summers before I pitched up at secondary school. We were on holiday at my aunt's bungalow in Bournemouth. Next door was a building site. That's how it was in those days. So many homes had been bombed to rubble. People had nowhere to live. As soon as a house was built, you moved in, even if all the other houses on the street hadn't been finished. It was normal to be surrounded by building sites and to play on building sites. So I was mucking about next door, probably playing cowboys and Indians. I tripped over some bricklayer's wire and landed on my jaw.

Mum took me to the hospital, they looked at it and said it was fine. I don't know what it is with me and hospitals. They always look at whatever is supposed to be wrong and say, 'It's fine.' Off I went back home with an apparent all-clear. Within 24 hours my jaw had swollen up. For the next couple of days, whenever we left the bungalow, I refused to get out of the back of Dad's taxi because I was making the Elephant Man look like Frank Sinatra. Everyone on the street was staring at me and I just sat there feeling sorry for myself.

It didn't get better. It just got bigger and bigger, and by the time Mum took me back to the surgery, it was pulsating. As we were waiting to see the doctor, something happened. All of a sudden, there was this terrible smell. Everyone in the waiting room started to look accusingly at everyone else. Who had been so indelicate as to let one off in a surgery?

'It wasn't me,' my eyes pleaded as they all settled on me. But then, I felt it. My shirt, my lovely flannel shirt, was wet. My infected jaw had burst. This time they did send me for an X-ray, and realised that my jaw had fractured in three places. I'm telling you this story for two reasons.

First, because you need to understand that when I walked through the gates at Acton County Grammar, I stood out like a sore thumb. Second, after the jaw got better, I never felt any pain when someone punched me in the face. That's probably quite important. If I'd gone through life with a glass jaw, things might have turned out quite different.

In a school with a high proportion of toffs who expected the first years to be their fags, the last thing you wanted to do was stick out like a sore thumb. Very quickly, very predictably, I was bullied. My nickname was Trog and it still grates with me today.

A favourite pastime of the older boys was to hang me from the wire-mesh fence that surrounded the playground. They'd make me hold onto it with my hands and then they'd lift my feet up so I was horizontal. When my arms got tired, bang. They loved that, they really loved it. And I had never felt so low.

It wasn't long before I started to play truant from school and just walk around all day on my own. I used to walk up and down the riverbank on Dukes Meadows, up and down, up and down, starving and lonely, really desperately lonely. It was beautiful down there by the river because it was wild and green and the air was fresh, but I used to think, if this is what life is like, I don't want to be here. I don't want to be in this world. I felt almost suicidal.

I think it felt worse because it was so far, so suddenly, from a happy childhood.

That time in my life seems distant now. It is distant. It was 60-odd years ago. But I can still remember one day like it was yesterday. It was a Friday, the end of a long week. It was break-time and I was in the playground, alone, trying to look busy, trying not to look alone. I looked ahead and remembered I had years of this to go. There was no end to it. I walked out of school and I went home, feeling completely empty. No one was home. I found my mum's sleeping pills and I just sat there looking at the bottle. Then I took four or five pills. Mum and Dad couldn't work out why I'd slept for 48 hours. I suppose they thought it was just part of growing up.

It didn't help that the teachers couldn't communicate with me either. There was no Mr Blake. The only one I liked was Mr Hamilton, our metalwork teacher. There was the maths teacher who hated me because I hated maths. I just couldn't get it to go into my brain. I don't know why they don't work out which kids are good at maths and let them get on with it and which ones aren't and give them a break. We still haven't worked that one out today. It's mad. Obviously it helps in life if you can add up a few numbers but I could do that. How else do you think I managed to work out how much we were being ripped off when The Who started making proper money in the 1970s? But algebra? Trigonometry? Sin, cos, tan and all that stuff? Do me a favour. Horses for courses.

Then there was Mr Watson, the form teacher who despised Elvis. Who could despise Elvis? I had the same English teacher for three years and all he did was chuck us a text book at the beginning of each class, light a pipe, put his feet up and work his way through the *Racing Post*. He never taught us a single thing. Then there was the music teacher, Mrs Bowen. She just wanted to teach us dots on pages and it didn't mean anything to me. Here's how to do a Bach chorale. This is a quaver. This is a crotchet. This is this. This is that. I couldn't stand it. Where was the music? And her response? She told me I'd never make a living at it.

All I wanted was to be left alone to play my guitar. Over the summer of 1956, I made my own approximation of a guitar and from the moment I strummed my first chord, I was absolutely focused on it. That was the trouble with school. I could focus on something if I wanted to. I could do anything if I wanted to, but the system didn't allow any latitude. You had to sit still in class. You had to follow their stupid rules. You had to do what they wanted you to do when they wanted. I couldn't do any of those things. I took about a year of this shit – bossed about in class, picked on outside it – before I answered back. One morning at lunchbreak, one of the bullies was having a go, so I picked up a chair and hit him with it hard. After that, they all backed off. The chair had turned the tables.

I don't think I ever became a bully myself. I learned to defend myself and I learned not to put up with any shit, but I never actively looked for trouble. Pete seems to think I did. It fits his narrative of what happened further down the line. So he claims to remember me fighting a Chinese guy in the year below me at Acton. I swear there wasn't a Chinese guy in the whole school.

Now, I'm an incredibly peaceful bloke really, and I think I'm fair as well. But in those days I was quite volatile. My fight-or flight fuse was shorter than a hummingbird's dick – and it was always fight. I also had a lot of energy, so when the red mist came down I was like a bomb going off. As soon as I got the whiff of someone about to attack me, I'd get the first blow in. When people worked that out, I was left in peace, and when I wasn't, well, then usually they deserved it.

• • •

The only fight I remember actually starting is one that I regret to this day. I was 14, the age when you're still finding your macho feet, and this friend and I were having a bit of a ruck in the common room. It started playfully but then he was squaring up to me, telling me he was going to have me. I just lost it. The red mist came down. Before I knew what I was doing, I'd leapt across a bench and started throwing punches and kicks. I nearly killed him and immediately I felt dreadful about it.

To make things worse, he was friends with a gang called the Acton Teds. They were a heavy mob – Acton Acton, not grammar-school Acton. They came from Acton Lane on the Vale council estate over on the other side of the British Light Steel Pressings railway line. That line has long since gone but, back then, it was the Berlin Wall of 1950s west London gang culture – a line I had to cross every time I went to see my mates. And the guy I'd half beaten to death was a member of this gang. Brilliant.

So he told his mates I beat him up and now I was on their hit list. They were going to get revenge and they were going to get it sooner than I thought. The Sunday after the fight, I was up on Ealing Common watching my friends playing football. I wasn't very good at football myself. I just used to go and watch, to have a laugh and a joke. Halfway through the first half, seven of these Acton Teds came up in all their Teddy Boy clobber. Their leader was a guy called Johnny Craft, a cooper from Fuller's Brewery, and the Williams brothers from Acton Lane were there, too. They wanted to have a little chat.

You can't run.

If you run, you've got your back to them. If you run, you're dead.

More importantly, I wasn't a particularly quick runner. So they formed a ring and little Johnny Craft – he was about my size but he was a cooper so he was a tough guy – says, 'You beat our mate up.'

'I know,' I told him. 'I'm really, really sorry,' not just because I was really, really sorry but also because there were seven of them.

Unmoved by my apology, Johnny explained that it was my turn now and started hitting me. I refused to fight back because the only thing more dangerous than trying to run for it was to start fighting back.

That's what they wanted. It would mean they could all pile in. So Johnny, exasperated, brings out this great big wooden cosh and starts whacking me with that. All his mates are telling me I have to fight and, in a terrifying moment of oh-fuck epiphany, I realise I have no choice. Passive resistance isn't working. So I hit him in the face.

His nose explodes.

There's blood everywhere. His mates look even more pissed off than they did a minute ago.

Oh shit, I think to myself. Why couldn't I have hit him where it wouldn't have bled so much? Why didn't I just kick him in the nuts? Now the circle is closing in and I find myself facing Mickey Dignan who you'd know, if you knew anything about the Acton Teds, had a terrible reputation as a knife man. True to his terrible reputation, he's pulled out his penknife, so now I've got real problems.

Roger Harry Daltrey RIP.

Cut down long before his prime.

And all because I lost my rag in the common room last Wednesday. About ten minutes later than I could have done with, I was saved by some older guys playing football on another pitch. They saw what was going on, came over and pointed out that seven against one was a bit unfair. The Teds from the Vale backed off. Mickey put his penknife away, whispering that I was a marked man as he did.

And that would have been the end of that if I hadn't started going out with Barbara Mason. Barbara was my first girlfriend and she was a beautiful, lovely girl. Way out of my league. She had been attracted to me because I was in a band and I sang. She lived in one of the East Acton prefabs hastily erected by the government in an attempt to solve the housing crisis, and the only way to get to her house from my house was to walk right past Mickey Dignan's house. At that age, at any age, you'd do anything to get to your girlfriend's house, especially if she was a year older than you, and several inches taller. So I was wearing turned-up collars and fucking hats and everything right in the middle of summer, just to make it to Barbara's in one piece.

I had to learn a kind of rabbit sensitivity. I also went round telling everyone I was carrying an axe, which wasn't very rabbit-like, but they believed me. It was all about image, which I suppose put me in good stead for my life as the frontman in The Who.

• • •

On 1 March 1959, the day I turned 15, I was slung out of school. It had probably been on the cards for a while. I'd been caught smoking. I'd been caught playing truant. I was disruptive in class because I just wanted to be left alone by these teachers. And I was the unofficial school tailor, which I guess they hated more than anything. I'd charge a shilling to 'update' uniforms. Mum had a sewing machine and I was pretty good at it. I still do my jeans today. My customers would come in with their grey baggy trousers and leave with drainpipes. I'd add jauntily angled school badges to their jackets. They'd go from proud parents' grammar school cherub to the very latest in late fifties youth fashion.

There was always a queue for Daltrey's Personal Tailoring Services Ltd, which must have been infuriating for the authorities. I was, literally, tinkering with the very fabric of the establishment.

The final straw was an air-gun pellet, which I didn't fire. Here's what happened, your honour. Back then, we watched a lot of war films and we were kids so we used to spend a lot of time pretending to be soldiers. We were armed with air guns. They weren't particularly powerful air guns – you could barely shoot from one end of the room to the other – but I imagine health and safety would have something to say about them today and, in this very particular case, they might have had a point. But as I said, we were kids and I was a kid who didn't like rules, and one of the rules was that you weren't allowed to bring air guns to school.

So I took my air gun to school.

We were in the changing room mucking about after football and my mate, not me, fired my air gun. The pellet bounced off a wall and hit another friend in the eye. It was a freak accident, a one-in-a-million shot, but all hell broke loose and, of course, because it was my air gun, I got it in the neck. That was fair enough. If I hadn't taken it to school, the accident wouldn't have happened, but I didn't pull the trigger. The bloke who did never got pulled up, but I got six of the best on my bare arse. That teacher should have been reported for sexual abuse. Much more upsetting, my mate lost the sight in his eye. That was the point at which the headmaster, Mr Kibblewhite, decided I was expelled. 'We can't control you, Daltrey,' he said. 'You're out.' And, as I left his office for the last time, a parting gesture: 'You'll never make anything of your life, Daltrey.'

Thanks a lot, Mr Kibblewhite, I thought.

On the afternoon of my fifteenth birthday, I had to go home early and tell my parents the good news.

They were devastated. I think we might have ended up in a fight, me and my dad. Not fists, but wrestling with each other. He wasn't a violent man at all, but that day he was angry. I just didn't see what the problem was. I'd be all right. If anyone had ever once sat me down and explained that school was for me, not the teachers or the system, and that there were reasons why I should stick at it, it would have been totally different. But no one ever did. My life was settled until I was 11 and then I had to go to this school. It felt like I was being punished. It never occurred to me that it was a successful thing to do. I think that's what it was. The first school had the vision of doing as well as you can in your 11-plus exam.

And I did. I passed with flying colours. The next school had no vision at all. So when rock and roll music came along, that became the vision. I decided I was going to do that. Dad had other ideas. When he'd finished shouting at me, he sent me straight off down to the employment office. Within a week I was working on a building site.

• • •

If it hadn't been for Elvis, that could have been it. The labourer's life. But the first time I saw Elvis, aged 12 or 13, I knew what I wanted to do. Of course, Elvis was Elvis. Elvis the Pelvis. The King of Rock 'n' Roll. He was completely out of reach to a boy from Shepherd's Bush. Nobody could be like him even though we all thought we could look like him. We couldn't afford Brylcreem to slick our hair back in the style of the King, but with the help of a bar of soap we could get close enough. But then along came Lonnie Donegan and the first time I saw him it was different. There he was on our little black and white television in March 1957 and he looked nothing like Elvis. He was wearing a tuxedo and a bow tie which was definitely not cool. But he was singing an Appalachian folk song called 'Cumberland Gap'. Even though I didn't understand what it was about, I got it. His music felt primal. I felt a frisson.

I wouldn't have known what it was called then but I read an article about it recently. Scientists at Eastern Washington University studied our response to music. Two-thirds of us have an intense emotional reaction to unexpected stimuli in our environment, particularly music. If you're immersed in a piece of music and you have 'openness to experience', you're more likely to experience this frisson. That's exactly how I've always felt about music. It was like that when I was listening to Lonnie and it's been like that every time I've sung to an audience. I'm not just singing it. I'm feeling it. And on a good day the audience isn't just listening to it. They're experiencing it on some deep, primal level.

The music had already begun to change before Lonnie and his skiffle band. I remember when I was about six, you started to hear more American music on the afternoon shows. My uncle used to play the drums in a little jazz band and he really loved Hank Williams. That was the first time I'd heard country. But when Lonnie came along, singing all those traditional folk songs, like 'Bring A Little Water, Sylvie' and 'The Midnight Special', it was different. He did it with a bit of oomph. When Lonnie used to put his head back and wail, I thought, that's what I want to do. I didn't feel like that with Elvis but even I could do a pretty good imitation of Lonnie. He was less controlled, more primal, and that suited me.

It was in that tradition of skiffle that I decided to make my first guitar when I was 12. This meant I had to get a summer job, which was not unusual for kids of that age to do in those days. I managed to get a gig at a laundry. I began at the bottom, which meant working on the 'in tray'. Blimey, I couldn't believe the filth and dirt some people lived in. After one of the longest weeks of my 12-year-old life, a week trying not to breathe through my nose, of being on the brink of fetching up every time a new load came in, the boss told me I was moving up. Moving up, my arse. I got moved to the washers. My job was to untangle the newly washed, soaking-wet sheets as they came out of the washers and they weighed a ton. I had to keep up with the women doing the ironing and they were on piecework. Keeping those women fed with untangled sheets was some of the hardest work I'd ever done. Boy, I paid a hard price for that guitar, but by the end of the summer I had enough cash to buy the bits and pieces I needed to get started.

I was copying a really cheap instrument lent to me by one of Dad's workmates. It was, very loosely speaking, a Spanish guitar. I cut the body out of plywood and bent thinner bits of plywood around the sides. I didn't have a clue how to join the body onto the neck, but I managed it somehow. Then I scouted around Hammersmith's music instrument repair shops for fret wire, struts, tuning pegs and a half-decent bridge. After a considerable amount of effort and experimentation, I had made what could almost be described as a guitar. It certainly looked like one and it worked like one. On a good day, it even sounded like one and that was enough.

I was off, playing every minute God (and my bloody teachers) gave me, and a few more on top. It's amazing how you can apply yourself if there's no trigonometry involved. The 'guitar' was more like a cheese grater stuck to a block of wood, so I had terrible bleeding fingers, but within a couple of weeks I'd mastered the three chords you needed to play pretty much anything you heard on the radio. A couple of weeks after that, I had played my first gig, channelling Lonnie with Elvis hair. The gig was the youth club dance and I didn't feel nervous. I just climbed up onstage and went for it. 'Heartbreak Hotel', full belt.

If you asked me to explain how a skinny little boy struggling to cope with his miserable life at school had the confidence to get up in front of an audience with a plywood guitar and perform, I couldn't begin to tell you. It was weird then and I still don't fully understand it now. But I survived and so did the guitar. Then, a week later, it folded in half. Bit of a design flaw and a bit of a problem because I was now in a band. Well, not a band. A skiffle group. I was in a skiffle group and my plywood guitar had given out after six weeks.

To the rescue came my Uncle John, who happened to be a carpenter for the Bedford Park Estate. He had watched me struggling to make Guitar One and now he was going to help me make Guitar Two. This time, we got the joint between the neck and the body right, and this one was French-polished. The action was better. The intonation still wasn't perfect, but I only needed to play the magic three chords. It did the job and, most importantly, it didn't fold in half after six weeks. In fact, it lasted almost three years. And from then on, whenever I wasn't working, I never went anywhere without that guitar around my neck.

Outside school, life was okay. I didn't talk to my parents much, but when I wasn't practising with the band I would hang out with my old Shepherd's Bush mates and my older cousin Graham Hughes. He wasn't one of the future nuclear physicists. He was at art school. He'd go on to become a successful photographer, producing many album covers for The Who and my solo work. But, back then, the important thing was that he had lots of records. He introduced me to rock 'n' roll. I moved on from Lonnie to Little Richard and, by the time I was 15, I was ready to make my first electric guitar. I was going to be a rock star, although there would be a few bumps in the road ahead.

THREE

THE
SKIFFLE
YEARS

One week after I escaped from the hell of Acton County Grammar, I found myself working as an electrician's mate on a building site just down the road. This was more of a deliberate career move than it might look. As an electrician's mate, it wouldn't take long to acquire the skills and trouser the materials needed to make that electric guitar. And it felt great. There I was out in the fresh air, free at last from calculus, and I got to watch those mugs traipsing in and out of school while I lived the high life.

That is an exaggeration.

I was earning two quid a week. Most of that went to my furious mum but there was still enough left over to buy cigarettes. They used to sell them in fives for the kids. Horrendous to think about that now, isn't it? The problem was that I was an electrician's mate, and an electrician's mate doesn't do any electrician's work. All I was doing was bending the pipes that the electrical wires would go in. And I thought to myself, this isn't electrical work. This is bloody plumbing. One of the things you don't need to know when you're making an electric guitar is how to bend bleeding pipes. Also, it was March. That fresh air was bloody freezing.

Six weeks later, I walked out, went back to the employment agency and asked for a different job. You could do that back then. The bloke behind the desk looked at my last school report, which I imagine made grim reading, and eventually said, 'You're obviously good with your hands. Go down to the sheet-metal factory in South Acton. They're looking for a tea boy.'

A tea boy? What's that all about, I wondered. How good with your hands do you need to be to serve a cup of tea? I did what I was told, though, because I could see potential in this particular tea-making appointment. After all, there would be metal in a sheet-metal factory, wouldn't there? And there would be tools, too. With a bit of luck, I could be a tea boy who made electric guitars when no one was looking. So off I went down to Chase Products, a factory that specialised in making computer cabinets, to present myself as the new brew-maker-in-chief.

It turns out that 'factory' was an optimistic way of describing it. It was a not very glorified shed with these big old pot-belly boilers which we used to have to light every morning and feed with coke all day. It was like stepping into a Dickens novel. The only difference? Our shed was built from asbestos sheeting.

In the middle of it all was old Frank Altman, the foreman, and, well, for some reason he just took a shine to me. Before I knew it, I was an apprentice tea boy earning the princely sum of £4 10s a week selling tea and sandwiches to the welders and the other men. The job came with some responsibility. Everyone wanted something different. A quarter of cheese, a ham sandwich, a bacon roll. If you got it wrong, then you'd upset the welder, and you did not want to upset the welder because the tea boy's other job was to file the weld. If the welder was upset, the weld was rough and bumpy – not easy at all. If you got it right, the welder was happy, the weld was smooth and you got tips. I'd take the orders at the start of the shift and then pop round to Marco's corner shop – you name it, Marco's sold it. And they'd always look after you because they wanted your business. It was win–win.

After a month of tips and free sandwiches, I decided I could improve on my situation. I'm mad buying this stuff from Marco's, I thought. If I get the rolls from the bakery, and the ham from the butcher and the cheese from the corner shop, I can make my own bloody sandwiches in the paint store round the back. They'd be fresher than Marco's and I could take all the profit. So I had a whole little business going and all the lads were happy because Daltrey's Sarnies Consolidated was an even more professional outfit than Daltrey's Personal Tailoring. I was quite the little entrepreneur.

In the afternoons, I went from tea boy to filer. We were making cabinets for computers the size of lorries. It wasn't exactly Apple. It wasn't precision engineering. There was a lot of filing to do. I filed bits of metal and the welders welded them together. The key was to file well enough to keep your welder happy which, as we've already discussed, was the key to a happy life.

I've said in the past that my time at Chase Products, in that asbestos-lined shed in South Acton, was the happiest of my life. I've also said I couldn't wait to get out of there. Looking back on it now, I think both things were true. It was dreary, monotonous work but there was routine. You clocked on for your shift, then off for tea, off for lunch and off to go home. There was structure. Life was simple. Innocent.

One of the problems with the rock business is that you never know what's going to come through the letterbox next. Those few teenage years in the factory were the last time for a long time that anything in my life was remotely predictable. It was also a happy place to work. The trick was that we used to sing. We sang all day, every day. We used to drive the guvnor mad. He wouldn't let us have a radio, and I'm glad he didn't, because then we wouldn't have sung. I can't tell you what a difference that made.

There were the young apprentices like me and the older lads, many of them not long back from Korea and the war in Malaya. We had our adolescent angst and they had their veterans' shell shock, and we held it all together with singing. One of the paint-shop guys could do a mean Sinatra, and a beautiful Nat King Cole. He was just great; he had perfect pitch so I used to sing along with him until I had it perfect, too. We used to do all the Everly Brothers songs. We had a regular barbershop quartet going in that shed.

In 1968, The Who was performing at the Hollywood Bowl, and we were on the same bill as the Everlys. I couldn't wait to meet them. All those years playing their songs and here we were at the same gig. It would have been a big moment. I might even have told them about the barbershop choir in the tin shed in South Acton. But it didn't happen.

So we did our bit. Keith and his entire drum kit ended up in the moat between the stage and the audience and Bobby Pridden, our sound guy, set off several military-grade smoke bombs during 'My Generation'. As the dust settled, we heard sirens. Half the Los Angeles Fire Department arrived, accompanied by most of its police force. Bobby was carted off to jail and released only after enduring a lengthy lecture on the hazards of fire in a desert environment. The rest of us were sent packing. I didn't see the Everly Brothers play. I didn't even meet them backstage.

The idea of sharing the bill with the Everly Brothers was unimaginable at the start of the decade. But I loved those impromptu sessions on the factory floor. You couldn't have called it rock 'n' roll, but we got some pretty good rhythm going with our improvised drum kits of hammers, presses and guillotines.

It's one of the sadnesses in modern life that no one sings like that any more. In those days, everyone did. You'd be walking down the road and people would be singing on building sites, at roadworks, in garages, everywhere. When you're singing, you're happy. Singing changes your brain. It reduces cortisol and increases the release of endorphins and oxytocin. Some people have to take drugs to do that. Why not just have a bit of a singalong? Singing in groups is even better. Scientists, not musicians, have found that our heart rates sync up when we sing together. You don't even have to be any good. Don't believe me? I refer you to the University of Sheffield's memorable 2005 paper: 'Effects of group singing and performance for marginalised and middle-class singers.'

'The emotional effects of participation in group-singing are similar regardless of training or socioeconomic status,' it says, which I could have told them but, wait, here comes the interesting bit... 'However, the interpersonal and cognitive components of the choral experience have different meanings for the marginalised and middle-class singers. Whereas the marginalised individuals appear to embrace all aspects of the group singing experience, the middle-class choristers are inhibited by prevalent social expectations of musicianship.'

I think it's fair to say our merry band of veterans and reprobate youths fitted more into the 'marginalised' bracket. We certainly weren't middle class. So the downtrodden masses benefit more than the posh kids I left behind at Acton County Grammar.

The last time I heard anyone singing at work outside of the Caribbean was in Majorca a couple of years ago. I was walking up this mountain for a bit of morning exercise. Halfway up, I pass this builder's van, and there's a couple of Spanish lads there unloading bags of cement. It's a blazing hot day right at the end of August and one of them is looking very pissed off with his lot in life, but he nods an *hola* as I walk past. As I'm coming back down the mountain a little while later, they're unloading the last bags of cement and the one who had looked pissed off looks a lot chirpier. Then he takes a deep breath and starts belting out our 1970 single 'Substitute'.

'I was born with a plastic spoon in my mouth,' he's singing in this heavy Spanish accent. 'The north side of my town faced east, and the east was facing south ... la, la, la.' I laughed my head off at that. It was just brilliant. I'm sure he felt better. He was certainly laughing, too.

I wasn't only in the shed for the singing, though, was I? I was there for Guitar Three. And this one was going to be a Fender. Or a close approximation of a Fender. Or a not-very-close-at-all approximation of one. I had heard Buddy Holly play one, and even on our little black and white television, the noise he got with 'That'll Be The Day' was just amazing. I couldn't buy one, of course. The price was astronomical. It cost more than a house. Only Buddy Holly could buy one. I would simply make my own.

One afternoon, tea made, sandwiches distributed, cabinets filed, I got off shift and took the Tube to Charing Cross Road to stare wide-eyed at a Fender Stratocaster hanging in the window of a music shop. Fender was so clever. He hollowed out the back of the guitar so it just sat on your hip. It was like a tailored suit, and I learned that by staring at it through the window. I took all the measurements and hightailed it back home.

I had bought two pieces of mahogany, and now that I had handsaws and vices available, I could join those two pieces together. I also had a friend down at Burns Guitars of Acton Lane and, somehow or other, a few of their pick-ups and machine heads made their way from his shed to my shed. Wood shavings on the floor in a sheet-metal factory are rather difficult to explain but no one asked too many questions.

Within a week, I had my very own bright-red Fender. It was streets ahead of my patented folding plywood guitar but there was still one serious design flaw. I hadn't realised, when I was measuring the thing through the window, that the glass was magnifying everything just that little bit. My 'Fender' was just that bit bigger than Buddy's Fender and that little difference meant the thing weighed a ton. It didn't sound like a Fender either, but it didn't sound bad.

One night in 1957, when I'd sang 'Heartbreak Hotel' at the local youth club, people had come up to me afterwards for a chat. Singing was like a magic friend-maker, and some of those friends wanted to start a band. If you're looking for formative moments, little events that made my life go one way rather than a thousand others, then this was probably one of them. On went the light. Singing is fun. Singing makes friends. I want to be in a band.

Harry Wilson, who had been my best friend since my first day at primary school, became the drummer in the line-up. Big Reggie Chaplin volunteered to have a go at the tea chest bass. Ian Moody played ... I can't really remember what he played. The washboard, maybe? His principal job was to stand there looking cool. He was a face – a neighbourhood face – and he gave our group an edge. Even then, it was about front. There he stood, tinkering away on whatever piece of kitchen apparatus he'd borrowed from his parents' house, looking cool. His older brother was the king of the Shepherd's Bush Teds and Ian got his hand-me-downs. When he'd grown out of them, I got them.

In those early years, our skiffle band was my life outside school. Then, when I got chucked out of school, it became my life outside the factory, and it became more serious. We'd progressed from skiffle to very basic versions of all the big hits. We did a Little Richard medley with 'Lucille' and 'Tutti Frutti'. That's a good example of how rock 'n' roll got sex past the censors. For bonking, read 'a whop-bop-a-lubop a whop bam boom'. Not exactly subtle but the men in suits at the BBC think you're talking about ice cream. Every teenager on the planet knows you're not. Rock and roll is about sex. The clue is in the name. Most of its creativity came from the songwriters coming up with euphemisms for a shag. It might all seem pretty obvious now but in those days the establishment, the men in suits, didn't have a clue. *Good Golly Miss Molly, sure like to ball.*

Our two main preoccupations, besides practising, were arguing over the name of the band and arguing over who called the shots. It was all about pecking order. Everything was decided on a push and shove. It was alpha-male volatile.

The slightest technological advancement could change the power balance. Our equipment was shoestring. If a string broke above the nut or below the bridge of the guitar, we used to tie it back together with a fisherman's knot. Any money we scraped together went towards kit upgrades but it was very gradual. I still had my 'Fender'. Reg Bowen not only had an electric guitar but also an amp. *The* amp. The *only* amp. So our rhythm guitar player at the time (his name escapes me) went out and bought a bass on hire purchase. Everything shifted constantly.

Mostly, we played weddings and local church hall teen clubs. We did a weekly spot at the Fuller, Smith & Turner brewery's social club in Chiswick. And, after a few months, we were calling ourselves the Detours and we were doing all right. But after a few months our bass player said he was leaving. We weren't earning enough and he was never going to pay off that never-never bass. So one night at Reg's house he said he was off. Our only bass player with our only bass guitar. I chased him all the way to the bus stop, but even with my considerable skills of persuasion I couldn't get him to change his mind.

A few days later, I was walking home from work and I saw this guy gambolling towards me with the biggest guitar I had seen in my life. I recognised him from school. It was a kid two from the year below me called John. It was a kid who played bass.

I didn't really know Pete Townshend or John Entwistle at school. I mean, I spotted them. You couldn't help it. They were two people you couldn't hide in a very large crowd. John never blended in anywhere. He was big and he was tall. He had a strange gait. He walked like a big, tall John Wayne. If you put him in a line of a thousand people, all the same height, all the same weight, all wearing balaclavas, I'd still be able to pick him out in a flash because of that walk.

Pete was also special in his own way. As a result, he had an equally tough time keeping a low profile when he arrived at Acton County Grammar. Like me, he was skinny, but where I had the funny jaw, he had the sizeable nose. That's not a criticism. It's been taken as a criticism in the past and it sounds like a criticism, but it isn't. I think he's got the most fantastic head. If I were a sculptor, that's the kind of head I'd want to sculpt all day long. And he's really grown into it. Back then, though? Well, he and his impressive sneezer made a target for the bullies. Tall and skinny, he looked like a nose on a stick.

I hadn't seen either of them since I'd left the year before but now, here was John, walking down the road with a bass guitar. I use the term 'bass guitar' in the loosest possible way. He'd built it just like I'd built mine but his was not much better than my first foldable plywood effort. It was the shape of a football boot and it looked like it wouldn't last the afternoon. But I needed a bass guitarist so we got chatting.

John told me he was already in a band – a trad jazz band, so he played bass and trumpet.

'You getting any work?' I asked.

'Local youth club in the church hall,' he replied.

'Getting paid?'

'No. You?'

'Of course we are,' I lied. 'We're getting bookings. Yeah, we're going to start making some real money. Definitely. Soon.'

It was the summer of 1961 when John joined the Detours. We had a few more months to wait before Pete arrived.

• • •

The sixties didn't start swinging until 1963. Before then, it was just the same as the fifties. More so, even. Elvis had stopped being cool and started doing his terrible movies. Bill Haley was old hat. Music was quite conservative, quite drab. Frank Ifield, a yodelling lounge singer from Australia, topped the charts for most of May and June 1962. His next two singles also went straight to Number 1. That should tell you everything you need to know about the early sixties. But life was about to change.

From 1963, there was this energy. It was all happening. It was happening because of music. That great period of rock bands – The Beatles, The Stones, all those Birmingham bands, all those Scouser bands and, yes, us, I'm sticking us in there, too. What are the chances of that kind of chemistry ever coming together again in music?

It came from little bands starting up, playing skiffle in the streets. Kids learned they could do something in music, even if it was nothing more than scrubbing a washboard with thimble-covered fingers or plucking on a string attached to a broomstick on top of a tea chest. Once you take part, you take an interest. So the music moved from the streets into the pubs and then the clubs. And then pirate radio spread the music. There was music before – of course there was – but it didn't speak to a specific age group. There was no room for that teenage slot. There was no teenager. Before the sixties, you were a child and then you were a man. You went to school and then you went to work. That changed. Our generation changed it. Why us?

I think it was to do with the war. What happened in the sixties started in the forties. The generation born during the hostilities, right up to 1950, those were the magical years for musicians, artists, scientists, everything. That's what happens when you start off with a fallow field. So much had been destroyed, there was only one thing that could happen. To build. We were a generation of builders. There was no choice. We had grown up with very little and, for all their attempts to make the best of it, we had been brought up by parents who were struggling to recover from the war. They didn't have anything left to give.

You can't blame them, really. After the victory parties were over and everyone had stopped kissing each other in fountains, what were they left with? Spiralling debt, housing shortages, unemployment. The men came back from war knackered. They were strangers in their own homes. A lot of them just caved in. That's what we grew up with. I wasn't the only one with a dad sitting in a taxi shedding a silent tear every Remembrance Sunday.

As children we just got on with it but when we became teenagers that channelled into adolescent anger. It began with the Teddy Boys. They were about five or six years older than us and their attire stood out from the drabness of everyday dress like headlamps. They wore long drape jackets and coloured shirts with cutaway collars turned up at the back. Some of them went further. They had their jackets made in bright blues and pinks and customised with black velvet collars. That was the start of the youth revolution. It might not have gone much further but, once society recognised the commercial value of teenagers, that was it.

There was money to be made so everything changed very quickly. Look at it today. It's interesting how much of the economy is now focused on youth. It's a complete reverse. Back in the sixties, there was no plan. It was just a feeling born out of the arrogance and vigour of youth. When you're young, you're bulletproof. You're full of energy and, in our case, it came out in the music. The anger and the energy, the demand to be heard, affected all these bands and it made the whole much greater than the sum of its parts.

I think that was true for us much more than the other bands we were coming up with. Pete used to say that, as individuals, we were three geniuses and 'just the singer.' Thanks Pete. Whatever he thought, what we added up to as a band was much more than what we were as individuals. As individuals, we were different. We came from different sides of the tracks. Pete was much more middle class than I realised. John was a trainee tax officer. Keith was working class like me, but if you're going to try and pigeon-hole him any more than that, good luck. A lot of the professional early sixties groups from the south were middle-class kids who came from middle-class backgrounds rebelling against middle-class values. We weren't like that. We were different from all the other bands. We were different from each other.

FOUR

THE DETOURS

P ete describes us as 'four people who should never have been in a band together'. Given our differences, given all the fighting and the fallings out, it's a miracle we stuck it out through that first decade. Of course, there were many, many times when we almost didn't, but I'm not as surprised as everyone else that we survived. Even in the darkest days, I was never going to give up. Not in a million years. Unlike Pete, it was all I really had.

Mr Townshend auditioned for the band in January 1962. Until that point, it was me and Reg on guitars, John on bass, Harry on drums and Colin Dawson on lead vocals. I was just finishing the second year of my apprenticeship at the factory. John was embarking on his career for life at the Inland Revenue, all pinstripe trousers, tie, waistcoat and City boy umbrella. Pete had stuck it out at Acton long enough to pass his O-levels and now he was in his second term at Ealing Technical College and School of Art.

John had been saying for a while that Reg wasn't good enough and that he knew someone who was much better, so one evening, he brought Pete to my house for a tryout. Pete says he remembers two things about that night.

First, there was a 'lovely blonde girl' leaving the house in floods of tears, giving me an ultimatum: 'It's either me or the guitar.'

Second, there was a villain on the hop hiding under my bed while he played. Now, the lovely blonde girl would have been Barbara and, it's true, we were arguing a lot about the amount of time I spent practising, and it's possible she was storming out when Pete was walking in. But I don't think the villain was under the bed. He was probably just sitting on it. Let's call him Jack. He was a mate and he was in trouble with the Old Bill for something, so he was staying round my house just in case they knocked on his door.

He was part of one of the big criminal families in the area. There were always these families. It was just like *The Godfather*, if *The Godfather* had been set in Acton. You didn't want to be out with them, so I harboured Jack while the heat blew over. You had to do stuff like that and you never grassed. But that's as far as it went with me. I had a few mates who were robbing banks and they'd try to convince me it was the thing to do because it was so easy. It was their get-rich plan. That, and winning the Pools. They didn't always get away with it, but enough of them did and a lot of people on the street admired them for it. I suppose robbing banks was their stage, their spotlight and their adrenaline kick. But I was never tempted to do any of that stuff myself. I had to harbour Jack, but that was as far as it went.

I was getting my kick from being in a band. I've often wondered what would have happened if I hadn't had music. Would I have been tempted into that world? It's easy to say you're an honest sort when you're not desperate. We can only live life as we know it and, since the seventies, I've lived a life of privilege. If it hadn't worked out like that, I might have been a prime candidate for criminal enterprise. Expelled, stuck in the factory, skint. Pissed off. But I still reckon I would have stayed honest. I think that was the bit of my dad that kept me out of it.

I tried to get Jack on the straight. I got him a job in the Acton shed for a few weeks, but he couldn't stick it. I don't think he realised how hard we worked. He saw that we were a lot tougher than he was, so he didn't try the hard-man thing with me after that. It didn't stop him turning up at the Marquee Club on one of our Tuesday nights with a sawn-off shotgun, threatening to kill someone. I remember it clearly. It was a couple of years after he'd been hiding at my house. He marched into the dressing room and announced that he'd had a ruck with someone.

'I'm going to kill him,' he said, and brought out a sawn-off 410 from under his coat. I just took it straight off him. I grabbed it before he could say anything else or do anything else. I think he was quite surprised by that. He just stood there while I gave him a proper bollocking. I told him he'd ruin his whole life, and then I gave him his shotgun back, minus the cartridge, and went onstage. Nothing happened that night. Jack didn't ruin his whole life that night. I'd like to tell you it was a turning point, that my intervention saved him from himself. But it only postponed the inevitable. He spent the rest of his life in and out of jail.

I was telling you about Pete's audition. A small moment in rock history, even if we were just a bunch of teenagers messing about on guitars. He remembers the blonde and the villain. I remember realising we'd found our man. Pete was only 16 but he just had ability. On a technical level, he was just better than us. He knew all these clever chords that were diminished, missing thirds here, adding sevenths there, all strange shapes. Majors with one note dropped or augmented to give a distinctive droning sound. They were flash chords and he knew it. Even then, he was confident.

It was his style that really made him special. He played banjo in the trad jazz band he was in with John, so when he moved to guitar, some of that banjo style came with him. The way his right hand moved, the rhythms he was playing – the overall effect was unique. The two of them playing together in that bedroom – that was the moment we went up another gear.

Up until that point, we were very, very straight. We were a cover band. We covered everything in the hit parade. And because Colin wanted to be Cliff Richard, we did everything like Cliff Richard did it. Nothing wrong with that. Cliff was what everyone was listening to, but when Pete came along it opened up a new road. He was in straight away.

The problem was that Reg owned the only amp, and even though he still let us practise at his house after he was out of the band, it was still just one amp. We had to run all the guitars and mics through that one measly little box. It was never going to blow the bloody doors off.

It was Pete who suggested we could go up to Laskys, 42 Tottenham Court Road, and buy extra amps on hire purchase. Today, Tottenham Court Road is all coffee shops and boutique furniture stores, but back then it was the ultimate sweet shop for boys who dreamed of playing in a proper band. It was just full of electrical stores selling equipment very, very cheap. You could buy valve-driven amplifiers, speakers, everything you needed, and you could haggle. And it was just up the road from the best music shops in London. On Saturday afternoons you'd get loads of young bands up there and that week it was our turn.

We steamed off up there and steamed back again with a 25-watt ex-War Department amp each. Imagine the excitement as we plugged them in. Imagine our disappointment when we realised they were just about loud enough to fill Pete's mum's front room. The speakers were worse. They were ten-inchers and they made this tinny little noise but, in a moment of marketing genius, I thought to myself, 'Well, it's all about front. It's all about image. We might have little amps, but we can make them look big.' So I made these great boxes out of plywood, and covered them with Fablon, that lovely, stuck-on, polished, wood-grained plastic.

Then I stuck them on legs. They looked like G Plan sideboards with a sort of painted gauze front. And although I'm laughing now just remembering it, trust me, people used to say, 'Fuck me, they must be good. Look at the size of their kit.'

Of course, it helped when the gear wasn't quite so shit, and that didn't take long. Not long before I turned 18, I'd cobbled together enough money to buy a proper guitar. Me and Pete had 12-inch speakers and John had the full 15-incher. Like most things in life, those extra inches made all the difference. We had the beginnings of a proper PA. We were loud. Ish.

We also had yet another change to the line-up. In August 1962, we swapped our drummer Harry Wilson for a bricklayer called Doug Sandom. It hadn't been the plan. Harry was going on holiday so we were only looking for a temporary replacement. The temporary replacement didn't turn up for his audition. For some reason, Doug turned up instead. We agreed he'd play the second set at the Paradise, a club in Peckham. Doug was better for us than Harry, my best mate since the first day of school, so he got the job full-time. I felt bad for Harry, but the band had to come first.

That wasn't my overriding memory of the Paradise. I mainly remember the fighting. Close your eyes and imagine paradise. Fluffy clouds. Harps. Angels. Now imagine the exact opposite and you've got the Paradise Club, 3 Consort Road, Peckham. We were there because John knew someone who knew someone who booked venues in south London and, the first week we played, there was hardly anyone in the audience. Just a few girls. At around ten o'clock, their boyfriends turned up with bloody noses and black eyes, having started a brawl at a rival club. The next week, the gang from the other club turned up to settle the score.

I suppose fighting was common, but it was nothing like as violent as it is today, and they almost always left the band alone. My trick was to find the toughest bloke in the whole place and buy him a drink. That usually worked like a charm. We did have a bit of a fracas in Nottingham much later in our career when a load of Hell's Angels turned up and demanded that we play 'some fucking rock 'n' roll'. There were a lot of them and four of us so you would assume it was a good time to adopt a conciliatory tone. That wasn't Pete's approach.

Emboldened by brandy, he started back at them. I don't know what he said but he said something wrong. All hell, appropriately enough, broke loose, bottles flew, mostly at him. One of them hit Bobby Pridden, and he was out for the count. The rest of the band scarpered and I was left up on the stage talking to the pissed-off leader of the Hell's Angels. He was a big fella and he had a ring through his nose. We had a chat and I'm still here, so obviously the chat went well.

Back in 1962, we settled into a routine. Every morning I would go to the factory, John would push a pen around his desk at the Inland Revenue, Doug would lay some bricks and Pete would do the art school thing and lie in bed. I'd finish work at six and head round to Pete's. Sometimes I'd have to drag him out of bed. He wouldn't have dragged himself out. I think he was smoking dope all day and would have quite happily smoked it all night, too. Or was that art school chic? Either way, we were lucky we had me, chief timekeeper, bloke who didn't want to spend the rest of his life filing metal, and we were lucky we had Betty, Pete's mum. She was an absolute treasure.

Without her, we might have spent a lot longer playing Wednesdays in Paradise. Without her, we might have amounted to very little. She was the first person to have faith in us. She saw that we had something. You could say that she had a nose for it.

She also wanted us out of her house. There is only so much rehearsing a parent can endure and, when she'd reached that limit, she got us our first agent. With it came our first rehearsal space. Peace and quiet at last.

On 1 September 1962, Betty frogmarched Bob Druce, a local promoter, to Acton Town Hall to see the Detours headline at the Gala Ball. Even though our triumphant gig made it into the illustrious *Acton Gazette & Post*, he wasn't convinced. But lukewarm Bob wasn't going to stop Betty getting her peace and quiet. So there was some more frogmarching, this time to the Oldfield Hotel in Greenford, and after that we found ourselves on the west London pub circuit. It worked like this. You turned up. You played. If you were rubbish, you got packed off in a hail of bottles. If you weren't rubbish, you were asked back. And that suited us because by now we were pretty good.

We started building our own audience.

Mondays, we'd play the White Hart Hotel in Acton. Thursdays, it was usually the Oldfield. Sunday afternoons it was Douglas House in Bayswater.

That Bayswater gig was also courtesy of Betty Townshend. It was an American officers' club that she'd got onto through Pete's dad, Cliff, and there were several reasons we loved it. For a start, we got 20 quid for two hours. They would request a whole cornucopia of American music – everything from Johnny Cash to the Coasters and Roy Orbison – and if we played the Dixieland classics well enough to bring tears to the homesick servicemen's eyes, we got enough free drinks to see us home in a zigzag. This was also our first glimpse of the American Dream. American beer, American whiskey, American pizza.

We were only a few years out of rationing, England wasn't famed for its cooking and supermarkets were virtually non-existent. We'd grown up with only the little food our parents could put down each day. So we were all as skinny as rails with eyes as big as the plates the pizzas came out on. We'd never seen pizza before.

We were just as wide-eyed when we started touring the States later in the decade. The contrast was ridiculous. You take off from the Land of Suet, you touch down in the Land of Steak. We'd never seen anything like it. For a long time I used to smuggle back suitcases of steak. I've stopped now.

When we weren't playing for the Yanks, our fee was £10 a gig or £12 10s if we were playing one of Bob's south coast venues, which we did frequently. It was on one of those long trips to Margate, Folkestone or Dover that I broke our beautiful new van. Okay, it wasn't beautiful and it wasn't new either. It was an old Post Office Austin with sliding doors that Bob had got us in return for another 10 per cent. The main thing was that it worked ... or it did until I hit a railway bridge. I can't remember exactly why I hit a railway bridge.

Contributing factors would have been (1) I didn't have a full driving licence (2) I was young and therefore (3) I was driving too fast. And (4) We had half a ton of gear in the back.

The front of the van went round the corner but the back continued on. There was a loud bang and some groans from my bandmates, and then we didn't have a van for a few days.

But we still had Betty. You remember the winter of 1962–3? No? Well, I'll tell you. It was snowy. Not 'I'm dreaming of a white Christmas' snowy. Siberian snowy. Yeti snowy. Sod this, I'll see you in May snowy. But right in the middle of it we had a gig in Broadstairs and, even though we didn't have a van and there was a full-scale blizzard, we weren't going to cancel. I'm telling you this because when people talk about The Who, you hear a lot about the bad behaviour. As this story continues, you're going to hear a lot more. But beneath all the pissing about, there was commitment, real commitment. Everyone remembers the sex, the drugs and the rock 'n' roll. I remember that night. A bunch of teenagers (and Doug, who was pretending to be a teenager but was actually married and in his early thirties), and one of their mums, her white knuckles on the steering wheel in a blizzard. Going to the gig in Broadstairs.

Every few miles, we'd stop and switch around. Two in the front with Betty and three in the back, lying on top of the kit, our noses three inches from the roof. Pete's would have been a bit closer. I don't know how she got us there because it was like driving on the Cresta Run. The snow was ploughed up twice the height of the van on either side. One slip and we'd have been walking the rest of the way.

Somehow she did it. I don't know how many mums would have been that supportive. I have no recollection of the gig whatsoever. Let's just assume there were hundreds of people in the audience and that we stormed it. Let's forget that there were only ever about 50 people under the age of 80 in Broadstairs at one time and only half of them would have been allowed out on a school night. The point is, we got there, we did our set and we got home again.

Note to those worried about the broken van. Not a problem. It had a huge dent in the front, which we fixed with the help of a lamp post opposite my mum's house, a heavy chain and a flying start in reverse. I sorted out the door with some two by four timber, a hacksaw and some sheet metal. Any further dents, Pete painted red to look like dripping wounds. Good as new, except the rest of the band had to climb through from the driver's seat.

• • •

In January 1963 we had another personnel change. Colin left. He was a bacon salesman and he had a company car. He wasn't going to give up the day job and the bacon for a decidedly long punt at rock 'n' roll. And I was ready to take the lead vocals. Or, rather, the lead vocals were ready to take me.

At St Mary's Hall, Putney, every Sunday night we had begun to support other bands and that had an effect. From the wings, we'd watch Screaming Lord Sutch – the "third Earl of Harrow" – who used to be carried through the crowd and onto the stage in a coffin. He was a showman, a precursor to Alice Cooper, and we learned from that. Then there was Johnny Kidd & the Pirates. They were a real act. They had a pirate ship for a backdrop and they were the first band I ever saw using ultraviolet lights. Johnny had an eye-patch and leather trousers, which went down very, very well with the girls. He had style.

He also had a three-piece band – bass, drums and Mick Green on guitar. Mick had this stunning way of playing – he half plucked, half strummed. He was half lead, half rhythm. Pete saw Mick play and, within a week, he'd got those techniques bang on and, for a while, we became a Pirates clone. And that's when it became obvious that I should sing. We had Pete and John on guitars, a perfect partnership. And we'd swapped out all the straight stuff, all the Buddy Holly, Del Shannon and Roy Orbison, for Johnny. Johnny was dirty. Colin couldn't sing Johnny but I could.

• • •

It wasn't all beat-up vans and Siberian road trips to Broadstairs. There was still a bit of time for girls. Barbara and I split up when she was 17 and I was 16. She'd been attracted to me because I was in a band and I sang, and then she was attracted to someone from her work because he had a motorbike. You win some, you lose some, but I knew from the first time I performed that I would win more than I lost. I never had to ask anyone out because they mostly asked first.

That's just the way it was. There's something about opening your mouth as a singer, and I don't know what, precisely, but women find it attractive. They always did. Look at what Elvis did to them. You've got the knickers hitting the floor from 20 miles away. Right up until the US army got hold of him, squared him up and he came out singing like Doris bloody Day. Maybe even after that. And look at Adam Faith. He used to walk into a room and you could hear the knickers going *schooop*. He wasn't a great singer. He was a good actor, though, and he only had to open his mouth and the girls would go crazy.

On paper, you would not have put someone like Barbara with someone like me. She was The Girl About Acton. She had that early sixties look: tight white skirt, white high heels, beehive haircut. She was a serious chick. And she wanted me, the bloke from the factory that wasn't even a proper factory who happened to be in a band. And then she didn't because some other bloke had a motorbike. I was gutted for a bit and then I went out with another Barbara. It was just a coincidence.

Barbara Two had her own flat. She lived on her own and that gave me a lot of freedom. Much better than standing in the door of a prefab in Acton of an evening making polite conversation with parents. Even though, for the record, Barbara One's parents were absolutely lovely.

After six months, things finished with Barbara Two, too, and then my memory gets a bit vague. Perhaps I was just enjoying myself. Embracing the revolution.

It's hard to explain to people today what a difference the Pill made but it was like someone had let the genie out of the bottle. Women went absolutely crazy, and it wasn't as if men were going to hold back, was it? And then I met Jackie, and Jackie got pregnant. That was the trouble with that particular revolution. The Pill wasn't easy to get hold of in 1964. It became easier later in the sixties but at the start, you assumed everyone was on it and that wasn't always the case. It was my fault. I never asked Jackie if she was on the Pill. I just assumed she was.

I first met Jacqueline Rickman at St Mary's Hall in the autumn of 1963. Pete was going out with a girl called Delores and Jackie was her friend. She was wonderful but neither of us was ready to have a kid.

Unfortunately, the sexual revolution was way ahead of the social revolution. If you got someone pregnant, you spent the first few days getting shouted at by your parents and her parents, then you got married, found somewhere to live, and that was you for the rest of your life. And that was me. Jackie got pregnant. I got shouted at by her mum and my parents. Then we got married and on the night of the wedding in early 1964 I moved into her mum's place. Not long after I turned 20, I found myself living with Jackie and our newborn son Simon in one room, six storeys up a council block in Wandsworth.

At first, I was absolutely determined to make it work. It wasn't what we'd planned but it was the situation we found ourselves in, so that was that. The problem was that, after years of slogging away in pubs and clubs, things were starting to go well with the band. And life in a band on the up isn't compatible with a new family. I'd be away for weeks at a time. I'd get home in the middle of the night and would be trying to sleep in the morning. I'd have some money one week and no money the next. I was not the reliable father figure my son Simon needed and I wasn't the caring husband Jackie deserved. That's what I would tell myself then, as a young man trying to talk himself out of his responsibilities. Years later, it's still not something I feel at ease with, even if it all worked out okay in the end.

Back then, I used to spend hours looking out of the window of that one-room flat. I could see across Wandsworth, all the way to Battersea Power Station and beyond. And I could see the van parked down below. I swear it was calling me, tempting me, and that beat-up old van just became more attractive by the day. It represented my dream. To be in a band. To play music. And, after a lot of hard work, we were finally beginning to get somewhere.

FIVE

THE HIGH
NUMBERS

The changes had come quickly. First, in the spring of 1964, we got a new manager. Helmut Gorden was a Jewish German doorknob manufacturer who wanted to be the next Brian Epstein. He was a nice guy and he had money that he was determined to waste on a rock band, so it made sense for us to be the rock band upon which it was wasted. He bought us a new van – not *new* new, but new second-hand and it had windows. He bought us our first professional amplifiers, and he got us into the recording studio. It was never going to go much further than that, but we owe him a huge debt of gratitude. He was obviously trying to make money out of us, which I don't think he ever did, but he got us through those years.

Second, our music was changing. We weren't just a covers band any more. We were starting to become a fairly good, fairly original outfit. We were resolving our musical differences. I like that term. It's so polite. What it really meant, for us, was me and Pete telling each other to fuck off and Doug attempting to play the elder statesman. But by 1963 there were new forces in motion. Everyone wanted The Beatles, of course, so we did The Beatles. We did 'Twist And Shout' and John did 'I Saw Her Standing There'. I used to be more into Johnny Cash songs, which seemed to suit our energy better, and they went down really well, but then, slowly but surely, we started introducing Jimmy Reed, John Lee Hooker and Sonny Boy Williamson. We did 'Big Boss Man', 'Boom Boom' 'Help Me', those kinds of songs.

But then we started to notice The Rolling Stones. We were on the same circuits as them and they became a huge, huge influence. We'd been aware of the blues, but we hadn't realised it could be popular. All we wanted to be was popular. The Stones showed that those two things – blues and popularity – weren't mutually exclusive.

That's how it was back then. It was uncharted territory. Everything we tried was new. Today, the whole music industry is geared towards adolescence, but in the early sixties it was all being invented. First, it was all straight, clean-cut, something your parents might approve of. We were so innocent. We were so much younger, less worldly than teenagers today. But then, as we found our voice, it got looser, wilder, freer. It was an incredibly exciting time. Nothing stayed the same from one week to the next.

That's why Pete wanted to play a full blues set immediately. He was always impatient to try the next new thing. I wanted to do the blues, too, but I was also very aware that we couldn't just change overnight. We had our audiences, built up painstakingly in all those long trips in clapped-out vans. They wanted to hear the hits. This was their *Ready, Steady, Go*. I knew we had to go slowly.

Maybe it's because I came from the street much more than Pete did. Maybe it's because I realised more than Pete what those nights out were to our audience. What it meant for people working from seven in the morning at a factory, slogging away all week, to go to a place where they could do all the things they wanted to do. If we'd gone and played them a load of strange music, they would have been insulted. If we went too far off on our blues trip in a great big sweep, we'd have lost them, and if we lost them, we were fucked.

Fucked for Pete meant carrying on with his art degree, which meant lying about in bed all day smoking dope, turning up at the occasional lecture to imagine the world from the point of view of a sponge.

Fucked for me was something quite different. I wasn't at college. I wasn't having my arse wiped by the state. I had a whole different outlook on life. So, musical differences.

We stood up to each other, and Pete could be very spiteful with his language sometimes, which took me straight back to those dark days at grammar school. But the thing was, I recognised his talent. I'm quick to see a path through a problem once I've focused on it. If I get too scrambled, my brain goes haywire, but once you get me to focus on something I'm absolutely 100 per cent driven. Pete could be all over the place. His default position was scrambled. I suppose I was the ground for his sky. Sky is great but you need the ground, too.

We both got our way in the end. We changed from a cover band to doing more blues and more original stuff, which we both wanted, but we did it gradually, which I wanted. Each week, we'd slip in a couple of new songs.

Within a couple of months, we weren't playing full blues but we were close. To keep people guessing, we'd switch in some Tamla Motown and some James Brown. Or some more obscure stuff like Garnet Mimms. Because the problem with blues is that it's all the same thing. After a while, it can be like listening to paint dry. I love it, but you have to imagine your on a dance floor and you're on a night out, and it's your only night out that week, and everything you hear is on a 12-bar riff. Stick some James Brown in and, woohoo, you're all right.

The final gear change happened one Thursday night at the Oldfield in late 1963. We were drafted in at short notice after the scheduled act had cancelled. We agreed on the condition that we could play what we wanted to play. That night, the audience got a full rhythm and blues set. And we stuck to the same set list the next week. We had changed. Our audience had changed with us. Who knows if I'd been right or Pete had been right. The important thing was that they were still with us. That was the important thing.

We were developing the way we performed as well. We were finding ways of expressing our aggression. The phrasing of things, the punch of the chords, more on-beat than swing. Our word for it was drive. Let's drive, we used to say before a gig. Drive. Drive. Drive. I used to feel like we were trying to drive our music through the audience to the back wall. I've always done that, even at Woodstock, with no back wall and half a million people stretching over the horizon. I had to drive the curvature of the earth. It's no good to play *at* an audience. You've got to play *to* them. You've got to try and move them. You have to drive through them. And it works.

You ask people who saw us from the back of Wembley Arena. Even in the days before big video screens, they'll tell you they were moved. At least I hope they'll tell you that. It's something you're putting into the music that does it. It's an energy. You can't pin it down but there was an energy that we emitted and the audience received.

That really all started to happen very fast when Keith, the Gingerbread Man, came along. Doug wasn't changing. He was still playing jazz drum, but two weeks after he left – his missus had had enough of him being in a band – we were playing at the Oldfield Hotel in Greenford and this kid comes up in the interval and tells us his mate can play drums better than the session guy we had with us. And then forward steps Moonie, ginger-topped after a failed attempt to go Beach Boy blond.

'Hello,' he said, cocky little bugger.

Keith Moon was born in Wembley on 23 August 1946, although he always pretended it was 1947. He was a hyperactive child whose favourite hobbies were *The Goon Show* and engineering explosions. Predictably enough, he got on with the education system even less well than I did, failing his 11-plus and ending up at Alperton Secondary Modern. His art teacher described him as, 'Retarded artistically, idiotic in other respects', and his music teacher said he had, 'great ability, but must guard against a tendency to show off'. In other words, he was born to be our drummer.

The session drummer that night chucked him his sticks and we went straight into Bo Diddley's 'Road Runner'. 'I'm a road-runner, honey, and you can't keep up with me.'

Keith could. More than that. Halfway through, he started to do his syncopations. It's all mathematics, isn't it, drumming, but his mathematics were from another planet. And it gave springboards for John's little bass guitar flicks and Pete's power rhythm. It just took things up to the next level. The final gear.

Immediately. That night at the Oldfield Hotel.

Keith always claimed he was never officially asked to join the band, but I remember clearly, at the end of that gig, telling him we'd pick him up next week. That means you've got the job, mate. It was April 1964, and that was the last time our line-up changed until 7 September 1978. Keith was the last in and he was the first out, bless him. He gave us 14 years of headaches and laughter in more or less equal measure. From then on we found ourselves locked in this incredibly intense experimental phase. There is a tape of us playing at the Marquee a little later in the year and we do Howlin' Wolf's 'Smokestack Lightning'.

Classic blues. Then, halfway through it, we go into jazz. It wasn't planned. It just happened. The gear changes were so smooth. It was like we were telepathic and it was extraordinary to experience. That's how crucial it was that the four of us ended up together. We were 19 years old but we were playing like we'd been at it for years. We knew each other. We followed each other. We communicated with each other through the music.

And something that gets missed in all the war stories about The Who ... we respected each other.

• • •

The first time I became aware of the mods was in the autumn of 1963. My sister Carol had a boyfriend from Lewisham and he had a scooter. Pete was very taken with his black shorty PVC coat. He was also very taken with my sister's mod dance moves. That was how it all started. A PVC coat, herringbone-tweed bell bottoms emphasising the bell, and my sister's minimalist twist. Pete got into his mod phase for the same reason most boys get into anything – because of a girl, my sister. But I think he became a proper mod.

I was trying to be a mod but really I was whatever the fuck you wanted me to be that didn't involve sheet-metal work. And if we're being honest, and we're not attempting to develop an elaborate cultural thesis to explain everything, it didn't matter what you called yourself. We were young. Most of us were working class. We had a bit of money to spend on clothes and fags and going out. No national service. No rationing. We wanted to have a laugh. We wanted to enjoy our freedom. All the stuff written about the mods ... it's all with hindsight. It makes it sound like there was a plan. It over-intellectualises it. But there wasn't a plan. All it was was fashion. You can take one bloke with sideburns and an Elvis jacket and take him through three shops, and he's a mod. But he hasn't changed.

The fashion wasn't coming from art school. It was being created from the streets and it was incredibly transitory. Things would be in fashion for two or three weeks, then out. Way out. There was a period, for example, when ice-cream-sellers' coats were the thing. Overnight, everyone was wandering around in white coats down to their knees. Hardly any of them were selling ice cream. Three weeks later, gone. The trend was to change the trend.

Having said all that, we did find ourselves at the forefront of a movement in society and that gave the band momentum. If you're at the forefront of any movement, quids in it will rub off on you. And we got lucky there. Pete Meaden really took us down that road. He came into our lives shortly after Keith, hired by Helmut Gorden to make a supergroup out of The Who. I first met him in early 1964 at the Glenlyn Ballroom in Forest Hill. We were supporting The Stones that night and I was chatting with Brian Jones at the bar. He was raving about a version of 'Route 66' they'd just recorded. Meaden had been business partners with The Stones' manager, Andrew Loog Oldham, and he was there, too, all dressed up like the ad man that he was.

After we'd performed we carried on chatting. He said he thought our band was great, but we had no image. Without any image, we were just another wannabe Stones. 'Don't be the black sheep,' he said. 'Be the red sheep.' That was his mantra. Be the red sheep. He was three years older than me, which is a lot when you're 19. So I listened to him. We all did. And the next minute, I'm wearing a white seersucker jacket, a button-down-collar shirt and a pair of black and white shoes (Hush Puppies, modified with paint). A red sheep. The minute after that, he convinced us to change our name from The Who, which he thought was tacky, to the High Numbers, because that week the mod fashion was stolen bowling shoes. The higher the number, the bigger the feet and the bigger the feet, well, you can work it out.

Then he made me get my hair cut at Jack the Barber's. A mod, even a pretend one, can't have long, curly hair. It was awful, God it was awful. I may as well have had the clap. But a mod with short, curly hair wasn't much better. I used to go through jars and jars of Dippity-Do, an industrial-strength American hair gel, to keep it straight. As long as there weren't too many encores, one big dollop could keep me on the straight and narrow through a gig. I was like Cinderella, with a curly mop instead of a pumpkin.

That was all down to Pete Meaden. He knew how to present us. He knew it was all about image. It always had been. Take Dean Martin, cultivating the laid-back alcoholic crooner look with a glass of liquor in one hand and a fag in the other. People loved him for that, but he was stone-cold sober. The liquor was apple juice. In our world, The Beatles were the first pop band. The Stones were their antithesis. We had to find our own niche, something fresh. And that's what we were starting to find with Pete at those gigs in Forest Hill. They were important. They were close to the heart of the mod birthplace around Lewisham and Bromley, those places. It gave us a base.

• • •

In the summer of 1964, we found new management. Or, rather, it found us. We were playing our regular R&B night at the

Railway Tavern in Harrow. The derelict hotel was burnt down by arsonists in 2000 and, predictably, there's a block of flats there now. They called it Daltrey House. The one next to it is Moon House.

Back in 1964, the Railway Tavern was our sweaty little low-ceilinged, smoke-filled home on a Tuesday night. At the time, these places always seemed at least eight times bigger than they were. You go back to see them 20, 30 years later and they're just these tiny little rooms. But the Tavern was always packed. It was just this mass of people, and in those days people used to dance. There would be maybe one row of people along the front just standing there watching, but everyone else would dance.

Our PA had come on a bit more by now. We'd borrowed and begged amps, swapped kit, found cheap bits and bobs. We still weren't making a huge racket like when we became famous, but our noise suited that room at the Tavern. It was loud and the atmosphere was dangerous, which we liked. And then in walked Kit Lambert, attracted, he said, by all the Lambrettas parked outside. All the local mods loved him because he immediately started buying them drinks. And Pete loved him too because he was the son of the composer Constant Lambert and his godfather was William Walton. I would have been, like, 'Who the fuck's Constant Lambert?' But then I grew to love Kit, too, because he was a charmer.

Christopher Sebastian Lambert was 29 when he saw those Lambrettas and walked into our world. He had the air of a well-to-do British officer because he'd been one. After Oxford, he served in Hong Kong before joining two friends from university on an expedition to discover the source of the Iriri River in Brazil. It didn't go well. One of the friends had the extremely dubious honour of becoming the last Englishman to be killed by an uncontacted tribe in the Amazon. Kit was held by the Brazilian government on suspicion of his friend's murder until a campaign by the *Daily Express* led to his release. He returned to England and became an assistant director on *The Guns of Navarone* and *From Russia with Love*. It was quite a start to a flamboyant life. And then he walked into our gig looking for his next adventure.

'We're trying to make a film of the new thing coming in,' says Kit. 'We're looking for bands and you're the best thing we've seen. We want to make a film about you. Do you want another drink?'

Kit wanted to show us to his business partner who was over in Ireland working on a film with John Huston. We agreed to do an audition at St Michael's Church Hall on Askew Road in Shepherd's Bush. This was the church where my mum and dad were married. It was also the church where, as a child, I'd sung in the choir. Now, it was the place where we'd find new management. So a couple of weeks later we were setting up our kit and in walks Chris Stamp. Talk about drop-dead cool. Talk about a Face. His brother Terence was the film star, and he had an image, but I've got to tell you, when you saw them both in the flesh, Chris had the edge. He was only a couple of years older than me, but he had this dangerous streak that Terence never had. He was so sharp. He was East End sharp.

After the audition, we all went to a Chinese restaurant and Kit announced that he wanted to manage us. He'd already got hold of our contracts with Helmut Gorden and Meaden, and he had a proposition.

They'd pay us a salary of 20 quid a week and they'd take 40 per cent from the gigs. It didn't take us long to make up our minds. It just seemed obvious. We'd gone along with Meaden's ideas. We'd done his single, 'Zoot Suit', and it hadn't even made the charts. We also knew he had no money. Kit, on the other hand, was loaded. Or we thought he was. He had to be, hadn't he, the way he was flashing the cash around? I only found out a long time later that he had to flog one of his father's paintings to pay our wages.

• • •

So I was 20, still a kid really, and I was at the crossroads. As things had moved on with the band, I had a very real chance to fulfil my dream. Or I could abandon it and stay with my young family. The second option was the safe one – and, I'll admit, the honourable one – but it just wasn't in my nature to take the safe option. You think you can do anything when you're young. But in some ways it still isn't in my nature now. I hope I've become a bit wiser with the years, but I still believe in luck and in taking chances. I wanted to be a musician. I wanted to give it everything I had. And that meant I had to leave.

A few days after I'd walked out, my dad came to see me. I was unloading the equipment for a gig at the Railway Hotel in Wealdstone and he came up and told me to get back with

Jackie. I told him, 'Dad, I can't do this marriage bit, this is my life. This thing.' And he just went bananas. He was raving at me right out in the middle of the street, and then he threw a punch. He wasn't a fighter. It took a lot to get him worked up. Even when I'd been expelled, he didn't hit me. That night outside the Railway Hotel was the first and only time it happened. I loved my dad, he loved me and my behaviour was terrible for him to endure.

It wasn't something I felt good about either. I was a complete arsehole. I was an uncaring bastard. I know that now and I knew it then, but maybe that's what it took for this band to happen. I was completely driven. I was driven to do what I did all that time and nothing in the world would have changed it. I was like the guy in *Close Encounters* building that bloody mountain in his basement and not knowing why. At the end of it, you realise why. And you realise that, even though you were a complete arsehole and an uncaring bastard, it wouldn't have happened any other way. There were no half-measures.

I'm not sorry I did what I did. I took the chance and went for what turned out to be the right thing. Once I'd made the decision, it just made sense. I knew I could do better, and that, when I did, I could take care of Jackie and Simon. I could provide better for them. And I did. As soon as I could, I looked after them. From the 1970s, we all used to go on holidays together every spring. Her family. My family. Old wounds healed and we all had a better life. This life – the one-room council flat, the job in the factory, the nights out gigging – this was no life. More importantly, if I hadn't walked out, The Who would never have been, not with me in it anyway. The world would have been full of Townshend solo albums.

I never spoke to my dad about it again after that, though. I felt deeply upset. I knew I'd hurt him and that stayed with me for a long time, even though he never held any grudges.

When I left, I left with one small suitcase and a guitar. I had the suit of clothes I stood up in, plus a few shirts. If you look back at all the pictures of the band, you'll only ever find me in four sets of clothes. I haven't changed. I'm still a really simple bloke that way.

• • •

That summer, I lived in our latest, greatest van. It had come with great promise, this van. It had been part of Kit's sales pitch.

'You're going to need a bigger van,' he'd said, 'because we're going to have lights, and the gear is going to be big. And I shall buy you that van.'

He did buy it, but it wasn't quite what we'd hoped for. The van that turned up was a fourth-hand 30 hundredweight removal truck. It had no windows in the back so I had them cut in, and I put style over substance. It was only when the rest of the band took their seats that we realised the windows were far, far too high. Pure Spinal Tap. Everyone went crazy, but I didn't mind for three reasons. First, it looked good and, as I've already said, looking good was nine-tenths of the law. It's best to have style and substance but if you can only have one, go for style. Second, it had a little bed space above the driver's cab. Third, the others refused to travel without a view. They decided to travel separately with Kit in his VW. They got to stay in hotels. I got to stay with Cleo.

Cleo. The girl who was unfortunate enough to share the little space above the cab with me in that dreadful old banger. She was West Indian and she was and probably still is the most well-spoken girl I've ever met in my life. And, believe it or not, I've met a lot of well-spoken girls in my time. She was also, entirely coincidentally, Constant Lambert's goddaughter. Her whole family was really tied up in the theatre. I didn't know who they were. I just fell in love with her. I thought she was drop-dead gorgeous. And she was into her music. She was always trying to turn me on to ska and bluebeat.

We used to go down to see her family in Brixton. I was the only white boy in the neighbourhood, but there wasn't a bad vibe. They welcomed me and I felt at home. It didn't have anything to do with colour. It was the struggle, the struggle of being at the bottom of the pile. Their music came from a different place from all these crooners. It came from a primal sense of wanting to leave your name on the wall and then get the fuck out of here. That's what we identified with. Well, I did anyway. It spoke to me. I wanted to leave my name on the wall. And I wanted to get the fuck out of here, too.

I really did love Cleo. I loved her for her music and I loved her because she was prepared to live in a van with me. Thinking back now, I have nothing but fond memories of that summer.

• • •

On 9 August 1964, the High Numbers did quite a prestigious gig at the Brighton Hippodrome. We were supporting Gerry and the Pacemakers, Elkie Brooks and (drum roll) Val McCullam. 'Who the fuck is Val McCullam?' you ask. Which is exactly what we asked. The promoter was this bloke called Arthur Howes. He arranged package tours around Britain and he said, 'Look, boys, you can come on board and do your bit but you also have to support Val.'

'Who?'

'Val. Val McCullam. She's a big deal.'

'Righto.'

So that night in Brighton, Pete, John and Keith were on in the first half with this Val bird, and then they were on in the second half with me. The following Sunday, we were in Blackpool with The Beatles and The Kinks. First half, Val and the boys. Second half, me and the boys. I can't remember at which point we worked out that part of Arthur's deal with Val was because he wanted to shag her, but it was pretty early on. I suppose we got off relatively lightly compared to Val.

And that was the summer and autumn of 1964. We drove all over Britain together, me and Cleo, on the way to whichever gig was next. When it got dark, we parked up on the side of the road in that rusty old lorry which was, increasingly, covered in lipstick messages from fans which were, increasingly, very similar to Keith's handwriting.

Life was just a wonderful adventure. We saw the Lake District for the first time. We got as far as Glasgow for a gig at the Kelvin Hall Arena with Lulu – 16 years old and already a great soul singer – and joined her whole family for a party after the show. We travelled the length and breadth of the country without breaking down once, the odds of which must have been longer than the odds of me and Pete still stepping out onstage together 50 years later. And you know the amazing thing – and it never does cease to amaze me to this day – it was all done with just a map and an address scribbled on the back of an envelope. No sat nav, no Google Maps, not even a postcode. How did we communicate with no mobile phones? How did we do all those shows, all that relentless touring with barely a landline between us? It was magic.

And this was happiness. I'd escaped school without becoming a bank robber. I'd left the factory. I'd left the council flat. I was 20 years old, I was doing the job Mrs Bowen, my music teacher, never thought I would do.

SIX

THE WHO, INNIT?

The first time a guitar died was an accident. It was September 1964 and we were playing our regular night at the Railway Tavern. The only difference was a new collapsible stage which was a few inches higher than the upturned beer crates we usually performed on. Pete was in the middle of his repertoire of moves when he stuck the guitar through the ceiling. The place went quiet. Some girls sniggered.

So he covered up the mistake by smashing the guitar to pieces. This pissed me off. Pete will tell you it was art. That he was taking the work of Gustav Metzger to a new level. Gustav who? Bollocks. He's journalising. The hole in the ceiling had nothing to do with Metzger and everything to do with the sniggering girls. It was heartbreaking. When I remembered how much I'd struggled to get my first guitars, it was like watching an animal being slaughtered. An expensive animal, that we'd have to replace with another expensive animal before the next gig. And we had to pay for the hole in the ceiling.

The following Tuesday, Keith kicked his drums over and that was it. From then on, the audience expected us to break our instruments. It was our thing.

Don't get me wrong, I saw quickly what it was doing for us. And even though it started as an accident, it soon became much more than that. The press got excited about the idea of these youths smashing up their kit. With the aid of a few ex-army smoke bombs, it was a good visual. It had impact. But they were missing the real point. It was about the noise. What had started as a mistake fitted into the ritual of what we were doing.

Very quickly, Pete wasn't just smashing his guitar. He used to stick the neck of it right up into the amps and through the speakers to make all kinds of surreal noises. It was animalistic. It was sacrificial. The guitar used to scream, and it used to go on for about five minutes until it was wrecked. The critics missed it, but the fans got it first time; they understood through the energy it created. The critics were writing about what they were seeing, but they weren't listening. That became the problem with the smashing of the guitars; I felt that in the end people had just come to see that; it stopped people listening.

And, you know, I'd love Pete to smash a guitar now just like he did, but he'd have to tell the crowd: don't just watch, listen. And they wouldn't, would they? The sight of a septuagenarian going to town on an amp stack would be all-consuming. But at least we could afford it now. Back in 1965, his artistic expression was very expensive.

I was already having to contend with Keith and his flying drumsticks. The first flash of recognition and he had become the pin-up of The Who. Wherever we went, all the girls were screaming, 'Keith, Keith, Keith'. He loved being loved, which you can't blame him for at all. The problem was that I had to stand in front of him. I was the frontman. It was my job. And Keith decided the drummer should be at the front.

To make his point, he would throw drumsticks at the back of my head all night, every night. The idea of having the drummer at the front of the stage with the rest of us tucked up round the back was ridiculous but he was serious about it. Completely serious. When the flying drumsticks didn't work, he became the master of upstaging. He was fabulous at it. He'd do anything to steal the limelight. Most of all, he wanted to sing. He couldn't sing. Well, he could but not terribly well. But if you ever want to see a drummer with pure joy on his face watch Keith Moon singing 'Bellboy'. He's gone. He's in pure heaven. Occasionally, when we were all in a good mood, we'd let him do 'Barbara Ann'. And then we wouldn't for the next few gigs. He'd sing anyway, as loud as he could. You can see it on the old tapes. Every song, Pete and John are doing the harmonies, I'm singing the lead. And so is Keith.

Apart from the drugs, the lack of money and Keith's big head, things had been going quite well. For starters, we'd worked out what we were going to be called, which is always important. We'd been the Detours until February 1963 when it became clear that we were getting confused with another band called the American Detours. I can't remember exactly who came up with 'The Who' in the first place. We were round at Pete's mate Barney's flat chucking around all sorts of silly names. The

Group. No One. The Hair. Pete liked that one. I think someone made a suggestion that Barney didn't hear.

He said, 'The Who?' Someone else said, 'That's good. The Who.' And that was that. Or it was for the next year or so. Then, for four months in 1964, we were the High Numbers. Then Kit arrived and said, 'No, we're going back to The Who. It's a much better name. Much more graphic. You can do much more with three letters than you can with God knows how many there are in the High Numbers.'

It was a lot of toing and froing, a lot of confusion for anyone printing the gig posters, but it was worth it. Within a couple of months, Kit had come up with what I think was the greatest rock poster of all time. It wouldn't have worked half as well with God knows how many letters there are in the High Numbers.

It was the end of 1964, and we'd got Tuesday nights at the Marquee. This shouldn't have been that big a deal. It was the Marquee. Proper West End. We'd played in town before, but this was big. This was where The Stones played. But Tuesday nights? Dead. Tumbleweed. Nobody went out on a Tuesday. But Kit did his poster.

The Who. Maximum R&B. Tuesdays at the Marquee.

With an image of Pete, his arm stretched up, like a swan. Kit brought ballet to that poster, and that was half the battle won.

He had another trick up his sleeve.

'We're going to go out,' he said, 'and we're going to find a hundred of the trendiest mods we can find, and we're going to make them the nucleus of a fan club. We will have a hundred faces.'

So we went round Shepherd's Bush and we gave out all these free tickets to the trendiest mods we could find. Then we did the same thing in the West End, except we couldn't find a single bloody person on the street on a Tuesday to take them. No mods. No Teds. Nobody.

I was so anxious that night. I'd played empty rooms before but an empty Marquee would be a new level of emptiness. But the poster and Kit's ruthless marketing skills saved us. That very first night, all our Shepherd's Bush mob, loyal, wonderful people that they were, turned up. And then a few stragglers came in. A new crowd. The following week, there were a few more. Quite quickly, it spiralled. Word of mouth spread about this Tuesday night in the West End, where this band was playing all this stuff with feedback and wild rhythms and improvisation. The jungle drums in those days were so much better than the internet these days.

Within three or four weeks, the line was round the block. It was the first real, tangible sign that we were a success. We were the mod band. We were the hot ticket at a hot club 'up West'. Until the Small Faces came up and spoilt it, bless them. They were real East End mods, and Steve Marriott, in my opinion, was one of the greatest rock-soul singers we've ever had.

But in early 1965, it was us and that felt good. Kit had done his job as our manager. He'd found us a home. He found us the beginnings of a fan club. He knew how to sell us. If one of us did something new onstage, he'd spot it and tell us whether or not to keep it. Usually, he'd want us to keep it. He had a masterplan – sometimes I wished he'd shared it with us, but we had complete trust in him. If he said jump, we'd jump. And he did say jump. He encouraged us to be wilder and wilder. Everyone in the pubs and clubs loved him, even though he came from a different walk of life. It might have had something to do with the fact that he always bought everyone a drink. But we loved him because he understood the show. He saw that it wasn't just about the music. It was the whole package.

Each week, we would add a new song. During the day I would spend hours with Kit, going round the record shops, trying to find new styles of music. We used to have bets on which records would be hits and which would be misses. He had a nose for it and I did, too. Nine times out of ten we'd pick the same ones and we'd be right.

On 15 January 1965 we released our first proper Townshend-composed Who single. Pete said recently that 'I Can't Explain' was written by some 18-year-old kid who can't tell his girlfriend he loves her because he's taken too many Dexedrine tablets. He also said it can't be beaten for straightforward Kink copying. It still made the Top Ten and we still open with it today. It's a great track. But the recording of it, a few months earlier, wasn't straightforward at all.

We had turned up at Pye Records in Marble Arch in September 1964 for our big studio debut. We were ready to play our first home-grown track, in our new, unique, English style. But Shel Talmy, the hotshot American producer, landed us with these three-part-harmony Beach Boy backing vocals, which Pete still curses to this day. Worse, he'd brought in Jimmy Page to play lead guitar.

'Oh shit.' That was my reaction. Pete had a slightly more protracted one, but what could we do? I wanted Pete to play. I wanted us to be the band we were, not the band some Yank wanted us to be. If it was up to us we would have said no. But there was no option. In those days, it was a live recording. There were only three tracks. Putting Pete's solo on afterwards would have been enormously difficult and could have lost the whole texture of the record. He would have played a great solo like he did every night live, but it would have left the sound sparse. You can't do rhythm and solo. You can get away with it live. Pete had a technique for that, but in the studio this was our first proper recording. Talmy had created huge hits with The Kinks and he was going to have his way. It was either that or nothing.

We did it in one take, and then Talmy said we had to do a B-side. He threw this song at us called 'Bald Headed Woman'. I scribbled out the lyrics, which didn't take long.

Yeah, I don't want no bald headed woman
It'll make me mean, yeah Lord, it'll make me mean.
Yeah, I don't want no sugar in my coffee.

And repeat. Job done. I didn't realise what the song was about at the time, but it was bluesy and I was right at home with that. Two hours later, we were out. Jimmy sounded nothing like Pete, but it was enough to get us into the charts for the first time.

Our first appearance on *Top of the Pops* meant my first appearance on an aeroplane. In those days the show was filmed in a church hall in Manchester so Kit booked us on a BAE flight up from London airport. Look at me. Part of the jet set.

I found myself sitting next to Marianne Faithfull, who was also booked for *TOTP*.

'Are you all right?' she asked as the plane took off. I was fine but it was lovely to have Marianne there to hold my hand.

Our next single was a more harmonious experience. Pete had 95 per cent of 'Anyway Anyhow Anywhere' written by the time he brought it into the Marquee one afternoon that April, but he didn't have the bridge worked out. We worked at it together onstage before the audience arrived. It started out as a song about a blissful free spirit because Pete was obsessed with Charlie Parker at the time. By the end of the day, it was about breaking through locked doors, not caring what was right or wrong.

That was my contribution. I gave it a bit more street, a bit more attitude. At that age, you think you're right all the time. That lyric, 'Nothing gets in my way', was all about how we were going to make our own lives, and I think those words suited it really well.

And, of course, it had Pete's feedback halfway through. It was new. It was revolutionary – so revolutionary that Decca sent the first pressing of the record back because they thought they had a faulty disc. But it was us. It was our stage act on vinyl.

We were in the charts. We were getting on television. The BBC had deigned to allow us on the radio. And then we had our first international tour. Two nights in Paris. It made a change from Shepherd's Bush. It was very, very foreign. I don't know what we must have looked like to the Parisians. They had great style, of course, and we must have looked like we were from outer space. The venue was the Club des Rockers, a small hall above a bar up by the Moulin Rouge, and there was no stage. We were crammed into a corner and the audience was right in front of us, at eye level, in our faces. Bon soir.

We started playing 'Heatwave' and they all just stood there, staring at us, hardly showing any emotion. They were French. We were English. No English bands had an easy time in France. Perhaps they hated us? Perhaps this was their way of showing Gallic disdain? So we reacted like we always did in those situations. We put on a bit of attitude.

'Daddy Rolling Stone'. 'Motoring. 'Jump Back'. Still nothing. We put on a bit more attitude. Is it going to go off? Is it going to go down? Are we going to walk off in abject silence?

This went on for the whole 45-minute set and then, as soon as we finished the angriest, snarliest, wildest version of 'Anyway Anyhow Anywhere', they went absolutely crazy. Our first gig abroad. Success. The local music magazine reviewed us. They said, 'The audience understood that a new style of rock was being created.' I'm not sure that was true. I'm not sure they had such a philosophical response. They were just completely shell-shocked.

Of course, Kit didn't have any money to get us home, but he spoke beautiful French so he talked our way onto the boat. Or he borrowed the money off Chris Parmenter, the A&R man from Fontana Records. Kit was all about blagging. He used his aristocratic accent and his Belgravia address to open all sorts of overdrafts. He had cards at Harrods and the Christopher Wine Company and accounts with several banks, all in the red. When things got really tight, he'd take a cheque to a casino. If he won, he'd have enough to pay off the bailiffs. If he lost, the cheque bounced anyway. He was a gambler, but he could talk his way out of anything. That's how we got back from France. But then, when he got home, he'd been evicted from Eaton Place. That should have been a big clue that finances at New Action, Kit and Chris's management company, weren't up to much.

Pete, on the other hand, was already going up in the world. He was sitting in his flat in Belgravia listening to opera, distanced and worried about the forthcoming album. He had the money. He had the publishing. The cash from the gigs was just pocket money for him. It changed us. We were becoming a group and its writer. That was always inevitable, I suppose, but it wasn't a dictatorship and I was never just a foot soldier. I still put the shows together. I've always decided on the running order. I have an instinct for getting the songs in a sequence where the musical senses in the body are taken on a journey. If you put songs in the wrong place, you break that journey, and we never did that. In the early days, we knew so many songs, we didn't have a set list. I just used to shout them out and they'd go into the next song. I'd get the feel for which song needed to follow the one we were doing while we were doing it. I'd think where was I in my head, what was I feeling, and then how could I take that feeling and emotion to another level without breaking the link. It was intense, a whole other level from just banging out one hit after another.

A lot of bands split up because of imbalance. Or, worse, they end up in front of a judge arguing who wrote what when. It didn't make a huge difference to me. I have been a bit bothered over the years, not about the cash but about the acknowledgement. I made my contribution, I know what I added, and so it was hard reading criticisms of my vocals in the press. But, that's life. Why waste time worrying about it? Instead, I just accepted it.

I made the conscious decision that if my job was going to be the singer of Pete's songs, and if Pete's songs were genius, which they were, then I would be happy with my lot, thank you very much. I'd go whichever way he wanted. Of course, if there was something I didn't like, I'd still tell him. I've always told him, which isn't easy because, like most writers, he gets defensive. But that tension was important. It's what made us who we are. It was never destructive. And, whatever happened, I knew that we were never going to split up because of money. Pete was in his flat in Belgravia and I was still in a van with Cleo. Honestly, I was happy with that. I was living the van-based dream.

That summer, we were just working. Working, working, working. We played 236 shows in 1965. We were existing on three, four hours' sleep a night. Show, sleep, drive, show, sleep, drive. I think I had it better than the boys because they were still cramming into the back of Kit's Beetle. But then, at some point, Pete got a Lincoln Continental and Keith and John got a Bentley. They also got a chauffeur because neither of them could drive. That suited Keith. The boy from Alperton was in his own version of *Pygmalion*. He was Eliza Doolittle. Kit was Professor Higgins.

We used to go to a Chinese restaurant called the Lotus House on Edgware Road. Kit went in there with no money, we'd all eat and drink lavishly, and at the end of the night he'd sign the tablecloth. In those days that was acceptable tender, and he got away with it. Most people could manage that trick once or twice. Kit did it for most of the sixties. He did it with cheques and he did it with contracts. After seeing an up-and-coming guitarist play one night in 1966, he took his manager to dinner at the Lotus. The manager was Chas Chandler, the guitarist was Jimi Hendrix and, by the end of the night, Jimi was contracted, by tablecloth, to Kit.

That's how Kit rolled. People admired him. They just assumed, from the cut of his jib, that he was a trustworthy, upstanding member of society.

Keith didn't just admire him. He became him. It took about six weeks from the first time they met. After that, Keith could do a perfect Kit Lambert. All his mannerisms, everything. It was like sitting down with Kit. He mimicked him for laughs but it quickly became more than that. All that 'My dear boy'. He wasn't speaking posh sarcastically. He really decided to become grand. He got the Bentley. He got the wardrobe. He became an aficionado of fine wines and brandies. Those long nights at the Lotus House became like masterclasses. Kit and Keith would work their way through all the vintages, comparing tasting notes, before Kit scribbled his signature on the tablecloth.

That's something people get wrong about Keith. He was never just a boozer. He was a connoisseur of booze. When we were filming *Tommy* in the 1970s, I remember he went into a bar in a hotel in Portsmouth and he asked for a Rémy Martin and a mixer. The barman pointed out that it didn't matter what brandy he used if he was going to mix it. He wouldn't know the difference.

So Keith made him a bet. He told him to line up all the brandies on the shelf and add ginger. 'If I can tell you which one is the Rémy Martin,' he said, 'then you buy the drinks for me and my mates for the rest of the night. If I can't, you can have my car.'

The barman agreed. Keith went along the line of brandies like he was in a Bordeaux wine cellar. And he picked the right one.

• • •

So that was the summer of 1965. A lot of work, some largely constructive arguments and Keith working tirelessly on his knowledge of brandy. It was a harmonious summer. This is something you don't hear very much about us. People assume we were fighting all the time. It's not true. Most of the time we were larking. A lot of the time we were talking about the music and the direction. The fights and the flare-ups? Most of it wasn't real. Most of it was image. It's all about jeopardy. We were a dangerous band, always teetering on the brink, always on the verge of a fistfight. That's what people want from their rock bands ... the constant potential for destruction. You couldn't have another band that just got on. The Beatles were already the best of mates ... or they were in the early years. And that suited their style of music. It wouldn't have suited ours. Where's the drama? Where's the danger? We did things differently.

Some of it wasn't just for show. Sometimes the fights and flare-ups were real. But they were, usually, a good thing. They kept the engine turning. They didn't happen very often and the rest of the time we were having a great time. Look at the photographs. Mucking about. Larking. There was some scowling, too, but that was just a bit of attitude for the cameras. In June 1965, *Melody Maker* wrote, 'Every so often, a group is poised on the brink of a breakthrough. Word has it, it's The Who.'

And it was The Who. We were poised. We were on the brink. And then we went on our very first European tour and everything unravelled. It is possible that you've heard the story about the time I was slung out of the band. Out of my band. Several people have told the story before. But this is my version and it's the honest truth, swear on my life. No, swear on Pete's life, because 50 years is a long time and there's a very slight chance I might get one or two details mixed up.

We were on tour in Europe and everything was going wrong. Some of it wasn't the band's fault and some of it bloody well was. Early in the month, the van with all our kit inside got nicked from outside Battersea Dogs Home, which was ironic because Cy, our roadie, had been in there enquiring about a German shepherd to beef up our van's security. The kit we then had to borrow for the tour kept going wrong, even when Pete and Keith weren't smashing it up.

The first gig in Holland went well, but somewhere between Holland and Denmark they picked up a sack full of purple hearts and that was it. The playing went out of the window. The tempo started getting faster and faster. There was no control. It was a mess.

We got to Aarhus, Denmark, on Sunday 26 September 1965, and the hall was filled with 5,000 pissed-up Danish farmers.

The band was halfway through the second song when all hell broke loose in the crowd. Chairs were smashed. Bottles were flying: it was turning into a full-scale riot. That was the second shortest show we've ever done.

It made headlines in the next morning's newspapers but we'd already moved on to the next show in Aalborg. That was where everything really unravelled. Maybe it was a combination of the drugs they'd taken and the nerves, but the show was a mess. I tried desperately to get the lyrics in and the vocal loud enough, but they just played louder and faster. It was a cacophony and something had to give. A band of musicians with this much talent and it was all getting flushed down the toilet.

So I decided to flush something else down the toilet instead.

While the band smashed up the stage at the end of My Generation, I stormed offstage and straight up to Keith's suitcase in the dressing room. I thought: I'm going to stop this once and for all. It took five seconds to find his stash, this great big bag full of pills in his suitcase. Black bombers. Purple hearts. You name it. And I just flushed the bloody lot down the toilet.

Of course, Keith came straight offstage behind me, wanting another pill. And he starts shouting, 'What's happened to them? What's fucking happened to them?'

So I told him I flushed them down the toilet.

This made him angry and he came slashing at me with the bells of a tambourine. I suppose I was lucky that was all he had to hand. So there I was, faced with a furious Keith and his percussive attack, and I fought back. And it wasn't a bad fight, but it was a fight and I finished it. The next day, we flew home. I was summoned to Kit's office and told I was no longer part of The Who.

SEVEN

BREAKING UP IS HARD TO DO

It had been three against one for a long time, and that had nothing to do with money and everything to do with a prodigious amount of drugs. Ever since they got into amphetamines and I hadn't, we'd moved apart. I'd tried purple hearts a couple of times, but they didn't work for me. All I did was chew my lip for a few hours. They gave me a dry throat and I couldn't sing. A guitarist doesn't give a shit if he's got a dry throat. He just drinks more booze, which is what Pete did. But I couldn't sing on pills. So it was a straightforward decision. I was either going to be a good singer, and care about what we were doing on a stage, because this was my life and I was going forward with this. Or I could chuck it in right there. I knew how tough the bloody competition was. There were some great bands out there, fantastic bands, and they never made it. I didn't want to be part of one of those bands. So I left the other three to it.

I've watched so many friends turn into absolute arseholes on drugs. And when you're in their company, it starts off and you're all mates, but then someone disappears to the toilet and they come back and then someone else disappears, and before you know it you're not sitting with your friends any more. It's like you're at a different party.

So many times in my life I've had to be tough with people stuck on drugs. The ones I was tough with are still here. The ones where I wasn't tough enough didn't make it. And that's something I think about often. It's something I think about when we perform today. The two of us that are left. But this put me in the minority, not just in the band but in the whole of bloody London.

Everyone in Soho was on these pills. You queued up for your ticket. Then you queued up for your drugs. It was that open (and still is). And when the government caught on and started fining dealers, they just switched to other pills. French blues. Dexies. Black bombers. Stronger and stronger. No bloody wonder Keith, the boy who had blown us away with his first rendition of 'Road Runner', couldn't keep the beat any more. I knew, right there, that I was the enemy. Rock 'n' roll had become all about taking as many drugs as possible until you died. And I was spoiling that. From their point of view, it was an intrusion on how they wanted to live their lives. They wanted to be free and I was spoiling it. The next day, we travelled back home separately and then I was told I was out.

For two days, I grieved. It was like a death. It was the end of everything. Five years slogging away, sacrificing everything, for nothing. And then, a couple of days after that, I pulled myself together and started making plans for a soul band. I called up old mates, planned a repertoire. It no longer felt like make-or-break because I would just carry on, like I always had. I wasn't going back to the factory.

And by now, I knew I could sing. All the pop songs were easy to sing – you just sing 'em. There's nothing deep about them. We hadn't got to the point where Pete's writing would demand something different, something I would feel less sure of.

In September 1965, I was still a confident singer. I knew my voice was having an effect on the audience and I liked being in a band, so I was just going to get on with it. My future wouldn't be with The Who, but I would be all right. We weren't earning money anyway so it didn't make much difference.

The situation didn't last long. They did a few shows without me, and they were getting booed off the stage. I didn't feel bad about that. They deserved it. But within a few days, Kit and Chris were knocking on the door saying, 'They need you back in. They've lost it without you.'

I'm not sure the band realised that. I suppose when you're in there playing, you think it's as good as it always was, but it's not the same if you're looking at the band from outside. All of a sudden, the chemistry's gone. I knew, once Keith joined the band, we had all the ingredients. If one of us wasn't there, it didn't work. It would have been the same if John had got thrown out. Or Keith. It was like that when he died. There was a hole we could never fill. It wasn't to do with his ability. It was his persona, and the way it fitted in. We were all individuals who made the one that was The Who. None of us could be replaced.

Luckily, they listened to the management. They agreed. There were conditions on both sides. They'd have me back as long as I didn't beat the crap out of them or flush their stash down the bog. I'd go back as long as they didn't take drugs before a show. I didn't care what they did offstage, but when we were onstage we were a team and we had to work together. This was going to be professional. We were going to be the best at this. They had to arrive *compos mentis*. It wasn't a lot to ask. That was the deal and they kept it well into the seventies, when Keith started to take stuff onstage again.

I'd like to say we'd put it all behind us and moved on but that would be a lie. I was back in the band, but the others begrudged my return. They were still pissed off, Keith in particular. And now he was released from the threat of violence, he would do everything he could think of to rile me up. He was a master of the verbal and he knew exactly which buttons to push to get me going. If anything, John was worse. John had a very spiteful streak. There were shades of Cousin Kevin from *Tommy*. I don't know if it was because he was an only child, but he could be mean and he could say smart-arse things that deserved a punch in the mouth.

In my world, the world I'd come from, you would have got a smack in the mouth for saying the things he said to me. He knew this. Keith knew it, too. They knew about my red mist.

After Denmark, they wasted a lot of energy trying to find the point at which I'd bite. It went on and on for months, years even, but I never did. It must have driven them mad. I had a trick, you see. It's a trick you need a lot when you're in the music industry. I used to imagine myself as a duck. An acid comment here, a trashed hotel room there – they were raindrops rolling off my duck's back. A Zen duck. That was me. Quack, quack.

• • •

On 13 October 1965, two weeks after we split up, two days before we got back together again, we arrived at IBC Studios in Portland Place to finish our much-delayed debut LP. I think the atmosphere was quite frosty, which was a good thing because we were going to record 'My Generation'. Pete had written the song six months earlier after the Queen Mother got his Packard hearse – yes, he had a hearse – towed from outside his flat because it reminded Her Majesty of Her Majesty's late husband.

That was just the sort of thing that could wind him up for a week. How dare she.

The first demo he played us was much slower. More of a chink-a-chink-a-chink Bo Diddley number. I didn't like it. Kit wasn't sure either, but he told him to keep going. The second demo had the key changes and the call and response, but it still didn't feel right.

Then we got to IBC studios and Keith just stuck it on the on-beat, which gave it the kick up the arse it needed. That was the thing about Moon – he was never a conformist drummer. He never practised. He just did it. When you tried to pin him down to a straight four-four time, it was impossible. He could do it but it killed him to do it. The whole reason for his genius was the absolute, utter anarchy. So he was off, on the on-beat, full of aggression. I tried to follow him and I stuttered on the first line. Next take, I corrected it, but Kit popped out and said,

'Keep it. Keep that in.' Pete had a long 'fffff' in the demo. 'Why don't you all fffffffade away'. But it wasn't a stutter. Not until Kit came out and said keep it. 'Keep that blues stutter.' And it worked. To me, it wasn't a sign of weakness. It wasn't a slip of the tongue. It was aggression, pure aggression, pushed forward by that on-beat. Bottled-up rage, barely controlled, spilling out onto vinyl, shouting out *I hope I die before I get old.*

Almost all the great things that happen in studios are accidents, and that's when you've got to rely on your producers to spot the ones that work and the ones that don't. Pete always hated Kit's production. I understand technically why Pete didn't like it. Some of the mixes Kit did were terrible. He was always a bit bass-light, which used to upset John, but recording circumstances were difficult in those days. We only had a three-track recorder – eight-tracks were still three years away – so we didn't have a lot to play with. But Kit was incredibly adventurous. He'd fly in, throw everything at the wall, tear it down and rebuild it. We'd do layers and layers. We'd do harmonies all over the place, building them up by bouncing one track onto another, on those three-tracks. This allowed us to get the backing vocal harmonies sounding like we were a 12-piece vocal group. The price to pay for this was that these things had to be mixed at the time of recording and that mix could never be changed. Put on too much echo and the result was permanent.

'My Generation' didn't need all that. It just needed a punch. It was another street song, like 'Anyway Anyhow Anywhere', and I think, Zen ducks aside, we were all in the mood for a bit of aggression. We were in the mood to tell everyone to f-f-f-fade away. So the stutter stayed, we crashed through the rest of the album and we went home.

The track was released at the end of October and the album came out on December 3. It should have been a great end to the year, but it wasn't quite like that. I was still the enemy. Everyone was talking about leaving. Keith and John were going to do their own thing. Keith asked Paul McCartney if he could join The Beatles. 'We already have a drummer,' said Paul. Then he was going to join The Animals. Then he was going to join The Nashville Teens. Pete was going to join a supergroup with Paddy, Klaus and Gibson.

The legal battles didn't help. Kit and Chris had fallen out with Shel Talmy. For five months, they were in and out of the High Court, trying to break Talmy's contract, and all that time we couldn't release any more music. Given that the average band lasts 18 months and we were far more volatile than the average band, five months was a lifetime.

But we just kept gigging. We played our last show at the Goldhawk Road Social Club on 3 December 1965. This had been our home turf since the beginning, so it's been described as an important moment. A turning point. The night we left our mod roots behind. It certainly wasn't a particularly salubrious night. Someone remembers a bouncer with a big stick on the end of a chain. But there was always a bouncer and they never needed big sticks on chains. They were massive. And I think the audience has made much more of it than we did. We weren't leaving them. We were moving on because we couldn't get them all in the place. I wasn't moving on from being a mod either because I was never a mod in the first place.

I've always been the same through my life. I never liked uniforms. When everybody else was wearing mod gear, I'd wear a leather jacket. And when they were wearing leather jackets, I'd wear a suede coat. We might have been the mod band. Dressing like a mod did the job for a while. But I didn't feel that we had to answer to anybody. I felt, and Pete did, too, that by the time we were making our own music, people were following us for that, not how we dressed.

I liked the mod thing in the early days. I liked the zoot suit. I liked the drape jackets, the Edwardian look, with the really stiff collars and studs. That was sharp and I liked to dress sharp. I got that from my dad. He had two shirts. One was his best shirt, the other was his work shirt. He changed the collar every other day, and he had cuffs but no sleeves. But he looked sharp. My dad always looked sharp. So I liked looking sharp, too.

But then it started to get into jeans and Fred Perrys, then the parka. It was all too much. It was stifling invention. People telling me what to wear was exactly what I didn't want to do.

So I was wearing what I wanted and I was living how I wanted. I wasn't in the van any more. I was going up in the world. For a while, I'd kipped in the office, which was a room in Kit's flat at Ivor Court, at the top of Gloucester Place.

Every morning, there'd be some boy making coffee in the kitchen. Kit would walk in, make some excuse about why he was there and send him on his way. I knew Kit was gay. I knew he liked young men, but he never hit on me. Not once. Perhaps

I wasn't his type. Perhaps he knew he wouldn't have got very far. After all, I was dating his father's goddaughter. But then, somehow or other, Cleo and I just drifted apart and I met up with a girl called Anna from Muswell Hill. She lived with her flatmate Gitta, so I shacked up in Muswell Hill with them. And that was my life. Driving to a gig, playing the gig, going back to Muswell Hill. Simple.

While I was doing that, Pete was making further forays into his own psyche. By 1966, he was really beginning to write his own songs and they were ... different. We'd had a string of decent enough hits. Whatever we did next, we'd still get on *Top of the Pops*. So Pete wrote 'I'm a Boy'.

Bloody hell. A song that was supposed to be part of a rock opera called *Quads* about a future where parents can choose the sex of their children. A couple have three girls but the fourth child is a boy. The mother isn't happy. So she brings him up as a girl. He questions his gender identity. It was, like so much of Pete's music, way, way ahead of its time.

One little girl was called Jean-Marie
Another little girl was called Felicity
Another little girl was Sally-Joy
The other was me and I'm a boy.

I found this very, very difficult. I was all right with the line 'My name is Bill and I'm a headcase' but the rest of it, a boy struggling to find his identity, was hard. Up until this point, the band had been moulded around what I did. Pete wrote it, but I sang it. I wasn't in charge but, onstage, I could do what I wanted. They fitted around me and so did the songs. It wasn't like that any more. My confidence had been knocked.

All I remember was that I listened more to Pete's voice on the demo tapes and how he was singing it. I tried to get his voice into my voice. I tried to sing it like a vulnerable kid. When I listen to 'I'm a Boy' now, I think it kind of works, but I didn't think it did at the time. Not at all.

I thought it sounded like I was singing down a tunnel. I've never liked listening to myself sing. I hate it when I'm out and I hear myself. You either listen to us at one of our shows or you listen to us on your own. If you want to kill a party, put a Who song on. If you want me to leave your party, put a Who song on. I don't want to hear it. It's bad enough when my voice crops up on television, which happens quite a lot these days and, usually, when you least expect it. The other day, I was watching a documentary about paddle steamers on the Clyde, and they used a bit of bloody 'Won't Get Fooled Again'. I mean, why?

So you get the picture. I've never liked the sound of it but I know when it's good. It's not the voice itself, it's the vibrations. And the vibrations didn't feel good once we moved deeper into Pete's brain.

As I've said, I already knew my job was to be a portal for Pete's words. Realising that, accepting it, embracing it, was what these years were all about. Between 'My Generation' and *Tommy*, it was all about finding that vulnerability. It wasn't easy.

'Happy Jack', a song about a bullied tramp, was even harder, and then we did 'Pictures of Lily', a song about a boy having a wank to an old black and white photograph. It was all about adolescent insecurities. It wasn't really my thing.

I just never had to fight for a girl. I've already told you, that's one of the great things about getting up onstage with a microphone. It just happens that girls like it and if you're 19, 20 years old, it's not a bad thing to happen. It meant that I really wasn't tuned in to insecurity the way Pete was. That doesn't mean I wasn't insecure. Deep down, I was just as insecure as everyone else. I could be a frontman onstage before thousands of people. I could hold my own with anyone. I could present the image of a rock star. But I wasn't confident about myself. Not even close. And I just hid it with bravado. That only began to change when I met Heather.

EIGHT

DIPPITY-
DON'T

The first time I woke up next to the woman I'd marry and spend the rest of my life with, she screamed, 'Your hair! Your hair!' This was quite a normal reaction with the birds. The Dippity-Do magic would wear off as we slept. My hair would be straight when we went to bed and it would be curly when we woke up. The poor girl would scream, I'd apologise and then I'd run off to the bathroom to sort myself out.

This time was different. I was halfway through the apology, getting ready to make the run for the bathroom, but she stopped me.

'What have you done to it?' she said.

'Nothing,' I replied. 'That's how it is.'

'It's beautiful,' she said. Well, that was it. Within a week, I was going around with curly hair. That's how it has always been with Heather. She gave me confidence. Not bravado, but real confidence. There's a huge difference.

She already knew who I was before we were introduced in New York in the spring of 1967. Chris Stamp had met her the year before and he'd decided to show her and her friend Devon, a beautiful six-foot-tall black girl, the publicity photos of 'the next big thing in rock 'n' roll'.

The girls took one look at our photos and announced that it would never work. We were just too ugly, Devon told him. Heather thought Keith was 'okay' and I was 'not bad' but the others? 'Poor Chris, it's never going to happen,' Devon said.

We first met when we were doing the *Murray the K Show* at the RKO 58th Street Theatre on The Who's first trip to America. Murray was a hotshot New York DJ. He was a weird, sleazy guy – he liked to call himself the fifth Beatle – but you played at his show because then he'd play your record on the station. The show itself ran five times a day and we played nine days in a row.

We'd go on, do three songs and then we'd have to sit around in the dressing room waiting for our next slot. That's when I first met Heather. There was a lot of time to meet people.

She had been a model on the show before and now she was here just hanging out with her friends. We said hello, we chatted a bit and that was it. I was with a girl called Emmaretta Marks. She was a backing singer for lots of different artists – she had a great voice and a bubbly personality. She went on to become an original cast member of *Hair* on Broadway. Heather was with a guy from Andy Warhol's Factory. It was like that. Everyone knew everyone. Everyone was always with someone but that someone changed all the time. It was a small scene, and we were all friends.

We were loving it, of course. We couldn't believe our luck. All these beautiful, exotic American girls and they were into us. Heather told me that British boys took American girls by storm. We were sharp dressers, she said. We strutted around like peacocks. And we were better in bed. That's what she said. And at the time, we didn't complain.

People call these girls groupies, which is a horrible name. They were much more than groupies and it was never just for the shag. These were real friends. They saved a lot of lives and I think we saved some of them. Because, despite all the people, all the noise and all the partying, life in the middle of that world could be lonely. And it was the same for them.

They were all models, dancers, singers – people who were connected in some way or in several ways to the arts. They were all living in that bubble, working hard then going to clubs and parties. It was companionship as much as it was anything else. We shared a lot and we used to have so much fun. They could all sing, and, boy, could they dance. They could all put on little shows in those dingy little dressing rooms. They made all that hanging around waiting to go onstage bearable.

Anyway, that's when I met Heather, that night in New York, and I didn't take much notice of her, beyond registering that she was a cracker. She thought we were behaving like a bunch of kids, which might not have been the best first impression, but it was true. After we'd talked for a while, she went off with the guy from the Andy Warhol Superstars and that was the last I saw of her for five months. Five more months of Dippity-Do.

• • •

The whole point of going to New York was to try to break into America. We'd never made much of a dent, partly because of our last American record company, which didn't get us at all, and partly because the English scene was way ahead of the Yanks. But now we had a new record deal and a tour lined up.

So a couple of months after we got back from New York, we were back in the States, first for a five-night stint ending in the Monterey Pop Festival, then for a ten-week, coast-to-coast tour with the squeaky-clean Herman's Hermits.

We began by flying to Detroit, Michigan, for a gig just up the road in Ann Arbor. It was a great place to start. It was the only place in the USA where our records had ever had decent radio play. Detroit was blue-collar. They were our people. They had a different accent but everything else was the same. They had the same traditions. They lived their lives the same way. And they came to our show and went crazy.

Then we went out to dinner with Frank Sinatra Jr and a load of Detroit mobsters. That was a culture shock.

A couple of nights later, we were playing with B. B. King at this club called the Fillmore West in Haight-Ashbury, San Francisco. Total contrast. The audience didn't know what to make of us. They looked puzzled, then they all sat down, then they went crazy. They were already well down the psychedelic hippy road. I don't think they knew what to make of a bunch of pasty boys from west London.

The day after that, we toddled off down to Monterey for the pop festival. And we were travelling in our first stretch limo and, to this day, the most uncomfortable car I've ever been in. Bone-breaking, it was, but we felt good in it. We felt posh.

The festival itself was pure summer of love. Everyone was feeling the vibe. Peace, love and understanding. And then we arrived and changed the vibe. We were scheduled to play the same night as Jimi Hendrix. This was bad news, because Jimi had stolen Pete's act.

We first met Jimi when he came to see us recording at IBC in London at the end of 1966. When we'd finished, we all went over to Blaises nightclub to see him make his British debut. Everyone was there and we could all see, immediately, that he was a threat. Everything Pete had been doing with his guitar since 1964 Jimi was doing. He was just so charismatic. It was unbelievable. His band was as carefully put together as ours was. It was perfect. Hendrix would turn on a dime but Noel Redding and Mitch Mitchell would match him note for note. They would know, immediately, where he was going and they'd go with him. You can't buy that. It's a gift. They had it and we had it. It's extraordinary when it happens, and when you see it you're touched. And everyone in Blaises that night, Clapton, Beck, us, we were all touched. Pete, of course, put it more strongly. He said he was destroyed.

Jimi did it all in a very short period of time. We first saw him in 1966 and he was gone by 1970. Who knows where he would have gone to with his music? He would have changed like we changed. He wanted his music to be more like jazz, he wanted to change but the audience didn't. They just wanted more and more and more and more. It's like Cream. The audience wanted more and more Cream music and the band couldn't keep it up. There was nowhere to go, and that's pressure. That's why so many rock bands implode.

Jimi wasn't there yet at Monterey. He was on the up. He was a star and he was backstage, face-to-face with Pete, arguing about who should go on first. Eventually, it ended in a coin toss, which Pete won. We went on first, thank fuck, and left the stage and the audience and our kit in pieces. Jimi came on next and set his guitar on fire, but it didn't matter. It was still a defining moment for us. The Americans saw us. They saw what we could do live. And I did it all wearing a bedspread I'd bought from the Chelsea Antiques Market. That was the way back then.

None of the rock bands had stylists or designers. Every tour, we all went off digging around the King's Road, looking for something, anything that would reinvent our look. The fringe waistcoat I wore at Woodstock came from a shop in Ealing. The Indian brave outfit I wore for our tour in 1975 was a set of chamois leathers, bought from a local garage in Sussex by Heather, hole-punched and stitched together by Daltrey's Personal Tailoring Services Ltd. Miles Davis' wife called Heather to ask which designer had made that costume. The next time we saw him perform, he was rocking the same look. I doubt very much he got it from his local garage. For me, it didn't matter where anything came from. The important thing was to be the red sheep, not the black sheep.

The bedspread worked that night in Monterey. I celebrated our success with a couple of drinks and a joint that Augustus Owsley Stanley III, the King of LSD, or 'Bear' as everyone on the

West Coast knew him, had given me. 'Never do anything more than a joint,' Owsley said as he handed it over. 'It won't suit you.' Owsley was the first bloke to mass-produce LSD. He churned out 500 grams of purple haze between 1965 and 1967. That's a million doses. And here he was telling me to steer clear, so I did.

The joint was the American version of the Camberwell Carrot, a great cheroot wrapped in the Stars and Stripes. It took most of the night to get through, but I didn't mind because Catherine James, Emmaretta's friend, had come back to my motel to help me. She was a beautiful blonde girl and everyone had been chasing her. I'd been with Emmaretta and she'd been with Eric Clapton when we first met, but at Monterey, she was mine to share that wonderful, mentholated joint with.

The others celebrated with 2.5-dimethoxy-4-methylamphetamine. Pete spent the entire flight back from Los Angeles to New York staring fiercely at my kaftan coat. God knows what was going on inside his head but he kept gibbering on about rainbows. That was a long six hours, and then I had to get them all through immigration at JFK for the flight back to London. That's not easy when everyone's tripping but there was no option. We had no money for another flight. Two good things came from that journey. Pete got the idea for 'I Can See For Miles' and he decided that drugs were bad.

For the next few days in London, we lived in the recording studio, working on our next album, *The Who Sell Out*. Then, on 7 July, we began our first full American tour, and it was wild.

• • •

For the Herman's Hermits tour of 1967 we had a private jet, which sounds very flash, but there were two small problems. First of all, it wasn't private – we had to share it with the Hermits, who were all right but they had their name plastered on the side, which pissed us off. Secondly, it wasn't a jet. It was a Douglas DC-8 four-prop and it was on its last legs. In a very former life, it had been some kind of cargo plane and they'd converted it into a tour plane with about as much style and panache as I'd converted our old tour vans. There were wooden bunks along the back and a few seats in the front.

Cruising speed was supposed to be 350mph but, because the plane had so many holes in it, it couldn't pressurise so we had to fly at a low altitude. It never felt like we were flying much above stall speed. And because we had to fly so low, it used to catch all the thermals. When we crossed the deserts of Arizona or Nevada, it was like being stuck on a rollercoaster at a particularly poorly maintained theme park. For several hours at a time.

We wouldn't have been the first musicians to go down in a plane someone hadn't coughed up enough cash for and we wouldn't have been the last either, but we never worried. If you're going to go, you're going to go, and if things like that bothered you, you'd never leave the house. That plane lasted half the tour, which is twice as long as any of us expected it to last. After an emergency landing on a foamed runway at Nashville after one of the engines packed in, it was retired, and we carried on by bus.

These days when we tour we travel in complete luxury. It's great, of course. I'm not complaining. It means there are no distractions. No one's tearing a hotel apart. No one's getting us thrown out onto the street at four in the morning. It means I can put all my energy into my performance. The first time round it was a party and that was great, too.

If we weren't travelling after the gigs, we'd go back to these fantastic little motels. They weren't five-star by any stretch of the imagination – they were more like military barracks – but they always had a pool in the middle, and we'd always end up seeing who could jump the highest into them. Keith always won because he just went straight off the roof. We were having the time of our lives. The gigs were going great – we were partying our way across America – and, of course, there were always girls hanging around. Most importantly, for the first time in almost two years, the others were beginning to treat me like one of the band again.

On 23 August 1967, in Flint, Michigan, Keith turned 21. He chose to mark the occasion by getting us banned from every Holiday Inn on the planet, and I wasn't even there. I'd seen him in the morning, and he was already pissed so I decided to spend the rest of the day in the company of a talented, beautiful guitarist called Patti Quatro. The next morning, I woke up to a long story and a longer bill. A drum company had delivered a cake with a girl in it. Keith had started a food fight with the cake and had knocked out two of his front teeth. Keith had been to an emergency dentist and required no painkillers to have his teeth fixed. Keith came back from the dentist and drove a Continental or a Cadillac (depending on who you ask) into the hotel pool. Keith was arrested, held for the rest of the night and then escorted to the plane by the sheriff, who warned him never to set foot in this town again. All in all, a fairly typical night out for our drummer.

The ban wasn't the end of the world – all publicity is good publicity and the ban only lasted until 1993 – but the $50,000 cost of draining the pool and fishing out the Continental or the Cadillac was.

We had already shelled out $1,000 for entirely understand-able reasons in Montgomery, Alabama, after a duty manager made the huge mistake of asking Keith to keep the music down. Keith had responded by blowing up his toilet with a bag of cherry bombs, small but very powerful fireworks shaped like a bomb from a *Tom and Jerry* cartoon. He loved his cherry bombs. He bought them by the sackful. 'That, my dear boy, is noise,' he'd told the manager who billed us for the damage and chucked us all out. When you travelled with Keith, you got used to changing hotels in the middle of the night.

Everyone assumes life on the road with Moon must have been hilarious but, when you think about it soberly, most of it wasn't. When he could stand up and let loose on one of his soliloquies, it was hysterical, but that was only about 20 per cent of the time. The rest of it, the pranks, the explosions, the general devastation, there was usually someone at the other end of it having a pretty miserable time. The last gig of the tour took place in Honolulu on 9 September and it was very nearly our last gig with Keith. I suppose you could say that about a lot of gigs, but this was a special one. He decided to go surfing as soon as we got there. He got the board, he got the shorts and he just announced he was off out. He was from Wembley, north London. He didn't know anything about surfing, but that wasn't going to stop him. This was part of his life plan. He used to have three posters on that bedroom wall in Wembley. The first was a surfer girl standing in front of a Ford Woodie with surfboards on top. The second was The Beach Boys. The third was Steve McQueen. He invented a life in his head in Wembley, and then he went out and did it.

By the time we'd got to Hawaii, he was already well over halfway there. He'd married Kim Kerrigan a year earlier and even though she was born in Leicester, she was the spit of any of those California surf chicks. He was already best friends with The Beach Boys. It would be a few years before he'd move next door to Steve McQueen, but on that beach in Hawaii he was going to do 'surfer'.

I'm still surprised he survived. It could easily have gone the other way. Because Keith, a Wembley boy through and through, did not understand that the waves don't just come in. He didn't know about rip tides and the razor-sharp coral underneath them. He came back out again some time later like the creature from the blue lagoon, bleeding heavily and half drowned, delighted to have ticked another thing off his list.

And then we went home, via *The Smothers Brothers' Comedy Hour* at CBS. One last chance for a final bit of publicity. Again, we have Keith to thank for that. We were due to play 'I Can See For Miles' and 'My Generation' and, at the end, Keith was to set off a smoke bomb. We rehearsed our little spot in the afternoon and it all went fine. After a lot of discussion, the studio fire marshal was happy with the extent of the planned explosion. But Keith wasn't.

In between rehearsals and broadcast, between the first and second bottle of brandy, he bribed the marshal. He wanted a bigger bang. That was his motto in life, and nothing, not even live television, would stop him.

The resulting explosion knocked me several feet forwards, covered the entire stage in smoke and dust and interrupted the live transmission for a couple of seconds. Keith was closest to the epicentre but escaped with a gashed arm. Pete took the full force of the explosion and spent the next few minutes tamping down his burning hair and wondering if he'd ever get his hearing back. He did, 20 minutes later, but it was never 100 per cent again.

It was an explosive end to an expensive tour. We should have been going home happy and loaded, but it didn't work out like that. I'd spent the whole trip being careful what I spent. I'd wanted to come home with more than I'd gone out with so I'd limited myself to a strict diet of one hamburger a day and a few other tidbits. I'd stuck to it right across the States and when I got back to LA, I went to see Frank Barsalona, our agent, to ask him for my share of the profits. 'There aren't any to share,' he said, quite apologetically.

I pointed out that I'd spent the last three months eating one hamburger a day. I'd hardly spent anything. And he just said, yes, but do you know what Keith spent?

I could imagine what Keith spent but I'm still suspicious about that. There was always some suggestion that the Continental/Cadillac never ended up in the swimming pool. Or, if it did, that our management exaggerated the size of the salvage bill to get their hands on our money. I wasn't there and most of the people who were there were too out of it to provide reliable witness testimony. A few years ago, I challenged Chris Stamp on this. I asked him straight if he'd seen the car in the pool. He said he had. He swore blind he'd seen it with his own eyes. I'm still not convinced. Given the extent of the swindling going on, who knows? At the time, I believed them. I believed Keith had blown all the tour money. Either way, I came home from our first big money-spinning trip with less cash than I'd gone out with. I had to borrow the money for my flight home.

It hadn't been a complete waste of time. We'd made bad headlines in the newspapers and good headlines in the music press, which was the right way round. We hadn't exactly cracked America, but we'd certainly put a big dent in it. That autumn, 'I Can See For Miles' made the Top Ten in the US charts.

I went home skint.

It was always good to get back from a tour. To reacquaint yourself with home comforts. While I was away, I'd let my mates borrow the beloved Aston Martin DB4 I'd bought at the end of 1966. The first morning back I took it for a spin. As I pulled away from the kerb, it sounded great – smooth as a baby's bum, as they say. When I got it up to 40mph, though, it started to crab slightly sideways. At 70, the back was trying to overtake the front. Something was definitely amiss. Something had happened. It was only as I came to park it that I worked out what. The Aston was only two foot longer than the Mini I'd pulled up beside. It was almost two foot shorter than it had been when I'd left. Great for parking. Not great for driving.

With sheepish grins on their faces, my mates owned up. They'd driven it up the arse of a coach full of women on the King's Road, showing off. And then they'd got it 'fixed'.

I was in my early twenties when I'd bought that car. I didn't have a regular girlfriend. I had nothing else to worry about. So I spent all my time hanging out with my petrol-head mates from Acton and Chiswick. There was George the Weld, Jaymo the Rub and my best mate, Nobby the Fibreglass Kid.

George had a repair shop just round the corner from Chase Products in South Acton. I say repair shop. It was another asbestos-lined shed in a yard he shared with Franie the Rag and Bone man (a real-life Steptoe, horse and all). We all spent every day in George's yard trying to keep our respective cars on the road, going faster, looking cooler. Alongside Franie's horse and cart, my Aston, my pride and joy, looked really cool. Or it did right up until my mates decided to take it up the King's Road. Losing two foot off that car felt like losing two inches off my dick.

And then, less than a week later, it didn't seem to matter so much. I found the girl I would spend the rest of my life with and my world was turned completely upside down.

• • •

If I'm honest, I hadn't given Heather another thought since we chatted in our dressing room at *Murray the K*. And then, not long after getting back to London, I was sitting in the Speakeasy Club just behind Oxford Circus. It was three in the morning, I was jet-lagged and I was reading a book. I can't remember which book – let's say Dostoyevsky – and then a girl's voice says hello.

I look up and all I can see is legs. Skirts weren't really very long in those days. They left a lot of space for the legs. I looked up a lot further, and there were those beautiful eyes again. Heather, five foot eleven of gorgeous redhead, was looking down, smiling, and she said, 'Don't you remember me?'

I could remember the eyes and the legs but not the name.

'I'm Heather,' said Heather. 'You're friends with Catherine. She's been trying to call you.' Catherine was the girl who'd introduced us and now she was about to have a baby. It's none of your business which of my fellow musicians was responsible but she needed somewhere to stay.

She'd been calling the number I'd given her after we met up a few times in New York but with a Mayfair code. She never assumed a rock star would be living in Maida Vale. She would have done if she'd known who was running our accounts.

'Course she can stay,' I said.

'Can I stay, too?' Heather asks.

'Course you can.'

It frightens me to think how differently things could have turned out if she hadn't found me at the Speakeasy. Jimi Hendrix had been after her that night. He'd been after her for a while. She was his Foxy Lady but never his. If she'd gone home with him instead, then my life would have gone down any one of a hundred other paths, and none of them would have been as good. I would have lost the best thing that's ever happened to me, and I would never have known it. Instead, I got Heather, and Jimi went home with someone else.

I'm tired of wasting all my precious time
You've got to be all mine, all mine
Foxy lady
Here I come.

Unlucky, mate. Of course, we were meant to be together, me and Heather. Her family's from my manor. We only really found this out recently when my daughter looked us up on an ancestry website.

Heather's parents emigrated straight after the war and brought her up in America. But her grandparents lived at 62 Stowe Road, Shepherd's Bush. Two doors along from my dad and his six sisters. Two doors.

What are the chances? What I really find mind-blowing is that my parents and her gran met each other loads of times. Christmases. Birthday parties. Weddings. And not once did they ever work out that they'd been neighbours-but-one. The families must have known each other. In those days you knew everything about your street. You knew what underwear everyone was wearing from what wasn't on the line. Doris is wearing her red bra today. But not one word, all those years. Okay, they're from the loose-talk-costs-lives generation but, really, you'd think it might have cropped up just once.

It was my good fortune that Heather was raised in New York on stories from the olde worlde. She had Glaswegian-Irish blood on her mother's side and Shepherd's Bush Irish on her dad's. Her parents were always building Britain up and so she loved being around British people. She liked the way we dressed. She liked our hair.

'It was a different type of boy than you met in America,' she says now. 'Even though you had comparatively terrible teeth.' She's talking generally. The reason most of us had bad teeth was an unintended consequence of the welfare state. It might sound like bullshit, but the truth is that NHS dentists were then, and maybe still are today, paid by the amount of fillings and extractions they could rack up per month. If the system works that way, everyone had bad teeth.

When we first met, Harold Wilson was prime minister and Heather was appalled by his black teeth.

'Well, he smokes a pipe,' I explained.

'You can't be a prime minister and have black teeth,' she said. Wilson's teeth aside, she looked kindly upon Englishmen and, in particular, upon Englishmen from Shepherd's Bush. This gave me the edge over Jimi. My daughter, by the way, traced the Daltrey family tree back to 1509. My ancestors were Huguenot lacemakers in Nantes.

Creative people, those lacemakers. And they got right up the Pope's nose. Rebellion is in my blood.

NINE

TOMMY

B y the end of 1967, The Who was starting to do more experimental stuff in the studio and we were starting to laugh a bit together again. We had survived the first climb of our rollercoaster ride, and the first fall. And now we were building up for the loop-the-loop. It had taken those two years, but I think that's when we were together again. It's surprising that any bands stay together for any length of time because of the ingredients it requires. You have to have a certain amount of madness. There's some madness deep down in us all. With the four of us, it was nearer the surface. Madness. Ambition. Ego. Paranoia.

The paranoia was the real killer. If you asked Keith if he felt undervalued, he'd say yes. The Ox (John) would then chip in and say he was more undervalued. And Pete would chip in and say, 'Fuck you all, none of you appreciate the pressure I'm under.' And I wasn't a stranger to deep insecurity. That was the nature of The Who. It was founded on each other's paranoia.

I can remember Kit once chalking up the definition of paranoia on the blackboard in Track Records' offices on Old Compton Street. 'A paranoiac,' he scribbled, 'might be loosely defined as someone who knows what is actually going on.' I don't think we knew what was actually going on, but we thought we did.

All this is why the average rock band completes its full life cycle in 18 months. Record deal. Hit record. Debut album. Difficult second album. Falling out. Break up. The End. But if you can survive that first stage of the rollercoaster, it makes something special, something that can't be touched. You always feel like you're on a precipice – that you could fall at any moment. But if you can keep it all together, you might just be in for one hell of a ride. For us, that was *Tommy*, the first rock opera. We didn't know it. Pete still had to pluck it out of his brain and I still had to find my voice, but it was just around the corner, waiting to change everything.

For now, we were in and out of the studio, recording *The Who Sell Out*, our 'pop art' album, a stepping stone between our earlier records and *Tommy*. The legal disputes had been resolved and Shel Talmy was long gone. A year earlier, Track Records had been set up to 'give us more control'. The deal was that Kit and Chris would get 60 per cent of Track and we'd get 40. A nice not-even split. It would never work like that – not at all – but for now, we were focused on the next step.

Talmy had always been happy churning out remakes of The Kinks. Like a lot of producers, he didn't see the point of fixing something that wasn't broken. He just wanted the same thing again and again. But he got the job done. We could go into the studio, lay down an A-side and a B-side and be in the pub two hours later. With Kit, it could take a whole day to do one track and it would involve eight hours of searching for inspiration. I always thought it was worth it, though. Something new would come out of it.

If you listen to 'Rael', you would never guess, or I hope you would never guess, that it was done in a studio in New York that was smaller than your bathroom. Recording it was pure musical adventure. All those harmonies, building and building from a nutmeg of an idea. It helped that Pete's lyrics were just so different from anything else that was out there.

> *The Red Chins in their millions*
> *Will overspill their borders,*
> *And chaos then will reign in our Rael.*

He wrote that in the autumn of 1967, six years before the Yom Kippur War, and half a century later look where we are with the world. History repeats itself. It repeats itself far too often and 'Rael' was prophetic. Pete was prophetic. The rest of us understood that. We could recognise it. It wasn't always clear and it was never easy, but we could see Pete's gift and that he was trying to do more than just write another pop song.

I'm not political in that sense, but I'm aware of what's going on out there. And I do try and think, how are they ever going to solve this rather than just going round and round making the same mistakes? I could see that what Pete was doing was a way of opening things up to get people thinking. 'Rael' was a ridiculous pop song but it was extraordinary, too. It was a big step on from 'My Generation'. Which was a relief. A huge relief.

They were still smashing instruments. That went on for a while. But it wasn't the only thing we were about. The mini-opera on *The Who Sell Out* was a taste of what was to come. And it pushed me further. I had to find different voices to match these different lyrics.

I couldn't just use aggression or blues swagger to get through it. I had to change. Mick Jagger has always sounded like Mick Jagger with his mock-American blues voice, but with Pete's music I didn't want to sound like Roger Daltrey, circa 1966. The more I changed, the more Pete became intrigued by it. He wanted to know how much further he could develop it.

It helped that I was growing up. I was growing into my own skin and I was growing my own curly hair. I had moved into a proper flat in St John's Wood with my proper girlfriend. We had an arrangement that suited me perfectly. I paid the rent. She bought the food. This meant I only had to find money – it was about £14 – once a month and there was always food in the cupboard. It was relative domestic bliss and it meant I had someone to mop my brow when I was ill.

And I was ill, almost as soon as she moved in, thanks to the photo shoot for that album. Each of us was shot posing in a mock advert. Pete got Odorono. Keith got Medac, a fictitious acne cream. John timed his arrival at the studio late enough to get the girl in a leopard-skin bikini. Smart bastard. I got the short straw.

I turned up at the shoot and David Montgomery, portrait photographer to the stars, said, 'I want you to sit in a bath of baked beans.'

'Okay,' I said.

They put me in this striped Victorian swimsuit in a Victorian tin bath, and then they got out these four huge vats of Heinz Baked Beans.

The beans had just come out of the fridge and they were freezing. They were still runny but only just. After ten minutes, I started shivering so they got a two-bar electric fire and stuck it right round the back of the bath. After five minutes, it started to get really hot. I should have moved the hot beans at the back round to the front, like you do in a normal bath, but I didn't think of it at the time.

I was in there for about 45 minutes, and I swear the ones round my arse were cooked by the end of it. I went home and bosh, pneumonia. I couldn't stop shivering but I had a burnt arse.

It's a great album cover, though, and it's one of my favourite albums. I love it because it's a real tribute to those days before the BBC hijacked pop music. What we hear now is what Mother wants us to hear. The DJs on the pirate ships were real music fans, and the competition between them made them all musically adventurous. Back then, everyone listened to them, and the music was real. It was an outlet for our generation's music, and the BBC hated that. They hated losing control. With the government, they did everything they could to stop the pirate stations or, at the very least, stop kids listening to it. And they succeeded. There's a lot I love about the BBC but there's a lot I loathe, and that's right at the top of the list.

On 20 January 1968, we arrived in Sydney for an 11-night tour of Australia and New Zealand. It was us, the Small Faces and Paul Jones, who had left Manfred Mann by then. Paul was a good singer and a good harmonica player, but he was a different class of rock star. He was Oxford-educated. The others spent most of the trip taking the piss out of him, but I got on with him. I got on with Stevie Marriott, too. I admired him. I thought he was one of the best British rock singers of all time. Him and Terry Reid. Anyway, that was the good thing about the tour. Hanging out with other singers, not just the usual animals in my band. The bad thing was everything else.

Pete opened proceedings by punching a reporter who asked him how he felt about the devalued pound. It wasn't a particularly friendly question to throw someone who had just flown 36 hours via Cairo, Bombay, Karachi and Singapore, and it went downhill from there.

Australia is like any other part of the civilised world today but, back then, it was like nowhere we'd ever seen. Every building still had a tin roof. There was no air conditioning. Wherever we went, there were screaming girls and, just behind them, a posse of their redneck boyfriends trying to beat us up.

We played two nights at Sydney Stadium, a massive old structure with a revolving stage that, in better days, hosted boxing matches. The idea was that you'd play a couple of songs facing one third of the audience and then some heavies would winch you round so you could play the next couple of songs to the next third, and so on. Halfway through the Small Faces set, the stage got stuck. None of the heavies could budge it. None of the technicians could fix it. It still wasn't working by the time we came on. Which means, if my maths is correct, two-thirds of the audience only ever saw the backs of our heads.

The whole tour was a disaster. The sound was shit. I couldn't hear anything. The equipment was shit and it was borrowed, so they didn't like it when we smashed it up, which we did because it was shit. The press had it in for us because we were young and British, we had long hair, filthy mouths and we were shagging their daughters.

And then one of us dared to open a can of beer on an aeroplane. It happened the morning after the gig in Adelaide. We had been put on a 10am flight back to Sydney. It's never a good idea to be around a rock band at ten in the morning and it wasn't long before a ruckus broke out.

Bobby Pridden, our sound man, had opened a bottle of beer. What was the big deal? Well, it turns out you're not allowed to consume alcohol when you're flying over the state of South Australia. Not in 1968, anyway. Who knew? But Bobby's beer was the fuse that sparked an inflight mini-riot.

First of all, I heard someone, probably Steve Marriott, telling the stewardess he was fifth in line to the throne and he could do what he wanted. Then, when the captain was called, Bobby concluded their heated discussion by shouting, 'How dare you call me a scruffy little man when your shirt isn't even properly cleaned.'

Well, that was it. The captain stormed back to his cockpit, sparked up the tannoy and announced that he was diverting the plane because of 'a disturbance'. The next thing we knew we were landing at Essendon airport. You would think they would just have chucked Bobby and Steve off the flight for their outrageous behaviour, but, no, all 19 of us, the bands and the roadies, were ejected. It was fabulous. We marched off the plane in a long line with our hands up in surrender and, of course, the entire press corps was there to catch it on camera.

Frankly, if you pissed your pants down under in those days it would have made the front page for a week. That's how much of a backwater it was. So this was a big story. It was tabloid gold and it would keep them going all year. '*Invasion of the pop singers*' was the front-page headline in the Melbourne *Age* the next day.

The captain of the next flight to Sydney refused to let us board, and we were only allowed on the one after that when we promised, crossed our hearts and hoped to die, that we'd cause no trouble, not that we had in the first place. Just to be absolutely sure, two dour security officials flew with us.

By the time we got to New Zealand, we'd received a telegram from the Australian prime minister, John Gorton. '*Dear Who's,*' he wrote, '*We never wanted you to come to Australia. You have behaved atrociously while you've been here, and we hope you never come back.*'

Pete took that literally and said, 'Right, fine, we're never going back.' That was a mistake. In the late nineties I went back on my own and I could see it had completely changed. I told him we were mad not to go there. When we finally did go back in 2004, he told the audience that he'd been wrong. And those shows went down great. Our audiences had dropped away a bit but that's what happens if you don't go back for 36 years. The second time we went, the numbers were great again. You're only as good as your last show.

Less than a month after we left Auckland, we were in California, setting off on the first of two big tours of America. Once again, I was on the hamburger diet, trying to save some cash. I was tired of renting a flat in St John's Wood. It was getting quite claustrophobic. You couldn't go outside. There were always girls outside, girls everywhere. Heather and I were in the top flat and every time you looked out they'd be there, in the front garden. It can't have been much fun for the neighbours either, but I was surprised how well they treated us. And the girls were all right, too – they didn't scream. It's just that there was no privacy at all. And, just up the road, the Walker Brothers had a flat, and they did have the screamers. Even at two hundred paces, it was loud enough to make sleep difficult.

The plan was to come back from the American tours with a grand to put a deposit down on a house outside London. Trying to spoil the plan, of course, was Keith Moon. If 1967 was the year he discovered cherry bombs, 1968 was the year of the Super Glue, the piranhas and the snake. The Super Glue is self-explanatory. I just feel sorry for all the hotel maids confronted with suddenly immovable furniture and toilet seats and wine glasses on the ceiling. The piranhas were John's idea. He was quiet and in the background, but he was very much a member of Keith's cohort. He had more of a mean streak than Keith, though. Look at the lyrics to 'Boris the Spider', which he wrote. He had a dark side. And it was him who put the piranhas in the hotel bath. I can't remember whose bath it was but I remember looking at the piranhas and thinking they didn't look very aggressive. John got sold a lemon.

The snake was definitely not a lemon. I was given it by this girl in Albuquerque, New Mexico. It was one of the stranger gifts I've been given but she was a Native American, and I was very grateful.

The bullsnake looked almost identical to a rattlesnake but it didn't have a rattle. Or a deadly bite. We used to carry this false rattler around in a pillowcase, and we called him Adolf. Keith kept borrowing him 'for a bit of fun'. He'd pop up with a grin, take Adolf out of his pillowcase and disappear. The next minute, you'd hear screams.

Adolf became a huge focus of attention on the flights, and he was an integral part – a fifth member – of our band for at least three weeks. The trouble was, we couldn't get him to eat. We tried everything, but he wasn't interested. He just kept trying to escape. He was an incredible escapologist. One minute, he'd be having a snooze in his pillowcase, the next he'd be gone, up on the pelmets, out of the tiniest crack in a window. It was almost as if he didn't like touring with us, and I knew how that felt. I liked that snake. Adolf was calm and quiet – two attributes which were in rare supply in the rest of the band.

We lost Adolf in San Diego. He was in the motel room and then he wasn't. We searched and searched but he was gone. I like to think that there's still a grotty room somewhere in the wrong part of San Diego where people go in and they never come out. And there's a 35-foot-long bullsnake who finally found his appetite.

When Adolf left, Keith fell back on his trusty supply of cherry bombs. At 4am on 5 April, we were thrown out of the Hotel Gorham in New York. It was a pretty whiffy hotel but it was nice. I liked it. I was having a good sleep. And then I learned that Keith had thrown cherry bombs from the ninth-floor window. He'd blown up a toilet and a nice old lady in an elevator. So we were all out. There was only enough time to dress, half asleep, grab my things and step out onto West 55th Street.

Worse, the Gorham let every other hotel in Manhattan know what had happened so it took until 6am to find a place far enough away and unscrupulous enough to take us. We ended up on the beltway out towards the airport. The next night, we were booked at the Waldorf. A step up from the Gorham. They insisted on a cash surety. We didn't have the cash. So we were thrown out before we even had a chance to unpack. And when Keith couldn't get back into his room to retrieve his luggage, he blew the door up with the cherry bombs he had left over from the night before. We were turfed out onto Park Avenue.

So that was the Waldorf, the Gorham, all the Holiday Inns, most of the Hiltons and some of the Sheratons. Once we got bigger and more organised, I started to stay in separate hotels from Keith. If I found somewhere at least a block away, I was guaranteed some kip. That was important, not just for my own sanity but also for the gig. If I didn't sleep, I couldn't sing.

Back then, I just got used to it. Half the time I didn't unpack, just so I had less packing to do when the manager or the police came knocking. Officially, the hotels minded. Unofficially, they loved us. I promise you, they loved us. We paid cash for the damage. They claimed insurance. They got the cash and they got some nice new interior decoration. Over the next decade, the Navarro managed an entire renovation. When they thought they needed a room remodelled, they would allocate that room to Keith. And Keith would then oblige by wrecking it in the night and paying for it in the morning. They were onto a winner.

• • •

Miraculously, I came home from the first US tour of 1968 tour with a bit of cash. I got back to Heather on 8 April, knackered and sleep-deprived, but I had that precious grand in my pocket. Just enough for the deposit on our first house. The problem was that I still had the sideways Aston and I was sick to death of it. So I took the precious grand to the car auction and bought a lovely old Mark 10 Jag.

Heather went ape-shit. She told me to take the Jag back. I tried to point out that you couldn't take a car back to the auction, but ten stressful minutes later I was taking it back. I called George the Weld and we went through the car's contract. We found enough wrong with it to get my money back.

I was out of the doghouse but I had to spend the next few months in a Mini. It nearly broke my back, especially as one of the gigs was in Inverness. But it meant I wasn't getting shouted at by Heather any more. The car after that was a sit-up-and-beg

Volvo, by the way. Keith and John had their chauffeured Bentley. Pete had all manner of sports cars. I just needed something to get me from A to B without breaking down or upsetting my beautiful Glaswegian-New Yorker.

With the change left over from the Mini, I managed to get a mortgage, and that summer, while I was off on another long US tour, Heather moved into our first home in Hurst, Berkshire. These days, the home counties are full of ageing rock stars. They've all moved out of town in search of peace, quiet and a place to keep their guitar collection.

It was not the thing to do when we did it. Elder Cottage was only 30 miles from London but it was a big step. Everyone we knew was in town. Nobody we knew was in Berkshire. Alvin Lee moved in round the corner and so did Jimmy Page, but when we went it felt like we were the first.

But I didn't give it a second thought. I wanted to live in the country. I think I always did. It was a deep psychological need. The happiest times of my childhood were when I skipped away to the river or found some overgrown bombsite to play in. It was pure wilderness. The wrecked basements had filled with water and become a home to frogs and toads, and me and my mates. It had all reverted to nature, forming a string of natural tunnels and hideouts. When I was older and unhappier, when I played truant and went down to Dukes Meadow out of sheer desperation to escape the hell of school, it was the peace and quiet of the river that made me feel grounded for the first time. During childhood, I had to find nature in west London and now I had a chance to find it for real.

The village was great. It had a butcher, a baker, a post office – everything for your everyday needs. The Green Man pub was its life and soul, just as it had been since the 1600s. We could just walk in and we were accepted. More or less. All the City gents used to get off the train at Twyford in their pinstripe suits and bowler hats and come into the pub to see the freak show.

I was just back from a summer in America. I'd come back with a brand new Chevy Stingray that I'd bought in Detroit, and which was already quite a sight for the locals. But in California I'd seen the last of the straightness going out and the whole hippy thing coming in. The frock coats and ruffled shirts were gone. The dandy was no more. I was growing my curly hair. I was out and proud. And I started borrowing all Heather's catwalk clothes. I took her boots on tour. I wore her white leather jacket. We made it up as we went along, which was brilliant. Fashion was getting more flamboyant in Haight-Ashbury, San Francisco, but Haight-Ashbury was a long way from Hurst. Those pinstriped regulars thought our threads were hilarious, but they got to know us and we all became good friends.

Pete would have hated the idea that these stockbrokers were getting on with us, but I didn't give a shit. It was a pub. Pubs are only ever as good as their landlords, and Jim and Anna at the Green Man were the best. There was no piped music. Conversation ruled and it was an absolute delight.

Our home was a 15th-century cottage with very low ceilings. Heather and Devon had to bend down to get inside but I was just the right height. It was romantic.

I was 24 and I suppose I was settling down. We all were. Keith had married his Leicester surfer girl Kim and they already had a kid. John married his childhood sweetheart Alison and they were living in domestic bliss in a semi-detached house in Acton (the address of which John had immediately changed to 'The Bastille'). And Pete had married Karen the year before. I didn't go to the wedding. Heather wanted to go but she had bronchitis, and there were too many people there with shows to do. We couldn't be responsible for wiping out half the country's vocalists. So I volunteered to stay home and look after her. That wasn't an excuse. She was very ill. But I'll be honest, I didn't like weddings. I'd already had enough bad experiences at them. I prefer funerals. I've always preferred funerals.

People go to weddings, they get pissed, they have an argument and it ends in a fight. At a funeral, everyone's happy to see each other, they're all saying nice things about the dead bloke, and then they go home happy.

Anyway, the point is we weren't teenagers any more. We weren't living the lives of wild bohemian rock stars night in, night out, any more – well, not when we were home at any rate. As a band, we weren't hanging out together either. When I wasn't touring, I spent most of my time in Berkshire. Rock years are like dog years. We were getting on a bit in rock years.

I was a commuter. I didn't have the pinstripe suit, but every day I'd drive in to IBC studios and, most nights, I'd drive back again. We started recording *Tommy* in September 1968 and we were supposed to be done by Christmas. Fat chance. It was March before we got to the final sessions. Seven months. Our longest time together in the studio by a long stretch, but *Tommy* wasn't like any other record we'd done before. It wasn't like any other record, full stop.

The main thing I remember is that I loved the idea. I loved it the first time I heard it. I can't remember exactly when Pete first mentioned it to us. He'd been scribbling away on the endless tour bus journeys around America and he'd told *Melody Maker* he was doing a rock opera called 'Journey Into Space'. He told *Rolling Stone* a lot of things, all in one go. But by September, he had a sketchy outline. Tommy was deaf, dumb and blind and he experienced life completely through vibration. I just loved that. Music is vibration. That's the whole point. It was an abstract idea, but I knew there was something in it and I just went with it.

When we started it, it was only going to be a single album. And as the songs came through, Kit guided it into the story it became. People tend to forget that Pete didn't write the whole of *Tommy*. It was his inspiration, but it was about as collaborative as anything we ever did. It wasn't at all formed at the start.

He used to turn up with demos every morning. They were brilliant but by the time it had gone through the studio, it had moved on. The story kept changing. Fragments of songs grew into whole plot lines. It was like putting a jigsaw together with no picture, no straight edges and half the pieces missing, but it was completely absorbing.

Pete would lay down the tracks and if anybody had a suggestion we'd throw it into the hat. I worked on the harmonies. I spent a lot of time trying to work out the voice. With Kit's help, it changed from something quite vague and philosophical into something set in the real world, in Britain. Pete gave the job of Uncle Ernie to John, which worked perfectly. Musically, John was very clever and his view of life was pretty dark, so he wrote the character in a particular way with a really ominous tone. That might have had something to do with the fact that John's dad left him and his mother in his early years. His mother married again and John never had a good word to say for his stepdad. I think it's fair to say he hated him. Uncle Ernie, a character we'd all seen as a bit of a joke, became a lot darker once John got hold of him.

It was Keith's idea to send Tommy to the holiday camp at the end. It was based on a very dark joke at the time. The concentration camp – a holiday that lasts forever. My apologies to my Jewish friends for our lack of feeling, but that was where humour was in those days. You wouldn't get away with it now. You wouldn't get away with that whole story today.

Pete never talked about where all this was coming from and we never asked him. We just let him get on with it. If we'd started to analyse it too much, it would have slowed his process. We'd still be in the studio now. And he needed the freedom.

It was only when we finished the jigsaw that we saw the complete picture. Even then, it's not exactly the clearest picture, is it? Some of the songs just don't fit into any plot. But I'll tell you what, even to this day, when you play *Tommy* in its entirety, it's so complete; it's so wonderful. The simplicity of it. The power in the lyrics. The journey. It builds and builds. It was still building when we took it out of the studio. And it was magical to play right from those opening chords. It was so unrock, but rock. It was genius. And Pete deserves everything he got from it.

It was only when we took it out live that I really got to grips with where I could go with my voice. We rehearsed it at the Southall Community Centre in March 1969 and, by the fourth run through, we'd worked it out. It was a live stage show and I felt like I'd been set free. Everything I learned to do with my voice came from *Tommy*, and it happened in those four rehearsals. I just changed. It was always in my voice. I'd been getting there with Pete's earlier songs but *Tommy* brought it out like that.

We had one weekend of student gigs in Scotland before we launched Tommy with a press preview at Ronnie Scott's in Soho. The journalists were all pissed before we got on. They all heckled when Pete introduced it as 'a story about a boy who witnesses a murder and becomes deaf, dumb and blind. He is later raped by his uncle and gets turned on to LSD.'

So we turned the amps up even louder and just went for it. An hour solid. Driving, driving, driving. No pauses for wild applause or critical derision. No breaks at all. They left with their ears ringing. None of them knew what had hit them.

TEN

ESCAPE
TO THE
COUNTRY

By the time *Tommy* was released in Britain on 23 May 1969, we were off touring in the States. We started well with three nights at the Grande Ballroom in Dearborn, Michigan, and another three in Boston, all building to a three-night, six-show marathon at the Fillmore East, New York. Ever since the first live rehearsals in Southhall, I knew we had something magical on our hands. This tour was going to take us to another level. And then came the man in the sports jacket.

It was half ten and we were playing 'Pinball Wizard' in the middle of the second show the first night at the Fillmore, when this bloke jumped up onto the stage and grabbed the microphone off me. I grabbed it back and told him to fuck off, but he kept struggling. As we were wrestling with it, I notice Pete crossing the stage towards us, doing a Chuck Berry duck walk. Perfectly on beat, he kicks the bloke in the balls, then I grab the mike and we finish the song.

The next thing I know, Bill Graham, the promoter, is on, pointing out that the bloke in the sports jacket, the bloke Pete kicked in the balls, is a plainclothes member of New York's elite tactical police force. He'd tried to commandeer the microphone because a fire had broken out in the Chinese supermarket next door. The building needed to be evacuated.

It's lucky he didn't get the mike. He would have caused a riot if he'd stopped us right in the middle of a song. Bill had been preparing to make a low-key announcement at the next break. That's how you evacuate a crowd in the middle of a gig. Calmly.

But the next thing we knew, there was a warrant out for our arrest. The copper was claiming he showed me his badge before we attacked him. I tell you now, hand on heart, he never showed his badge. And even if he did, which he didn't, I wouldn't have seen it. You're in a different world up there when you're performing. I wouldn't have had a clue what some random bloke was showing me.

It didn't matter. Pete and I were fugitives. We were on the run. We didn't go back to the hotel. We didn't dare. Instead, we called International Rescue which, in our case, was the network of girls we knew in New York. Pete stayed with Mandy Wilson. I ended up on the other side of town with Jenni Dean, another of our happy band of wonderful women. I woke up to the sound of Hispanic women shouting at each other through the tenement windows. Word came through the groupie grapevine from Kit and Chris that they had negotiated our surrender. We were to hand ourselves in at the Ninth Precinct police station, so we did. For nine hours we were stuck in the cage getting eyeballed by our fellow prisoners while Kit tried to convince the coppers not to charge us with felonious assault. They should have been glad nobody died but the authorities relished any chance to have a pop at a rock band.

Eventually, I got off without charge. Pete was done for third-degree assault and arraigned for a court hearing the following week. We got back to the Fillmore just in time for the 8pm show.

• • •

I always knew we'd never make it on records alone. You had to see us live. When people saw us live, we had them. By 1969, we had reached a new level of performance. Unlike any other band, The Who had a bass player who played like a lead guitarist, a guitarist who played like a drummer and a drummer who, instead of playing just four to the floor, gave you the whole score. Physically, I had been transformed as well. I was playing the character and I had absolute freedom of expression in sound and movement. Sometimes I was on my own. Sometimes I was synchronised with Pete's great windmilling arms and Olympic high-jumps. Keith was upstaging his own upstaging. It was ballet.

By the time we reached Chicago, the show had got longer. It was an hour and ten minutes, then an hour and 20, then it pushed beyond that. And there were no breaks. What we'd started at Ronnie Scott's had grown into one continuous 90-minute show, and at the Playground in Chicago it just all came together. The audience started off sitting down and then halfway through they all stood up. You could feel the tension building and then, at the end, they just went crazy. It was new for us and it was new for the audience.

By the end of the summer, the physical and emotional exhaustion of touring *Tommy* had taken its toll. We'd dragged ourselves to the furthest points of America and Canada, we'd flown home to share a fraught gig with Chuck Berry at the Albert Hall, and each night the performance just kept building. It was intense. The reward? *Tommy* became our first album to get into the Top Five in the USA. And then we had to do Woodstock. I say had to because even though it's gone down in history as a seminal moment in 20th-century culture, it wasn't much fun. Three days of peace and love? Do me a favour. It was crazy even before we arrived. Pete spent several hours in the traffic jams. Other artists didn't make it at all. The whole place was chaos.

Fortunately, I had a different mode of transport.

'Chuck will drive you,' Heather's mum had said while we were visiting them in Connecticut. Chuck and Helen, Heather's parents, were still young. They wanted to go to Woodstock. We wanted them to drop us off and leave as quickly as possible, but you can't have everything. So we all piled into their bright red VW Beetle – Herbie goes to Woodstock – and when we reached the traffic jams I told Chuck to drive us up the hard shoulder.

'Don't worry if the police stop us, Chuck. I'll sort it out.'

No one minded. Everyone just waved Herbie through.

We made it through in the early afternoon of Saturday 16 August 1969, at what we thought would be something to behold. On every news outlet in America, Woodstock was THE story. Nothing like it had ever been seen before. The crowd on site was estimated at half a million. Many more were still trying to get there despite the governor of New York declaring it a national disaster. If the governor of New York tells you something's bad, you know it's going to be good.

. The destination we arrived at was a little different. A Holiday Inn with a large sign ironically saying 'Camp Tranquility'. All the bands were there. Jefferson Airplane, Big Brother and the Holding Company, Grateful Dead, Hendrix … the musicians had the rooms and the roadies and technicians slept in the corridors. Everyone all just hanging around and waiting their turn to go to the site. And we waited and waited and waited. At about 7pm, we drove to the backstage area in the obligatory Hertz station wagon. And waited some more. You hope things will be running like clockwork but at festivals in those days, particularly inaugural festivals, they never were and they certainly weren't at Woodstock. We were due on in the evening but by four the next morning we were still hanging around backstage in a muddy field waiting. And waiting some more.

Even at the best of times, I hate doing nothing. Doing nothing while you're waiting to play to half a million people is the hardest thing in the world. It's not because of the half-million people. It's never mattered to me if I was singing to one man and his dog in a pub, 80,000 people at Hyde Park or half a million on a dairy farm in the Catskills. In my mind, I always treat it the same way. Give it everything you've got to give. And that's hard if you're waiting. It's the boredom laced with the tension. You have to be ready. You have to keep a grip. But you can't go over the boil.

Keith found it harder. He used to get terrible nerves. He used to throw up before gigs. He was terrified of that first stroll out onto the stage. It came a lot harder to him. I think that's what kicked off his alcoholism. The fear of going onstage. He'd have to have a drink to settle his nerves. The first drink was a brandy. The second drink was a large brandy and then it was the bottle. And he hadn't even gone on yet.

I imagine he found that 14-hour wait at Woodstock particularly hard. There was no food backstage. Everything was laced with LSD. Even the ice cubes had been done. Fortunately, I'd brought in my own bottle of Southern Comfort so I was fine right up until the moment I decided to have a cup of tea. That's how they got me. A nice cup of hallucinogenic tea.

Everything was breaking down. Everything and everyone was soaking wet. There were constant power cuts. People were climbing up on the stage, climbing up the lighting rigs. Pete said he saw a kid falling from one of the rigs and possibly breaking his neck. It was billed as an Aquarian Exposition – three days of peace and music. But it was chaos.

And then halfway through the night the organisers decided they weren't going to pay us. Our fee was $11,200, most of which we'd already spent on the flights for us and the crew. We needed the cash to get home and pay the bills, so we refused to go on until we were paid. There's a story about how a bank manager was woken in the middle of the night and put on a helicopter to crack the local bank's safe, retrieve our cash and chopper into Woodstock to pay us in crisp stacks of twenties. It's a great story but it didn't happen. Our tour manager just eyeballed the organisers until they gave us a cheque.

After all the arguments, the hallucinations, the mud and the chaos, we were finally onstage, sometime after 5am.

About a month earlier, I'd woken up from a particularly vivid nightmare. It was the kind you have when you're a kid. I was looking out on some barren, smoke-filled landscape. There were guard towers with searchlights scanning around and there were helicopters overhead. It was a subconscious approximation of Vietnam. Looking out into the pre-dawn gloom of Woodstock, making out the vague shape of half a million mud-caked people as the lights swept over them, I felt in my sleep-deprived, hallucinating state, that this was my nightmare come true.

The show didn't feel like it went well. The monitors kept breaking. The sound was shit. We were all battling the elements and ourselves. It didn't help when a political activist called Abbie Hoffman climbed onto the stage at the end of 'Pinball Wizard', grabbed Pete's mike and shouted, 'I think this is a pile of shit while John Sinclair rots in prison.'

Naturally, Pete booted him off the stage before threatening to kill the next person who tried to take his mike. Music and peace.

Somehow, we kept going and every time we felt like we were losing it, we dug in a bit deeper. Then, shortly after six, we got to 'See Me, Feel Me' from *Tommy* and the bleeding sun came up. Right on cue. You couldn't have topped it. After all the shit we'd been through, it was perfect. It was extraordinary. It was one of those moments you couldn't ever recreate if you tried. Once in a lifetime.

Except exactly the same thing happened again on 25 April 2015, a mere 46 years later. We were due to headline at the New Orleans Jazz Festival and it had been pissing with rain all day. A tropical storm had just been through and the whole place was drenched. It's always chaos when it's so wet. It plays havoc with the electrics and it's always disconcerting when you see an amp half-submerged in a foot of water. I got to the trailer, looked out of the window and told Mitch, my assistant, not to worry. I'd sort it out. He said, doubtfully, 'Okay, Roger.' Cynical young man. And I started shouting at the sky, 'Stop it. Stop now. We've had enough of this crap.'

And it did. Right on cue. Like someone had turned a tap off. Mitch didn't say anything. I didn't say anything but, to be honest, I was just as shocked as he was.

The sky was dark grey when we went onstage. It stayed like that right up until the end of 'Pinball Wizard'. As I opened my mouth to sing 'See Me, Feel Me', the sun broke through. Absolute magic. That's what I love about live shows. Things can happen. Some of those things are bad. Some of them are good. Occasionally, they're magic. That was one of those twice-in-a-lifetime moments.

Two weeks after Woodstock we played the Isle of Wight Festival. There was no Herbie this time. We went in by helicopter, which was significantly more rock 'n' roll, particularly given that a piece of board from the festival's makeshift H for helipad sign dislodged and flew up into the rotors as our pilot was trying to land. We did the last few metres of the journey 'at speed'. The helicopter was knackered but we were all fine.

That's not normally how things end up if you crash a helicopter. We went onstage, we played *Tommy*, we flew back to London in another helicopter. Job done.

Who paid for the helicopters? Track Records. Who paid Track Records? Us. After Woodstock, the money had really started rolling in. *Life* magazine had done an entire commemorative issue on the festival, and I was the lucky bloke who occupied the photo on the centre spread. Me and my fringe jacket. It was a new level of exposure and our careers rocketed almost immediately. For the first time, we had to start using pseudonyms when we travelled. Inevitably, this became another source of mischief. I'm not sure what the receptionists would have thought when Lord Elpus, John Fitzperfectly and Miles Apart checked in for the night but it gave us a laugh.

In 1969, Neil Armstrong took one small step for man and one giant leap for mankind. Friends came over to watch it with us because we were the only people in the village to have a colour television. It was a huge great cube of a thing providing 36 inches of the very latest in audiovisual technology. Everyone was excited. The moon landings ... in colour. What a moment in history. Only trouble was that space is black and the moon is white. Armstrong wasn't exactly making the most of the Technicolor broadcast either.

'What do you think of the colour TV, then?' I asked one of the old boys, jokingly.

'Fantastic,' he replied, genuinely enthralled.

That was the year people started to describe us as millionaires. I might have had enough cash for a posh television, but millionaires? That was a load of bollocks. It was bollocks because all the money we were supposed to be making was getting spent. It was rolling in and it was rolling out again on legitimate expenses and less legitimate ones. We had our 40-60 deal, but in reality it meant very little.

In 1969, cocaine arrived in the music industry. It had always been around, but now Chris and Kit started getting into it in a big way. Kit would have a line when he woke up. He'd come into Track Records at 11. He'd have a joint. Then he'd drop a few pills. Then he'd have another line. Then he'd go out for lunch. He was a drug addict and you don't want a drug addict running your business. Particularly if your business is rock 'n' roll. The bigger we got, the more money we made, but the faster and more wildly Kit spent it, the less of any percentage we saw. By the end of 1969, we were the biggest rock band in the world. We were headlining festivals. We were the first band to sell out six nights at the Fillmore West in less than an hour. We were filling opera houses. And we were barely breaking even.

• • •

Four days into the new decade, Keith Moon ran over and killed his chauffeur and bodyguard, Neil Boland, outside Keith's friend's pub in Hatfield. It was an accident. It was a panic reaction to escape a mob of skinheads. They'd followed him out of the pub, trying to pick a fight. They surrounded the car and started attacking it. Neil got out to clear the way. Keith drove away. In the chaos, no one realised Neil had fallen under the wheels.

I phoned Keith the next day to ask if he was okay. He said he was but of course he wasn't. He was obviously in deep remorse. They tried to do him for manslaughter. He got off with a charge of drink-driving, but he still had to relive the whole thing in court and I don't know how he got through that. He didn't get away with it, not by any stretch. He was haunted by it, and his drinking just got worse and worse.

When he wasn't with us, he spent all his time with Viv Stanshall and Legs Larry from Bonzo Dog, raising merry hell. Viv was a perfect partner in crime for Keith. He was a wonderful, colourful eccentric. He looked like something from Rupert Bear. On a quiet day, they'd walk into a Savile Row shop and ask if they had any really strong trousers. 'Really strong trousers, sir?'

'Yes, really strong.'

The bloke would come out with a pair of trousers. Keith would get in one leg, Viv would get in the other and, rip.

'Sorry, they're not strong enough.'

On a day when they had more energy, Viv would dress up as a priest and Keith would drop him at the top of Oxford Street. Then Keith, dressed as a Nazi officer, obviously, would do a few laps in his purple Rolls before doubling back to Oxford Street. With no warning to the afternoon shoppers, he'd jump out of the roller, scream at Viv and then start pretending to beat the shit out of him. Why? To see how people would react to the sight of an SS officer attacking a priest. Of course, nobody did anything. So Keith would stand to attention, give it the full 'Heil Hitler', jump back into the Roller and drive off. Viv would limp away and they'd meet sometime later for a celebratory drink.

The two of them thought it was hilarious. I'm sure it was hilarious at the time, even if it isn't with hindsight. But the underlying force driving Keith into all these japes was a need to be the centre of attention. He felt like he was nothing without the attention or the bottle. Remember what his teacher wrote in his report? Must guard against a tendency to show off.

He didn't have that guard. He was in a rock band. His whole life was showing off. When Neil died, it was a terrible blow, and a lot of people have said that that was the beginning of the end for Keith. There's no doubt it was a source of terrible guilt and it played on his mind, but the real catalyst, the thing that set him on a darker course, was losing his wife Kim. That really escalated things. After that, he lost the last few boundaries he had.

Keith and Kim bought Tara House in Chertsey in 1971 from Peter Collinson, the film director who did *The Italian Job*. It was, of course, an unusual home – an abstract bungalow with five pyramids on top, all sorts of *Tomorrow's World* gadgetry and a huge sunken central living room and a pub at the end of the drive. Kim described it as an upside-down egg box. It could have been their first proper family home – their daughter Mandy was four when they moved in – but Keith made it party central instead. He wasn't good when he wasn't touring. He never practised. He didn't even have a drum kit there. He got bored, he got depressed, he hit the pills and the bottle. Within six months, he'd driven the Rolls into the pond. He claimed he was just trying to bump-start it, but I'm sure he did it for a laugh. He'd smashed up the house a few times, too. When we took a break in 1972, he was bouncing off the walls.

His antics pushed Kim, the girl he always loved, away and, eventually, she started seeing Ian McLagan from the Faces. When Keith found out about it, he went berserk and smashed the whole place up, and he did it in front of his daughter Mandy. It makes me feel sick thinking about it. He was just completely off his head on brandy and pills.

That night, he broke Kim's nose, and that was the final straw for her. She walked out and she never came back. I don't know whether he had ever hit her before but he had been violent. He'd thrown a Champagne bottle at her at their flat in Highgate. The bottle missed but he'd thrown it hard enough that it had embedded itself in the wall. The next day, he put a frame round it and got our publicist to call the newspapers. It made a full page in one of the Sundays and people thought it was all a great laugh, but it wasn't a laugh at all.

The truth was, he idolised her and he was a jealous man. We were all jealous at that age. I used to find it difficult when Heather was chatting to some guy and he was clearly trying it on. But I couldn't say anything. Not after I'd just got back from some tour. But that didn't mean I didn't have it in me.

Keith was on a different level, though. He was an incredibly jealous man. Once, he paid some heavy 200 quid to break Ian's fingers. Pete found out and paid the same heavy another 200 quid to do nothing. It was Keith's jealousy that drove Kim away. When I saw her after the night Keith broke her nose, she told me she loved him and that she had put up with all his destructive behaviour because of that. But following that night, she had no choice but to leave. She left the house that night with Mandy and they checked into a hotel. It was final. That was that. He'd lost the thing he cherished the most. And he would never get over her.

• • •

About the same time Keith was moving to his egg box in Surrey (chosen partly, I suspect, because it had that pub at the end of the drive), I was heading south to something altogether more traditional. Heather and I weren't really in the market to buy a house. We had no money. We were happy enough in our cottage in deepest, darkest Berkshire. But there was no harm in looking. I used to go around with a friend of mine who ran an estate agent's. He'd go off and check all these houses and I'd go with him. One beautiful Saturday in late spring, he took me and Heather down to Sussex. We passed one For Sale sign on a bend in front of some farm buildings. Over a wall, you could see a house in the distance and Heather asked what it was. My friend said we'd have a look on the way back. They're clever, these estate agents.

We went on to look at Pashley Manor, a Tudor house once owned by Henry VIII, but I didn't like the vibe. If I don't like the vibe, that's it. I'm very susceptible to ground energy. I can't explain it but there are places I go to that I have to get out of. It's like someone has dimmed the lights. I just have to get away.

Anyway, I wasn't going to buy Pashley Manor, even if we could afford it, which we couldn't. We looked at a couple of other places and then we got back to the place on the bend with the For Sale sign. The friend turned off the main road and there it was: Holmshurst. We were shown around the house by a young kid whose parents were getting divorced and there was just something about the place. It was in good condition, but nothing had been done to it for a long, long time. The hallway was black as pitch, there was damp, the kitchen was terrible but nothing frightening. Then we walked up into the front room and I saw the view for the first time.

The house is on a hill looking west across the valleys and villages of the High Weald of East Sussex. You can see for miles and miles and miles and miles, no drugs required. The first time I looked out, I just stood open-mouthed and knew I had to live there. I thought to myself, 'With this view, I'm safe.'

I asked the friend how much it was and he said, '£39,500. A bargain. But whoever offers the money first can have it.' So I said, right, offer the money and I'll worry about finding it later. All I had to do was convince the bank manager to lend it to me. If everyone else assumed I was a millionaire, why wouldn't he? I went straight into the bank and managed to raise the loan. The offer went in first thing on Monday and by five that night it was accepted.

I called Heather, all excited.

She didn't sound over the moon. I asked her what the matter was.

She said, 'There's going to be an awful lot of cleaning.' Never happy.

We moved into the place that would be our home for the rest of our lives on 26 June 1971, and the first week in was wonderful. The road crew moved us in. We had a party every night. It was the ultimate hippy crash pad and it felt great. Holmshurst is a very special house and it grounded me. It was built for a Puritan. There's nothing fancy about it. It's a simple, functional place which suits me. I'm no Puritan but I do like to work. I do like things to be functional, on the level. And that was Holmshurst. But Heather was right, there was an awful lot of cleaning.

A few days later, my decree absolute came through from my first marriage and, the following month, Heather and I tied the knot at Battle registry office. We didn't have a wedding reception. There was no need because we'd already had one the year before. We had planned to get married in the summer of 1970. We'd organised this big wedding and everyone was invited. All the bands. All the music industry bigwigs and most of the village. We'd even got Ahmet Ertegun, president of Atlantic Records, to trudge out to this three-acre field in Berkshire in his never-before-used wellies. It was going to be a huge event.

The field belonged to a Miss Gwendoline Taylor, a very respectable lady from the village, but it was used by Eric Goody, a large and portly Mr Micawber character with rosy red cheeks and bright blue eyes, that twinkled devilishly beneath his flat tweed cap.

I first met Eric when he turned up on our doorstep about a month after we'd moved into Elder Cottage. He was wearing a white shirt, a bright red waistcoat and large brown dealer boots.

'I've come to meet the real Roger Daltrey,' he declared. Apparently, I wasn't the only young man with long, curly hair in the village. 'I've met the imposter. Now I'm here to meet the real one.'

Eric's accent was as broad as the Royal County of Berkshire and he spoke as if he were still living in Victorian times. We hit it off immediately and he invited me to his yard to see what he did for a living. What a place. In a large, covered agricultural shed he showed me all manner of gypsy caravans, barrel organs, steam engines and other delights. In pride of place was a 1911 London bus with its open-top deck and its open staircase at the back.

Eric and his brother Harold had, I think, been the first scrap dealers to summon the courage to knock on the doors of the stately homes of England and ask if they needed anything clearing out. The brothers ended up with one of the largest collections of horse-drawn vehicles and Victorian artefacts in the country. In period films, Eric was always in high demand as a horse-drawn coach driver. He'd started his working life decades earlier driving the mail coach between Reading and London, so his credentials were impeccable.

He was also the perfect man to help organise a party. With Eric and Gwen's help, we were going to have the wedding of the century. There was a big, old-fashioned circus tent in the middle of the field. We had all of Eric's old half-restored vehicles around the perimeters. There were pigs and chickens on spits, eels in jelly, coconuts in shies. There were fairground stalls and games, and the wonderful sound of the barrel organs. There was a hay trailer for a stage and Bob Kerr's Whoopee Band for the live music. It was all there. In fact, there was only one thing we didn't have, and that was the piece of paper that said my last marriage was over. We had no choice but to cancel the actual ceremony at the registry office.

It was too late to cancel the party so Heather and I just pretended we'd got married. All through the party, everyone kept asking about the service. We just told them it was lovely.

The next morning, as I woke up next to my beautiful 'bride', I made the perfectly valid point that if we'd had a big wedding party and everyone thought we were married, why did we need to bother?

'You Mick Jagger, you,' she said.

As soon as she said that, I thought we'd better get married. I was honest with her, though. If it was going to last it had to be a marriage with no issues because of the business I was in. I knew the reality. Life on the road, month after month, can be a very lonely place without company. And we were away on tour for five, six months at a time as one of the biggest rock bands in the world. To come back home and tell her I'd been a good boy – it would have been a lie.

Sexual infidelity should never be a reason for divorce. For a man, it's mostly just a shag, unless you fall in love. If a relationship is based on just that, it's crazy. People get married and they immediately start trying to change each other. If you're straight from the start and you really love each other, then you can be who you are all the way through. Otherwise, why would you get married in the first place?

So we had a wedding and then, a year later, we got married properly. The vast majority of marriages in my world don't last, but we're still together after all these years, and I've never regretted it. Not once. Heather might have from time to time, but I haven't. I was very, very lucky to bump into her that night at the Speakeasy.

What I do know is that settling down in Sussex came at the right time. I had that view across the fields. I had a wife and then a young family. I had a whole side of my life away from the band.

Pete, on the other hand, had the family but he was under pressure. He was the writer. He'd written *Tommy*. What was he going to do next?

ELEVEN

WHO'S NEXT

The idea Pete had was *Lifehouse*. An album and a film. Musically, it was an astonishing concept, but it was so out-there it was hard to grasp. In a world sometime in the not-too-distant future, pollution is so bad that the urban population has to live indoors wearing experience suits. Senses are stimulated artificially by these suits. People disconnect from their natural environment. He got that bit right, didn't he?

Everyone else lives hand-to-mouth in the fields. The experience suits are linked to the Grid, which keeps them fed and entertained through test tubes. They can experience thousands of lifetimes of experience in a day, which is great, but there's no rock 'n' roll, which is bad. Along comes a rebel called Bobby who hacks the Grid. He converts everyone's personal data into musical notes which he plays to them.

The music converges into one single note. With that note, they are free. They all vanish into Nirvana. The end.

It sounds pretentious now. Can you imagine what it sounded like in 1971? And it wasn't half as clear. Pete's always been sketchy on narrative, which is fine when you're making rock music but not when you're making a film. *Lifehouse* was an intellectual ever-decreasing circle. It was a mess.

I offered to try to write it into a proper script but this proved insurmountably difficult. I understood what he was trying to say. When we find the meaning of everything, when you find a higher being, it will be a musical note. I got that. But how do you make a film of that? How do you make a film of something that isn't there?

Every time we talked about it, it was all about the film and we just went round and round in circles. We sat around various tables at Track, at my house, at his house. Kit and Chris were there, too, and it went on for hours and hours. Keith and John would start drinking, just to make the time pass faster. On one particularly long evening, Keith just started taking his clothes off. Then he stood on his head and rested his bollocks on the table.

I tried to be more constructive. I kept saying, 'You've got these songs. Let's do these songs.' But for him, it was the whole thing at once. A project. A film and an album. The full multimedia experience. And we were just too stupid to understand.

I've said it before, and I mean it in the nicest possible way, but talking to Pete could be like walking through a minefield wearing a pair of clown shoes. And a blindfold. When he's fixated on something and other people don't get it, he's intellectually terrifying. His frustration sometimes manifests itself as spitefulness. He has a beautiful, kind side to him – and that's the side you see most often – but there's this other side which can just come out of the blue. He's like a scorpion with a warm heart. No matter how happily the conversation is ticking along, you're constantly aware of the sting in its tail.

It might have helped if we'd taken the idea into the studio to knock it about. There was always something in Pete's ideas and we could have helped. We could have worked it out. But he just couldn't do that. He took all the pressure of coming up with the next big thing on his own.

The hours and hours turned to months and months. Then we did some experimental shows in front of some students at the Young Vic. Pete's plan was audience participation. *Lifehouse* would be a participatory experience. A four-dimensional show. He said he'd seen Who concerts where the vibrations had become so pure that he thought the world was going to stop and we'd all fly off into a unified Nirvana. He wanted to recreate that.

It doesn't work like that. I said that at the time. It happens, occasionally, during a concert, but it's not something you can recreate. Pete thinks it comes from the audience. I don't. I love the audience and the audience feeds your ego. But that thing Pete's talking about, that vibration, comes out of us and the audience. It's a symbiotic synchronisation. The way each member plays together creates a harmonic and, when it happens, we do feel the audience move up a notch, which moves us up a notch, and it's magic.

Whether you could still do it without an audience, I don't know. I guess it would be harder in a completely empty room. There's an energy you're transmitting, and if there's no one to receive it then it probably doesn't work. But you don't need an audience to behave in a certain way. Pete got irritated if the audience wasn't right. If it was full of record execs or the same people from yesterday's front row or whatever, I never cared. I don't care. I play to the back of the room. I see a mass of faces and that's it. The music takes me somewhere and I don't care about the rest of it. If you start to worry about individuals, you flounder. I see it in footballers when they start trying too hard – they never hit the goal. When they relax and go with the flow, it works. It's the same onstage.

But the point is, it's not a tangible thing you can produce by interacting with the audience. When you get it right, you know it. The second time we played Charlton Athletic Football ground in 1976, we got it right. There were supposed to be 70,000 people in the audience but 120,000 turned up, the gates to the ground were ripped off and in they all came. It was raining all day and, by the time we hit the stage, it had turned into a fine misty drizzle. When I ran on, I skidded across the entire stage. 'Welcome to the Who on Ice,' I announced as I took off my boots and socks (you learn very quickly that the only way to engage with a soaked audience is to get soaked, too – it's harder for the guitarist but Pete managed it as well). After that, we just went for it. The audience responded. You could feel the whole thing reach another level. And then another level. And then another. It just kept going, a symbiotic relationship. Us. The crowd. You couldn't bottle it.

This was the first time we'd deployed our three big argon lasers. They were large, hugely powerful things. The only way we could keep them cool enough to stop them exploding was to connect them to a fire hydrant. The beam from each laser was passed through a prism that formed a Tommy album cover of green light over the audience. The light then descended slowly onto the crowd. The sensation for anyone in the audience was one of being lifted up through a roof of light. It all fitted with the music and it was transcendental, man. They felt our energy and we felt theirs.

So it doesn't matter what the audience is like, but it does matter that they're there and that we're creating energy together. That didn't stop Pete. He had us all turning up to the Young Vic to work with a participatory audience. We just nodded at him like you nod at a crazy person and treated it like an open rehearsal. It was all very puzzling.

• • •

While we were waiting for Pete's thoughts to crystallise, de-crystallise and re-crystallise into something we understood, Track put out our first live record. *Live at Leeds* is supposed to be our defining performance. *The New York Times* called it 'the definitive hard-rock holocaust'. I didn't think it was that good myself. We recorded it at the University Refectory on Valentine's Night 1970, and I couldn't hear myself over the band.

This happened a lot. John played too loud, Moonie was never quiet and Pete amped up to compete. They were all too loud at Leeds. I had to work off the sound reflected back and the only way I could hear myself was to oversing. I always knew when I was doing it, and I did it at Leeds. It was a shame because it's been a 'defining album' for the last 47 years.

The very next night was a more defining show. We did it all again at Hull and the balance was better. I could hear myself. They put it out a few years ago as an album and I think it's better. Maybe I'm just being oversensitive. You get like that when you've had to stand in front of Entwistle's amps for so many years.

John was a genius bass player, but he couldn't control his ego. He used to overplay all the time. Even Pete, who wasn't exactly a church mouse when it came to volume, used to complain about it. I used to have really big conversations with John about it. In the 1990s, we were taking *Quadrophenia* on the road and I worked in a solo in '5.15' to give John the spotlight. He very rarely got the spotlight and that wasn't healthy. A whole lifetime in a band, and everyone else basking in glory while he stands there, plucking away. Even for the most balanced ego in the world, that's not ideal. I understand that. So I put in this solo and gave John the same talk I'd given him a hundred times.

'I've got to tell you, John, it's all about the drama. If you're thundering away at the same level from beginning to end, nothing will change when you get to your solo. The only thing the audience will notice is that someone in the lighting department has, for some reason, stuck a spotlight on you.'

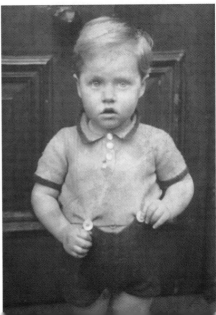

LEFT: *Mum and Dad on Hammersmith Broadway, 1938*
ABOVE: *Mum and me, 1945*

ABOVE: *Dad home from the war, 1945*
MIDDLE RIGHT: *Time for bed, I'm running away (with scratchy jumper), 1948*
BELOW RIGHT: *Outside 16 Percy Road, 1946*

LONDON COUNTY COUNCIL
THE VICTORIA J.B. SCHOOL

REPORT FOR YEAR ENDING _July_ 19 55

Name _Roger Daltrey_   Number in Class _49_

Class _1_   Position in Class _1_

SUBJECT	ASSESSMENT	REMARKS
ENGLISH		
Reading	Very good	
Comprehension	good	
Composition	V.good	
ARITHMETIC	Very good	
HISTORY	V.good	
GEOGRAPHY	V.good	
SCIENCE/Nature Study	Ex	
Physical Education	Good	
ART	V.good	
WRITING	Ex	
HANDWORK	Excellent	
Spelling	Good	
OTHER SUBJECTS Vocabulary	V.good	
Silent Reading	Good	
Music	Good	A keen member of the choir

RELIGIOUS KNOWLEDGE _Very good_   Attendance _Excellent_

GENERAL REPORT _A creditable year's work in many ways by an intelligent, eager and persevering boy. His attitude to school work is highly commendable. He is invariably co-operative, helpful and neat, and shows initiative._

P.H. Blake Class Master

J.B. Saunders Head Master

ABOVE: *My school photo, age nine, 1953*
RIGHT: *School report card, 1955*

ABOVE: *School journey to Paignton, Devon, 1955. I'm on the second row, second from the right, and Mr. Blake is seated lower left.*
RIGHT: *School uniform and a kiss-me-quick hat, 1959*

ABOVE: *John, Doug Sandom, me, and Pete. The Detours van with the working door, 1962.*
RIGHT: *Bored of just standing here: first mic swing at the Golf-Drouot club, Paris, June 2, 1965*

LEFT: *Blow!—me on trombone and John on trumpet, 1961*
BELOW: *At the Goldhawk Social Club, Shepherds Bush, March 1965*

TOP LEFT: *The famous van that got stolen, 1965*
TOP RIGHT: *Girlfriend Anna at my flat at Ivor Court, 1965*
ABOVE: *Rolling Stones Rock and Roll Circus, 1968. Pete, Brian Jones, Rocky Dijon, Yoko Ono, Julian Lennon, John Lennon, Eric Clapton, and me.*
LEFT: *Emmaretta Marks, 1970, after playing the New York Metropolitan Opera House*

ABOVE: *The Who live in Copenhagen, 1970*
LEFT: *The Who live at the Isle of Wight, 1970*

ABOVE: *"My Generation," Surrey Docks, 1965*
RIGHT: *Arriving in Finland, 1967. Chris Stamp with the band.*

ABOVE: *Pete, Kit, and me at IBC Recording Studios working on Tommy, late 1968*
LEFT: *Chris's Viking boat*
BOTTOM: *Track Record, "Giving It All Away"*

ABOVE: *Old mods outside Goldhawk Club, 1977.*
From left to right: Ian Moody, Tommy Shelly,
Irish Jack, Lee Gash, me, Griff in the hat,
Chrissy Coville with broken arm and a pint
of Becks. First of the 100 Faces.

TOP: *Bill Curbishley and me, 1975*
ABOVE: *"Back from the garage"—*
chamois shirt

ABOVE LEFT: *Brand-new Corvette Stingray, 1969*
ABOVE RIGHT: *Outside Percy Road, 1975*
BELOW LEFT: *Riding Ollie, 1974*
BELOW RIGHT: *Who cares if you catch anything?*
1979

BELOW: *Giving Jamie, age two, a bulldozer driving lesson, 1983*

ABOVE: *Heather and me at Elder Cottage, 1969*
LEFT: *"Flossie," 1979. Photo by me.*
BELOW RIGHT: *She likes me, 1989*

ABOVE LEFT: *Flying low*
ABOVE RIGHT: *On the set of* Tommy's *holiday camp with Ken Russell, 1974*
BELOW: Tommy

RIGHT: *Me playing Franz Liszt in the Ken Russell movie* Lisztomania, *1975*

LEFT: *The Moon and the Goon.
Me and Keith with Peter Sellers in
the stage version of* Tommy *at the
Rainbow, London, 1972.*
BELOW: McVicar, 1980
BOTTOM: The Comedy of Errors, for
the BBC. *Clockwise from bottom left:
Michael Kitchen, Dame Wendy Hiller,
Cyril Cusack, and me, 1983.*

ABOVE LEFT: *Discussing team tactics with Arsene Wenger, 201*

ABOVE RIGHT: *Bruce Springsteen and me, Madison Square Garden, 1980*

LEFT: *"Boys night out," 1985 wit Paul McCartney, Bob Geldof, ar Phil Collins*

BELOW: *Rehearsing in England for the* Quadrophenia *tour, 1973*

ABOVE: *The Who with Keith Richards and Mick Jagger backstage at Madison Square Garden for the Concert for New York City after 9/11, 2001*

BELOW: *At the White House reception for the Kennedy Center Honors with Chris and Calixte Stamp, Bill, Marcela and Catalina Curbishley, and Heather with President and Mrs. Bush,2008*

ABOVE: *"Please speak up, Ma'am, I'm in a rock band."* At the Royal Albert Hall for TCT, 2005.
CENTER: *Neil Young Bridge School Benefit, 1999. Bringing us back together.*
BELOW: Daltrey, Ride a Rock Horse, *and* Under a Raging Moon *album covers*

Madison Square Garden, New York, 1974

ABOVE LEFT: *Me and Pete recording, 1966*
ABOVE MIDDLE: Quadrophenia *in Hyde Park, 1996 — "I Eye"*
ABOVE RIGHT: *Two old geezers, 2005*
BELOW: *Pete and I closing the Olympics in 2012*

'Yes, Roger,' he mumbled.

'John, you do not need to play at solo volume through the whole bloody show. When the singing's going on, thin it out behind the vocal. When it gets to your bits, go for it. You've got the room to do it. But if it becomes just a cacophony, you're throwing it away.'

'All right, Roger.'

'And for Christ's sake, when you've finished your solo, turn it down again.'

We got to the show and, miraculously, John started out if not quiet then certainly not deafening. You could hear the vocal. You could hear everything. And then we got to '5.15' and the big bass solo. Up went the volume. Away went The Ox. Wow. A contrast. A beautiful moment. Except for the rest of the gig, with a wry smile on his face, he kept it right up at 11 on the dial.

Just for a laugh, or for payback for the years and years and years of volume, I put John with The Chieftains, the quietest band in the world, at my 50th birthday party at Carnegie Hall in February 1994. We were doing 'Behind Blue Eyes'. Find it on the internet. It's worth it just to see John jamming with a band you could drown out if you tapped your foot too loud. It's lovely. It still makes me smile.

Ego. That's the problem. It's a vital component of a rock band but it's also a killer. I think I rose above all that during my sent-to-Coventry probation period, which sounds egotistical, doesn't it? But I did become above all that, largely because I was out front. I was getting my share of the limelight. But ego could cause problems. It could escalate tensions. And it wasn't always just the boys turning their amps up.

I started twirling my microphone not because of my ego but because I didn't know what to do with my hands during the solos. It began in a small way on the Herman's Hermits tour when we started including the mini-opera in the act. We had this longer piece of music and I just felt it needed animating. I was stuck in the middle of the stage holding the microphone. That's quite a dull pose. You can only do so much choreography with one arm and there was no way I could outdance Mick Jagger. So, in the breaks, I tried a bit of twirling. Over the next few months, it got bigger and bigger. And that's when Pete started jumping.

So I did some more twirling. And he did some more jumping.

John just stood there, stoic. Keith was always thrashing away. But Pete and I got into a sort of dance arms race. It wasn't choreographed. It all just came from the music. And, perhaps, our egos.

I don't always catch the microphone. I had a perfect strike rate in the sixties but these days, now my eyesight isn't so good, it's more hit and miss. When I miss, it thwacks into my leg or my balls and hurts like fuck. But it sure helps me get the high notes.

I've only ever hit one person intentionally, and that was a bloke at the Chuck Berry gig, and he deserved it. The unintentional ones have been kit malfunctions. The microphone has left the lead a few times and that's been scary. It's just disappeared. It must go a hell of a way and, if it hit someone on the head, it would be pretty bad. Try not to think of that next time you're in the first hundred rows of one of our shows.

I never practised. I used to swing it a few times to get my arm in before the show because it weighs a pound or so. I used to swing it to work out how much energy to put into it. And I have to be aware, subconsciously, of where everyone is on the stage. I need to know my safe arcs. Poor Pino Palladino, our bass player for the last however many years. He was terrified at first. He's cool with it now because he knows it's safe. He can almost stand there without flinching.

I'm sure they were always nervous at first but, after a while, they came to trust me. Pete certainly does. And the thing to note here is that I've never hit Pete with the microphone. There's still time but it just shows that he's never pissed me off that much. It would have been relatively easy to knock him off during those months and months of *Lifehouse* deliberations. Or any of the other times we were at odds. A quick, off-centre twirl and crack. Gone. But it never crossed my mind.

• • •

In the end, the grand *Lifehouse* project, the next *Tommy*, fizzled out and we recorded *Who's Next* instead. I love that album. It's a good one, and the reason it's good is because Pete let us have the songs several months before we went into the studio.

Remember, he was always generous once we were in the studio. He let us work things through, to develop things from his demos. But because of the sketchiness and the way he worked, he never let us have time with the tracks beforehand.

I suppose that came from his family. His dad, Cliff, was a saxophonist in the RAF's dance band the Squadronaires. His mum, the indomitable Betty, was a singer with Sidney Torch & His Orchestra. Theirs was the itinerant life of the jobbing musician. You were told what to play and you played it instantly.

A rock band doesn't work like that. A rock band has to digest the music, try it this way and that way, and, before you even get to that point, the most important thing is that everybody knows the song. You need to know it long enough that you're not thinking about it. You need to live with it until the head goes away and the heart takes over. We never did that and I feel that's the reason we always suffered in the studio. Here's a song about X, Y and Z. Off you go, boys. I used to find that so, so difficult.

With *Who's Next*, we went out and rehearsed all that material. We played it onstage for about four weeks. We did some gigs up north. Then we went to New York and did some recording with Kit. I didn't think there was anything wrong with it but Pete's relationship with Kit was starting to unravel so he just binned all that material.

We came back to England and started from scratch. By that time, we were completely comfortable with it. And it shows in the record. You get your timing. You sing it like you feel it.

Take 'Won't Get Fooled Again'. It's just a brilliant song. Brilliant lyrics.

We'll be fighting in the streets
With our children at our feet
And the morals that they worship will be gone
And the men who spurred us on
Sit in judgement of all wrong
They decide and the shotgun sings the song.

This was right in the middle of Vietnam. Just one generation from everything our parents had been through and it was all happening again. This song put it all in a package, and it made you stop and think. It made me stop and think.

We recorded it at Stargroves, Mick Jagger's gothic country house in Hampshire. It was a big old house with a massive double-height hall and that's where I did the vocals. I'd listened to Pete's demo and at the bit where the vocal came in again after the drum riff, he'd done this leary, jazzy, smooth 'Yeeah'. Like dig it, man.

I knew the song. I knew it was angry. Really fucking angry. I felt it, so I just let out a scream of rage. And it was from the heart, not the head.

Everyone else was in the kitchen having dinner. They all heard that terrifying scream. The rest of the band must have thought the singer had died. Keith put his head round the door to check I was all right.

I was all right and it turned out to be a great record. We were in good shape. And then our accountant called a meeting. He said we'd had a fantastic year, which is what you want to hear from your accountant. He said we'd done all that touring, we'd done *Who's Next* and *Live at Leeds*. We'd made loads of money. And he was pleased to tell us that we were only £600,000 in debt.

If everyone assumed we were millionaires in 1969, they assumed we must have been multi-millionaires by now. But we were still spending it faster than we could earn it. It wasn't our living expenses. John was living on Popes Lane in Acton. I'd been in a two-up, two-down until that summer. It was all going on the tours. And, as we'd find out over the next few years, up Keith and Kit's noses. 'Profitless prosperity' is how Chris Stamp described it, which was a bit rich coming from him. He was certainly making a profit. But it was obvious that the more we toured the more we owed. So we decided to stop.

• • •

After however many years of non-stop slogging with The Who, we took our first break in 1972. A six-month sabbatical from the rock 'n' roll circus.

It was nice to have some downtime. Bandmates can get under each other's skin. You're tightly knit on the road. You have to be. But after months and months, you're tightly wound up, too. It becomes easier with age. It's really relaxed now. We're all friends and I love it. But that break in 1972 was a huge relief.

I know what you're thinking. Six months swanning about. Lazy rock star lounging around his nice old manor house with his nice new wife. I've told you, I hate doing nothing. If I'm doing nothing, what's the point of being here?

Week one: stripping the wooden beams of the black stain the Victorians had coated them with.

Week two: stripping the beams.

Weeks three and four: stripping the beams.

Week five: bored of stripping the beams so I built myself a home studio.

Week six: I was mucking about in the studio when Adam Faith called. He said he was looking for a place to record a new singer called Leo Sayer, so I invited them over. I always got on with Adam like a brother and what he'd found in Leo was like something else. He was just an amazing, amazing singer. Completely unique. And it counted for nothing because they were having trouble getting him a good record deal.

Leo's songwriting partner was Dave Courtney. Flippantly, I suggested they write me some songs. I'd put out a solo record, we'd see if anyone noticed and it might help Leo get his deal. The only condition was that it couldn't be anything like a Who record. Leo said fine, and off he went. I honestly didn't think anything would come of it. The very next week, just when I was summoning the energy to have another go at the beams, Leo and Dave turned up with ten songs. Bosh. Just like that. It was a choice between more beams and music, so we started recording immediately.

Daltrey was released in the spring of 1973 and it sold better than any of the earlier Who singles albums. At one point, it was doing 40,000 copies a day. But musically it was completely different and that was deliberate.

John and Pete's solo albums were much closer to The Who sound but I was always absolutely clear where my priorities were. Sadly, Kit and Chris didn't see it that way. Nor did the record company. I found out later that they held it back in America deliberately. They worried that if it was a success, I'd leave The Who, and, at that time, The Who was their biggest product. I didn't care about any of that. I've always had people telling me I should go solo, but I didn't want to be a solo singer. I didn't want to do a Rod Stewart.

Sometimes I look back and think I should have gone it alone. But it never felt right. I was part of this magical band. It wasn't the most popular band in the world but the stuff we did felt important. I felt rewarded.

Pete and I never spoke about my solo album, but I'm sure he thought it was sentimental shit. I know John thought it was crap because when it came on the radio he blew a raspberry. Keith was equally encouraging. My cousin, the photographer Graham Hughes, took this photograph of me with a halo of curls which he soft-focused to enhance the angelic look. I thought it fitted the whole *Tommy* vibe so I went with it for the cover of the *Daltrey* album. The shot then turned up in a teen magazine as a Pin-up of the Month double-page spread. The following morning, I received post from Keith. He'd torn out the spread and scrawled all over my angelic face in biro. It said, 'Yuk' and that was the extent of his review.

Did I care? Of course I didn't. It was an album I knew they would hate. That was the whole point. To make an album John would like, it would have had to be some sort of depressing death-metal record. And I would have hated it and he would have loved it.

The only thing that pissed me off about that whole experience was the way Kit and Chris reacted. They ran Track Records but first and foremost they were our managers. They were my managers. And when I took the record to them, they threw it up in the air, and we had this big argument in the basement at Track. They said it was too soft, too gentle. I said that was exactly the point. I didn't want to take anything away from The Who. I wanted to do something that might add another dimension for me. They just said it was rubbish.

That upset me. I just completely lost it right there in the office. When I'd calmed down, I realised something I should have realised much earlier. They didn't have my interests at heart. They were only interested in protecting their golden goose. After that, I knew they could never manage me again. It was Goodnight, Vienna. As soon as that happened, I asked Bill Curbishley to be my manager.

TWELVE

UNDER NEW MANAGEMENT

In the weeks leading up to the row, I had noticed this guy in the office. He was a big, tall bloke with a beard and short, straight, non-frizzy black hair (you'll see why that's important in a couple of pages), and I just got on with him. There was empathy. So I asked Mike Shaw, our production manager, who he was.

'That's Bill,' he said. 'One of our old mates.'

'Where's he come from then, Mike?'

'He's a Canning Town boy.'

'I like him. I think I'll make him my manager.'

'He'll be the best manager you ever had.'

'What's his story?' I asked.

'Keep it quiet,' said Mike, 'but every night, he has to go back to Pentonville. He's residing at Her Majesty's pleasure.'

In all the profiles and interviews of Bill Curbishley over the years, there is always a section about his seven years in the merchant navy. But Bill, the man who became my manager in

1972 and has been my manager ever since, was never in the merchant navy. He was in prison. The navy was just a cover story to protect his kids. Now they're older, he's told them the truth. And I can tell you the truth, too.

Bill was born in Forest Gate and he grew up in Canning Town. He was the eldest of six kids and his mum sent him to school a year early so she could go to work. Like me, he went to grammar school – smart kid to pass a year earlier than everyone else did. Like me, he didn't have the privileged background of the other kids at school. During the war, his dad had been a Royal Navy marine engineer, patching up submarines in Ceylon. Every time he fixed one, he got a bottle of rum in thanks.

When he came back, he took work on the docks and the drinking became more intensive. Money was already tight and then the post-war dock strikes left the family more or less destitute. Bill used to go out on Saturday nights with a pram to steal coal from the local bakery, just to keep his family warm.

'It was the first stepping stone to rebellion,' he said. 'By the time I was eleven, I knew the only way to get out was to fight your way out. And if that involved crime, fair enough.'

The crime Bill got sent down for was a bank van robbery in Erith, Kent, in 1963. At the time, it was one of England's largest armoured truck robberies, but Bill had nothing to do with it. The whole of the East End underworld knew who did but they kept schtum. So did Bill. Unfortunately, the investigating sergeant had it in for him (another story involving planted fake bank notes and a thrown pint) so Bill got fingered for it anyway.

At trial, the evidence against Bill was flimsy. The coppers claimed he had an association with one of the other alleged gang members. They had a witness who said she saw someone who looked like Bill driving the getaway car. And they put up a uniformed policeman who described a five foot eight man with bushy, frizzy hair running from the bank van to the getaway car.

Now, Bill was well over six foot tall and he was a mod. His hair was mod-short. Nothing frizzy about it. But in his summation, Justice Thesiger said, 'Well, you might think, members of the jury, that Curbishley when he was running from the bank might well be stooped over and look five foot eight and, with the wind rushing through his hair, it would look frizzy. And indeed bushy.' Unbelievable leading of the jury.

Bill was found guilty and got sent to Durham Prison to share a block with the Great Train Robbers. That could have been it for him – if you're flirting with the criminal life, getting locked up young can make it hard to ever go straight. But Bill spent most of his time in solitary. He studied while he was away. He got his A-levels, he did courses, he kept his head down.

After a few years, he was moved to Leicester. And then Reggie Kray had a word with his governor, told him Bill had been fitted up, and that governor got Bill moved to Wormwood Scrubs. So he was back in London, still protesting his innocence. Eventually, Bill's story made the front page of the *Sunday Mirror*. 'Are these two men innocent?' was the headline, followed by an account of how Bill and the other alleged robber, Billy Stuckle, had been wrongly accused. As if by magic, Bill was summoned to the parole board a few days after Christmas 1970.

They said to him, 'We're going to recommend you for a working-out scheme from Pentonville for three or four months, and then you will go on parole.' He said, 'Why?' So they said, 'Well, we think you're a suitable case for parole.'

'No you don't,' said Bill. 'You fucking know I'm innocent.' Under protest, Bill was out, out of his stint in the 'merchant navy'. Stuckle got out not long after and was dead within months of his release. 'In my opinion, it was the prison that killed him,' says Bill. It must be hard enough doing time when you've done the job. But when you're innocent? Well, Bill survived but he missed the sixties. He did seven years of hard labour and solitary and then he was turned loose without so much as an apology. He called Mike Shaw, one of his oldest friends from Canning Town, and the next day he was working at Track. It was a lucky break for him and a lucky break for me.

It was only a few months later that I had it out with Kit and Chris in the basement at Track and reached the decision that I needed a new manager. Bill had already tried to talk them round to my solo stuff. He'd told them, 'If we work his album and he has success it will be the best thing we can do for him and us. He will have self-confidence, he will feel himself. He should be made to feel equal.' And, as he puts it now, 'They fucking laughed at me. They said you can fucking do it if you want to.' So Bill said, 'Okay, I'll do it.'

From the minute I made him my manager, I started making money like I never had before. It was all down to him, because when he arrived Kit and Chris were already out of control. In fact, it might have all unravelled sooner if Bill hadn't learned the ropes so quick. He had no choice. No one else was running things. It was a mess.

I didn't go into Track that often, but the way Bill tells it they treated it like their own private cash machine. Kit would roll in around lunchtime, take whatever cash was in the safe and, if there wasn't enough, he'd have a cheque made out to himself and then head out to score.

The way it was structured was that Track would split label profits 50-50 with Polygram. That was clever. They managed the bands, put them on the road, produced the albums and released them. They made money at every stage. But they also controlled the artist's royalty, which would have been 15 per cent of retail. When they started signing other artists – Marc Bolan, Jimi Hendrix, Arthur Brown, Thunderclap Newman – all those royalties went into a separate account under Mammoth Records. Occasionally, they'd dish a bit out to Jimi and the others, but they always kept the bulk of it. And half the money coming in from the deals with Polygram.

As I've said before, we were supposed to be partners. Kit and Chris had promised the four of us 10 per cent each of Track. I still have the letter. It's been chewed up by my dog, but I've kept it to remind me. It would have been an enormous amount of money but none of us ever saw a penny.

Meanwhile, Kit had a 15th-century palace right on the Grand Canal in Venice. I never went but I'm told it's beautiful. Monet painted it. Ruskin was very keen on its encrusted oculi. It belonged to countesses, diplomats and Venetian royalty. And then Kit Lambert. Both Kit and Chris had large houses in Knightsbridge as well.

By the early seventies, Kit and Chris were heroin addicts. And when you're a heroin addict the fear of running out of money is real. So they were cutting deals with promoters where they'd get a smaller amount of cash upfront rather than a fair share of the total profit at the end. Like any addicts, they just wanted to get their hands on the cash. I'm sure they didn't sit down and say, 'We're going to steal this money'. I'm sure they told themselves they were only borrowing it but it's no different. It's desperation.

Bill puts it a different way. In his opinion, Lambert and Stamp always felt they were superior to the band. Moon was the clown, Entwistle was the anchor and Townshend was the genius, who they doted on and cultivated. I was someone they put up with.

If it had been up to me, we would have got rid of Kit and Chris sooner. We would have got rid of them the moment I knew for a fact they were ripping us off. I knew they were shifty for years but it's different when you have conclusive proof that the two people who are supposed to be managing you are stealing from you.

I got the conclusive proof not long after I'd come back from touring my solo album. Kit and Chris said, 'We've got The Who a three-album deal with MCA and it's a million dollars an album.' Great. 'And your percentage of every album is $529,325.' Hang about.

Our percentage for the record contract was 60 per cent. I knew that, no matter how often you run it through a calculator, $529,325 is not 60 per cent of a million dollars. It was even more ridiculous than that. The figure ran all the way down to cents. I might be a Shepherd's Bush boy but I'm not stupid. So I called them up and asked them to run through it again. They came up with the same number. I asked if they were sure and they said they were. So I called Ted Oldham, our lawyer, who confirmed the band was due 60 per cent of a million dollars per album. My Shepherd's Bush mathematics was correct. And he was quite clear. Kit and Chris were screwing us.

I spoke to Keith and John and told them I didn't want people I couldn't trust handling my business any more. It wasn't about the money. Even though we had families to support, it was never about the money. I always knew how lucky we were to have anything, to have found each other and to have found those two. I always valued their creativity and how much they'd done for us. I just didn't want them managing the band any more. I wanted to break the management deal, bung them 10 per cent and keep them on for their creative value. I wanted them involved but I didn't want drug addicts with their hands on the purse strings. Keith and John saw my reasoning, but Pete wasn't interested. He wouldn't sign the thing to get us out of the contract. I told him we had to do something about it. He said he didn't want to and that was that. Who money was pocket money for him.

So nothing happened until he went to America a year or two later and found out they'd been at his publishing money as well. I don't know how much they'd taken. It was none of my business but that's when the shit really hit the fan.

Rather than keeping them on in some capacity, they were out for good. Pete threw the book at them. In 1976, the rest of the band asked Bill to manage them. They'd watched Bill handle everything for me and they wanted him to do the same for them. I stayed out of that. I would have preferred to keep Bill all to myself. But I suppose it was inevitable. When everything came to a head, Bill was the obvious choice to manage the Who. And so Kit and Chris were out. They lost Track. They lost us. And we lost them. I always felt bad about that because I was the bastard that instigated the split. It wasn't the split on my terms in the end. It went much further.

I've never held grudges. I've always moved on. Forgiven if not always forgotten. But you have to clear the air and that never happened with Chris or Kit. Kit died in 1981 and he went to his grave thinking he'd been unfairly treated by the band. I saw him a few months before he died. He came for lunch down in Sussex and he was in a deeply melancholic mood. Bill saw him just before the end and Kit kept telling him, 'Just make sure you get paid.' He had that drug addict's paranoia. Bill gave him some cash and wrote him a cheque. He came back an hour later, bruised and in tears. He'd tried to score some drugs and they'd smacked him around a bit. So Bill gave him some more cash and arranged a car for him to get home. That was the last time any of us saw him.

He was only 45 when he died. He suffered a cerebral haemorrhage after falling down the stairs at his mum's house. It was a horrible end for a man who had meant so much to the band. Somehow, Chris survived. He cleaned himself up and became an addiction therapist in New York. We became friends again and, in 1992, remembering his love of the film business, I asked him to co-produce a film idea I'd had about Keith. (I still have the idea but, back then, pre-Tarantino, no one understood our script because it wasn't written with a linear time frame.)

Chris and I stayed very close friends right up until his death in 2012. He would mentor me when I lacked confidence. He encouraged me greatly to pursue my vision of how to present my upcoming solo tour of *Tommy* and The Who's next *Quadrophenia* tour. In 2008, when we received the Kennedy Center Honor in Washington, Chris was alongside me with his beautiful wife Calixte at the White House and State Department. He deserved to be there for what he and Kit had given us all those years before.

For many years we had spent holidays together in the West Indies and that's where Calixte, Chris's daughter Amie, Heather and I gave him a Viking burial. I have no idea why but on that particular morning I was driven to give him a special send-off. I built a boat of palm leaves and whatever else I could find on the beach while the girls collected flowers from neighbouring gardens to cover his ashes. By the time we were finished, we'd built a proper tropical/Viking burial ship, complete with a dried banana leaf mast. With the help of some flammable jelly, Chris had a burial at sea, from a beach off St Kitts.

And yet, despite all those years of friendship, he never admitted he'd done anything wrong by us. Not once. They made a whole film about the two of them a couple of years ago. *Lambert & Stamp*. I did all I could to help Chris and the producers compete the project. I gave them interviews and full access to early film clips I owned. And even then, in all the interviews in the film, Chris never explains the real reason we had to get rid of them as managers. That was the great shame about the film. It was supposed to be journalistic, but they only told half the story. The film's version of the truth is that we got rid of them because they were bad managers. Never once have I said that they were bad managers. They were the best creative managers a group could wish for, but they were addicts. If only Chris had just said, 'look we were out of our boxes ... there was so much cash about and when you're hooked on drugs you need a lot of cash, and, yes, we were spending your money'. Well, that would have been the end of it for me. But he didn't come close. And the film's record of a half-truth brings it all back to me and it left me angry.

Yes, they had been integral to our success. Yes, they had been on top of the world with us. And, yes, they'd been absolute pioneers in the rock industry. But when the money and the drugs started rolling in, the 1970s became like the Wild West for swindlers, and they'd taken the wrong path. They never got over it. Kit died far too young. Chris lived with it for the next 40 years.

THIRTEEN

FAMILY

In 1972, Heather and I had our first daughter, Rosie. Given the chaos and instability in my professional life, it was a godsend to do the family thing properly. I never had a relationship with my first family. I did eventually. As I've said, we all used to go on holidays together. Jackie and her husband, their two kids and our son Simon used to come away with my second family. We went to Florida and Portugal together. We went to the West Indies. The whole caboodle. But for the first few years I had no role with my son. And I deserved that.

It was different the second time around. I was happy. I was with Heather, the love of my life, and we were in the first flush of marriage when the kids started coming along. And although I was still away a lot, I had some time to be with them and I enjoyed it a lot. It was still hard going away and coming back – Rosie and then Willow, who came along three years later, always changed so much, even if it was a short tour. It was only when we had our son Jamie in 1981 that I really got to have a go at the hands-on dad routine. But all through those early years, it didn't matter how crazy things got on the road, I knew I was always coming back to stability. I got very lucky there. The other guys in the band all had quite troubled relationships and, as I've already suggested, that's the norm in my world. It could easily have been the norm for me. It's very hard to find a girl who would not just put up with all the rock 'n' roll crap but also stand up to you, stand with you, tell you what's what, help you navigate your way through the madness. Heather was my equal. She was and still is my partner in everything.

We had lots of neighbours with kids so it was very communal. There were always kids hanging around, other parents helping out, sharing the load. We had someone up in the cottages with two kids and it was an open-door life. It was idyllic.

• • •

You can't spend all your time enjoying yourself, though, can you? My sabbatical ended with *Quadrophenia*. First off, I want to say that I always realised, recording-wise, we were an acquired taste because of the material. But I also always recognised that what Pete was saying, how he was verbalising it and where it came from made it ground-breaking stuff. Although it felt like it at the time, it wasn't just a fleeting thing. Those feelings he conveyed in his music were timeless. You can be 16, 17 today, pick up *Quadrophenia* and feel like those lyrics are talking to you. I see it now when I'm performing. There are plenty of old codgers, rocking out to us like they have for half a century. But their grandkids are there, too.

And they're going nuts.

Second off, making *Quadrophenia* was not all sweetness and light. Pete's idea, his next big concept, came in a flash of inspiration when we were building Ramport Studios in an old church hall on Thessaly Road, Battersea. We built a lot of things in the 1970s. There was no point trying to keep any cash, not when the government was taking 98 per cent of it. So we had projects and one of them was Ramport. The plan was to build a quadrophonic studio – surround sound, very futuristic. The only problem was that we didn't know very much about building studios. It looked great and, when you played in it, everything sounded great. But the sound we were hearing playing back was a distortion of the true sound.

When we played it back in a different studio (built by someone who knew what they were doing) it didn't sound right at all.

Still, it gave Pete his flash of inspiration. 'There's this guy with double schizophrenia,' he said. 'It's the four members of the band and the music is the person.'

I got it. I got it immediately even if everyone else didn't. He went off to scribble and then, because Ramport wasn't finished, we went back to Stargroves to record it a few weeks later. Immediately, things started to go wrong.

On the first day, Kit turned up with a huge feast of food. It was typical Kit. Flamboyant and generous, though I'm sure we were paying for it. I had accepted that Kit wasn't going to get the boot and I was getting on with it. But Pete had other ideas. When Kit turned up with his elaborate feast, he flew into a rage. Maybe he was pissed off after all. Maybe it was more to do with that recording session in New York for *Who's Next*. That was what Pete cared about. The music. The process of making music. He would give Kit a pass on stealing from us, but if he interfered with the sessions, that was unforgivable. Pete never explained why that feast pissed him off so much, but it was the last time we saw Kit in the studio. He was replaced by Ron Nevison and I have no idea where he came from. We should have gone for Glyn Johns, who stepped in on *Who's Next* and did a brilliant job. Why fix what ain't broken?

Anyway, I was never happy with the original mixes on *Quadrophenia*. Things happened on the vocal tracks that were irreparable. They added echoes and effects that couldn't be removed. When you try and remix it, you can't really improve it very much. I remember when I heard it in our flashy quadro-phonic studio at Ramport for the first time, I thought it was amazing, but when I heard it on the record it just sounded flat. I know it wasn't me. I've always blamed it on the mix. That flashy studio wasn't tuned right.

I blamed it publicly. I told an interviewer, 'Since *Tommy*, we've lost our light and shade, I found it a lot less rewarding. Too loud.' Pete was, of course, unhappy with my comments but I was only being honest. I felt that a certain amount of power had been lost. The vocal had been smoothed out and that took the power away. And the way we appeared to respond to this loss of light and shade was to get louder.

That's how I knew I was right. Everyone was playing with a level of desperation. If it isn't going well, play it louder.

Pete knew it wasn't going well, too, even if he didn't admit it. The pressure on him was immense and he was drinking more heavily than ever. Onstage, he'd get through a bottle of brandy, and drunk musicians don't make good musicians. I'd like to hear some of the live recordings from that period and see if my memory of it is what it really sounded like. Because I hear everything from the front of the stage and it's a strange place to inhabit. You're naked to the audience. You never see the band. You can turn to them on a solo and work with them, but you could never do that with John because he was statuesque. You couldn't go near Keith because he was thrashing away and you'd lose the rest of the band. And, with Pete, it depended on the night.

All the time, the amp stacks were getting bigger. We'd moved from Marshall to Sound City in the late sixties. Then Pete and John worked with Dave Reeves to create a customised Hiwatt Electronics stack in 1968. That was upgraded to the Super Who 100 model in 1970, which became the DR103W model in 1973. Which, in short, meant I couldn't hear bloody anything of the vocals.

It was a crazy time, absolutely crazy. Even before we set off to tour *Quadrophenia*, we were struggling. The rehearsals at Shepperton were exhausting. That's what sparked the fight that ended with Pete unconscious on the floor and me screaming for an ambulance. Halfway through the rehearsals, I just got fed up with the film crew, who were supposed to be recording a promo for MCA, and hadn't even bothered to get their cameras going. 'When are you going to start filming then?' I asked. 'When I've lost my bloody voice? This is a hard piece and I am only doing it once.' Quite reasonable, don't you think?

Pete, fuelled by the best part of a bottle of brandy, went off like a firecracker. He was up in my face, prodding me. 'You'll do what you're fucking well told,' he sneered. This is not the way to talk to me, but I still backed off. The roadies knew what I was capable of so they sprang into action and held me back.

'Let him go,' screams Pete. 'I'll kill the little fucker.' They let me go.

Next thing I knew, he'd swung a 24-pound Les Paul guitar at me. It whistled past my ear and glanced off my shoulder, very nearly bringing a much earlier end to The Who. I still hadn't retaliated, but I was beginning to feel quite put out. He'd called me a *little* fucker, after all.

Finally, after almost ten years of Peaceful Perce, after another left hook narrowly dodged, I replied with an uppercut to the jaw. Pete went up and backwards like he'd been poleaxed. And then he fell down hard, cracking his head on the stage. I thought I'd killed him.

To make matters only slightly worse, our publicist Keith Altham chose that moment to bring the American managing director from our newly signed record company onto the sound stage. The bigwig's first sight of his big new signing was of the lead vocalist knocking the lead guitarist out cold.

'My God,' said the horrified MD. 'Is it always like this?'

'No,' said Keith. 'Today is one of their better days.'

I wound up in the back of the ambulance, holding Pete's hand, wracked with guilt. I was the one who had been attacked, but somehow I ended up feeling responsible. It was just like being back in the playground at Acton again.

Thankfully, Pete survived, but for the rest of my life I've had to listen to him blaming me for the bald spot on the top of his head. To this day, I think he believes I was the aggressor. He has a very selective memory at times.

It was pressure and alcohol that caused the fight and it didn't get any easier on tour. For the first time, we were trying to work with tapes. All very futuristic and pioneering, but you had to be able to hear the tempo and the rhythm. If you lost that, you were screwed. Poor old Keith. I don't know how he did it. Playing to click tracks was a nightmare. It was like putting handcuffs on us.

That all came to a head at the Odeon Newcastle on Fireworks Night, of course, 1973, just two weeks after the last fisticuffs. Pete attacked Bobby Pridden. Now, Bobby had been our sound engineer forever. He was still touring with us until earlier this year, which is remarkable because, after me, he is, geographically, the closest man to Pete during a gig. And when a gig goes bad, you want to be the furthest man, geographically, from Pete. Bobby has had more guitars, amps and tape decks thrown at him over the years than any man, even a sound man, deserves and on that night, it probably wasn't his fault. We were just trying to be too ambitious.

It was so hard to do the things we take for granted today. Everything now is digital. Everything is numbered. You've got a standby of this and a standby of that and you just push a button and off you go. In those days, you had to line up the tape which, for any kids reading, was an actual tape, and you had to get it just right. Even if you managed that, the tape could and very often would split. It was a nightmare. So many things could go wrong, and they did. Where we were with sound in the early seventies was where we were with my guitars in the late fifties. Sticky tape. Splints. Wings and prayers. And an ever-present propensity for the whole thing to fold in half.

Of course, that was the whole point of rock. We were being incredibly ambitious because nothing was ever too ambitious in rock in the 1970s. The Beatles were a little four-piece band in the middle of a stadium, which was ridiculous, but it worked because of the hysteria. Once the girls stopped screaming, it would have been four pinpricks doing not very much. We couldn't hide behind the hysteria so we had to do more. We had to fill the stadium. We couldn't rely on screens because they didn't exist. We just had lights and we had sound. That's why it became so insane onstage, why we were trying things we couldn't rely on and why septuagenarians Pete and I have to ask you to say that again, only a bit louder.

And it's why Bobby got a tape machine thrown at him that night in Newcastle. 'The Who – A Ridiculous Display of Unwarranted Violence' was the headline in the next day's Newcastle *Evening Chronicle*.

Tempers flared after drummer Keith Moon had trouble with headphones. He let the drumsticks fly as the sound engineers battled to fix them. Then Townshend intervened. He ripped out backing tapes and heaved over equipment into the side curtains. The three other members of the band – lead singer Roger Daltrey, guitarist John Entwistle and drummer Keith Moon – just stared. It was, in my opinion, an extremely childish publicity stunt with potentially damaging effect on the thousands of youngsters who invariably follow their idols in all they do. Otherwise, they were musically immaculate, as always.

To me, that's why the critics, however good they were, never quite got what we were about. It might have felt 'musically immaculate' to them but to us – and to Pete especially – the smallest glitch in the groove caused by a poxy tape machine felt like a major bump in the road.

It wasn't a publicity stunt. Not even close. It was pure frustration, spilling over. The next two shows at the Odeon passed without incident. Then, after three shows at the Lyceum in London, we set off for America and yet more disaster.

• • •

Tuesday 20 November 1973. The Cow Palace, San Francisco. The start of the US–Canadian leg of the *Quadrophenia* tour. The band's 1965 promise to stay off the drugs until after the show had been, how shall I put it, fraying. Before the show, Keith drank a bottle of brandy chased down with a handful of horse tranquillisers and something else we never quite discovered. Partly, he was an addict. Partly, he suffered from stage fright. People assume that someone like Keith, a natural performer, a natural show-off, couldn't possibly have nerves, but he did. He could be hard on himself and some nights he would be throwing up for hours in the room next to mine, waiting to go onstage. Sometimes it was too much of whatever he was taking. Sometimes it was plain old fear. He was close to the wire a lot of the time. That night, he crossed it.

The show started comparatively well. The click tracks were working. Bobby had nothing thrown at him. Then, Keith started to flag during 'Drowned'. He picked up again for 'Bell Boy' but when we reached his solo in 'Won't Get Fooled Again', he ground to a complete halt.

'We're just going to revive our drummer by punching him in the stomach,' said Pete in his usual sympathetic fashion. 'He's out cold. I think he'd gone and eaten something he shouldn't have eaten. It's your foreign food.'

You've got no idea what it feels like to be up there standing on a stage in front of 15,000 people, all hyped up, all screaming at you, and your drummer is face-deep in a snare. In the end, he just collapsed flat on his back. There wasn't panic. Even though you're in the shit, you know you'll get through. That's the beauty of rock. It's so irreverent, you can make a show out of almost anything, even an unmitigated disaster like this. If the drummer's out on his back for the whole show and people are chucking water on him, you can still make a show of it. As long as you're making a noise, as long as you're creating a performance, you'll get through it. Rock fans are not like any other audience. They're forgiving. They appreciate improvisation.

Still, it would have been nice to have some drums. A lifeless Keith, eyes rolled to the back of his head, was carted off by the roadies and chucked in a cold shower. A doctor injected him with something and he was back onstage. This time he got to the end of 'Magic Bus' and then you didn't need a doctor to tell you he was out for good.

'Can anybody play the drums?' asked Pete. 'I mean somebody good.' Up came 19-year-old Scot Halpin from Muscatine, Iowa, and we got through 'Smokestack Lightning', 'Spoonful' and 'Naked Eye' before finally throwing in the towel. We survived the night and, miraculously, Keith did, too, but I could have killed him. We all could have done.

The next day, we found him in the hotel reception languishing in a wheelchair. He wasn't exactly contrite. He was wearing a big grin and an even bigger fur hat he'd taken a shine to. Naturally, it came with buffalo horns. Whatever industrial-grade medication he'd taken, it had left him paralysed from the chest down. Like sherpas, we had to carry him onto the plane.

There was a day's rest before the gig at the Forum in Inglewood but Keith still wasn't quite right. The doctor had propped him up at the drum kit with a needle going into his ankle. It took him four days to get all his feeling back. First, it was his arms, which was useful for the performance. Then it was his waist, then his bits and pieces, then, finally, his legs.

The doctors were always there, on the fringes, ready to supply whatever was needed in whichever given situation. Yes, doctor, we'd like some uppers. Yes, doctor, now we need some downers. It was all perfectly legal and above board. Ethically, it was probably a grey area.

Most of what Keith took was on prescription. I used to smoke a bit of pot in the gaps between tours, but I kept out of it all until I damaged my shoulders and got stuck on painkillers. Horrible things and they took a long time to kick in. Then I got addicted to sleeping pills, which was worse. I couldn't sleep because there was just so much adrenaline. It's impossible to come offstage and have a decent kip. Not a chance. I used to de-stress with birds and booze, but that wasn't a solution any more so I got into Quaaludes, or Mandrax as it was called in Britain. First manufactured in the early seventies, it was a barbiturate-derivative depressant and it was horrible stuff. The side effects were horrendous: depression, fatigue, unpleasant dreams, ataxia, headache, numbed emotions, double vision, dizziness. It got pulled off the market and banned once people realised how potent and addictive it was. But I had to sleep.

We were doing longer and longer shows. We were hitting three hours, which required huge levels of energy and concentration, so I became obsessed by sleep. It became the thing in my life. And, as any insomniac will tell you, if you think about sleep, you worry about it and then it becomes even more elusive. I just lay there each night thinking, I have to go to sleep now. If I don't, I won't make it through tomorrow's show. It's going to be too late. I have to sleep. Now. Hurry up and go to sleep. Maybe I should have counted sheep.

The Mandrax was prescribed quite innocently by my own doctor rather than one of the mysterious tour suppliers. Those guys were too busy keeping Keith upright. The doc didn't want to give me the pills, but I was desperate. I told him

I wouldn't make it through the tour without them and eventually he relented. That's why there are so many casualties in our business. It's so intense, the temptation to take something to maintain balance is huge. First, you take the downers to bring you out of the clouds after a show. Then you need the uppers to put you right back up there in time for the next one. I never needed the upper. I never did the full Elvis. But kicking Mandrax was horrible. It's cold turkey for two weeks and you wake up through these endless, restless nights, feeling like you're falling off a cliff. I still have trouble sleeping. Even when I'm not touring, I struggle. There are times, usually in the very small hours, when I'd trade it all in for the ability to get into bed and fall asleep. I wouldn't, of course, but I don't think you'll find many performers who sleep well after a show. If they do, they're probably not doing it right.

By the time the tour moved on to Canada, Keith had regained the full use of his limbs. A fully mobile Keith is a dangerous animal and his brush with paralysis hadn't made him any more circumspect. On 2 December, our American record company MCA threw an after-show party at the Bonaventure Hotel in Montreal. We were playing the next night in Boston and I had a killer sore throat so I went to bed, miserable, with my Mandrax and all its accompanying side effects. I left the rest of the band to it.

At some point in the night, Keith decided to redecorate the entire hospitality suite with his own abstract ketchup art before Pete helped him shove a large marble table through a wall. After they'd thrown several other items of furniture into the pool, they scarpered off to bed. At four in the morning, the Royal Canadian Mounted Police arrived in force and dragged 16 of us off to the nick. There was no point telling them I'd had absolutely nothing to do with it – you could see they were in no mood for due process – but I did try to tell them they'd arrested Mike's nurse.

Mike Shaw had been with us since 1964. He and Chris Stamp were childhood friends and he'd been working as a lighting director in the theatre before he came to do the lighting for The Who. He was an energetic mod with a very dry sense of humour; he was a great part of the management team. But in 1965, just as we were beginning to make it big, he was taking the minivan back from a gig when he drove into the back of a truck just south of Stafford. He survived but he broke his neck and spent the rest of his life in a wheelchair. We did the best we could for him and he never complained, even though it was so hard for him. He continued to work for Track and he still came everywhere with us, but he could do nothing without his nurse. I explained all this to the cops that December night in Montreal, but they didn't care. They just wanted to beat the shit out of us, wheelchair or not. The authorities always hated people like us and these authorities were the worst we ever encountered.

We were all locked up in pens. I was with Bill Curbishley and, as you can imagine, he's quite cool under lock and key. As soon as he got in, he just lay down on the bunk and stayed there motionless, almost like he was meditating. What a professional. I was pacing around like a caged animal, which is not the way to do time. The others were all in the adjacent pens looking miserable. There was only one person missing. Keith bloody Moon. At some point much, much later, there was a huge ruckus and in swans Moon in his tiger-skin coat doing his best Noël Coward.

He looked at the meanest buzz-cut Mountie in the room and, with a dismissive wave of the hand, said, 'Could you make mine with two sugars, dear boy?' He then turned to the next Mountie along and said, 'I think you'll find I booked a suite.' I'm sure that didn't help expedite our release.

In the end, they held us for eight hours and only let us go when the local promoter agreed to pay $6,000 in cash to cover repairs. The whole thing was ridiculous. It was only a wall, a window and a couple of bits of furniture. I told you before, hotels saw us as a chance to refurbish.

We missed our early afternoon flight, just about made the late afternoon flight and arrived onstage at Boston Garden ten minutes late, which, all things considered, was a miracle. I remember we played one of the best shows on the tour. It's amazing what being let out of the cage after eight hours can do to your energy levels.

Unfortunately, getting locked up before every show wasn't an option. We limped on to the end of the tour – through Pennsylvania, Maryland, and then four nights back in London at the Sundown Theatre in Edmonton. When I finally made it back to Sussex on Christmas Eve 1973 I was knackered, but I was also relieved. I needed stability and I had my family at home waiting for me.

It wasn't just Heather and Rosie. The entire Daltrey clan invaded that Christmas. We'd sent a coach up to Shepherd's Bush to collect all the uncles and aunts, nieces and nephews, second cousins, third cousins and fourth cousins six times removed. We had a roaring fire and a roaring knees-up, singing all the filthy Cockney songs, just like the old days.

Some of my friends in the business found it hard coming off tour. Trying to readjust to a normal family existence after the madness of three months on the road was a struggle. Me? No problem. I was young. I lived in the moment. If the moment involved standing in front of thousands of people with a drummer passed out on his drums, I'd just deal with it. If it involved hosting a hundred aunts and uncles, nieces, third cousins and nephews twice removed, no problem. Some moments were better than others and, that Christmas, I had one of them. Mum and Dad were there and, at one point during that week of celebration, Dad looked me in the eye and said, 'Isn't it grand?' He was happy and that meant the world to me.

FOURTEEN

AND

ACTION ...

It had been on the cards for a long time. *Tommy: The Movie.* Ever since he'd gone off to the Amazon with two friends and a camera in 1961 to make an expedition documentary, Kit had fancied himself as a film producer. Chris had the same affliction. More than the album, the live shows and the full-scale opera house productions, he saw *Tommy* as his ticket into the movie business proper. And so he'd been going around separately from Pete, touting his own script. Then there were some other film people over from America and it all sounded like it was going to happen. Then it didn't, then it did, then it didn't again. Things are always off and on in the film industry, but because it was Kit and because it was not your average film, it always felt more off than on.

At some point in 1973, Robert Stigwood became the producer, Kit was holding various meetings and plans were all firming up. Then it all started to go weird in the backroom. There was a lot of brilliance but there was also a lot of drugs and, therefore, a lot of miscommunication. We were battling with *Quadrophenia*, trying to inhabit it like we'd inhabited *Tommy*. Making a film seemed like a distant item on the to-do list. And then, all of a sudden, Ken Russell arrived, things started happening very quickly, and I was cast as Tommy.

To be honest, I was shocked. I know I'd been singing *Tommy* for the last few years, but that didn't mean I had a clue about how to act it, particularly with Ken directing. Anybody who was in touch with anything in the 1970s was a Ken Russell fan. He was an icon, a hero, and we idolised him. And there I was not only meeting him but having lunch with him and his wife, the costume designer Shirley Kingdon, in their very posh house in Holland Park. He loved music and he completely got *Tommy* – he said it was 'the best modern opera since Berg's *Wozzeck*'. But I was completely straight with him. I said that I'd never done any acting before. I'd tried to be in the school play, but they'd chucked me out for being too disruptive. So I had no experience. I wasn't sure I could do it.

Ken was having none of it. He said I was Tommy, full stop. I explained that I could handle a crowd from a stage, but I didn't have a clue about how to project on film. In the end, I got off lightly because there was no dialogue. It was all singing. It would have been a whole different matter if I'd had to speak.

So that was it. I was going to be an actor and, once I'd calmed down and thought about it, I knew I was going to love it. It was a complete change and the timing was perfect. We'd had the difficult *Quadrophenia* tour. We'd had conflict within the band and with our management. I knew we were never going to break up but, four years after our biggest album, never a day went by without someone in the music press predicting our imminent demise. I needed that complete change.

Overnight, I switched from the hours of a musician, late to bed, very late to rise, to the hours of an actor, up well before the larks, still late to bed. I spent most of my time hanging out with the crew and it was great. If a band is like a small family that fights a lot, being on a film set is more like being in a large family that only fights some of the time. There are 50 or 60 people thrown together for four months.

There are the actors, the crew, the make-up girls. We all stayed in the same motel on Hayling Island, down by Portsmouth, and the intensity of life on a Ken Russell set meant we all developed a close bond quickly. And while I said I got off lightly, that's only very relative. The first thing I had to get to grips with was being deaf, dumb and blind. I spent a lot of time with the disabled extras we had in the film, and they taught me a lot. I already knew from Mike Shaw how difficult life in a wheelchair could be. You just need to push someone around for a day and you realise how hard it is, and how little things make a huge difference. Things like kneeling down to talk to wheelchair users at their eye level. No one's educated about it, are they? And because they aren't, it creates a barrier. How hard would it be to replace one, just one, trigonometry class for a lesson run by a disabled person, explaining what would make their lives easier? Because everyone would do it. Even the toughest kids would do it. And it would make a huge difference to society.

Anyway, I spent time with these guys on set and they were amazing. Just amazing. They taught me so much, not just with how to play Tommy but for the rest of my life. They helped me feel some of what they feel.

And by the time the shoot began, Tommy's complete sensory deprivation just took over. I went into a complete trance. I can't remember half of the stuff that went on because I was in such a daze. Sometimes that was a good thing. Sometimes, less so.

For example, I spent a whole day lying on the floor between Tina Turner's legs while she wiggled and shook her stuff. I had been a huge fan for years, but I can't for the life of me remember anything about it. I couldn't even tell you what colour knickers she was wearing. Or if she was wearing any at all. I can't even remember if I spoke to her. Tina Turner. A whole day.

Nothing. I must be the greatest method actor ever to have lived.

But then there was another day on the same 'Acid Queen' segment where I had to stand there while Ken tried to work out which tropical creatures I should share a sarcophagus with. I was wearing nothing but a loincloth. If they hadn't had the film classification board to worry about, they would have made me do it naked. And I thought I'd come a long way since that bath of cold baked beans in 1967.

First, Ken tried snakes. I quickly learned that snakes spray not only faeces and urine, but also, if you're really lucky, a very strong musk from their cloacal scent gland. For context, the musk is second only to a skunk's for potency but it's far more durable. Snakes spray it to mark territory, even if that territory is a sarcophagus. It stinks like you wouldn't believe. Ken didn't care. He just wanted to get the right shot, and, after a couple of hours with the snakes, he decided the snakes weren't right so he tried bugs. Then he tried butterflies.

I remember feeling relieved when the butterflies fluttered in but that was a mistake. They were not normal butterflies. They were giants: plate-sized with bodies the size of a fist. Into the sarcophagus they'd go and they were all over me, nice and dark, settled and calm. Then, after a lot of faffing around, someone would shout 'Action!' and the sarcophagus would open. Each time, as the butterflies flew up into a panic, they'd all empty their bowels. By the end of that session, I was covered in snake and butterfly shit. It took days to get the stench off, but I got through it with my brilliant method acting. Complete detachment from reality. Hardly noticed the smell. Away with the fairies, not the butterflies. Ken, by the way, never used any of the footage. He went with poppies instead. And poppies don't spray.

The other big test was to convince myself and the audience that Ann-Margret, the stunning Scandinavian-born Hollywood actress only three years older than me, was my mother. I did that by steering clear of her on set. Because you can't fancy your mum, even if she's a screen mum. She was an absolute treasure, though. No airs and graces, always smiling. Not a hint of superiority about her.

I doubt she even complained when they were shooting her big finale where she throws the bottle through the television and gets sprayed in foam and beans. On one of those takes, when she's writhing around, the crew watched as the foam turned pink first and then red. She'd caught a piece of glass and slashed her wrist. The blood went everywhere. I wasn't on set that day, but I saw the crew that evening and they were all still quite shaken. She needed 21 stitches but she'd stayed in character as the blood had flowed.

Proper actors have the same mentality as proper musicians. The show must go on. Ann-Margret was a pro. So was Oliver Reed. Ken liked to push his cast to the brink. It wasn't purely sadism. He was always in search of the fully committed performance. But there was still an element of brinkmanship about it and Ollie was never going to show he was near any brink. I'll give you an example. When we were filming the end scene at the holiday camp, it was an uncommonly hot summer's day. The set designers had sprayed a load of harbour buoys silver – they were like mirrors reflecting and magnifying the sunlight. By the time Ken shouted wrap, we were all burnt to a crisp. But Ollie had it worse. This was the scene in which his evil Uncle Frank was murdered by the angry mob. Ken had him lying in a puddle, playing dead.

After several takes, someone said, 'Ollie, it's lunchtime.' And Ollie replied, 'You go ahead. If that fucker thinks he's going to break me, he can think again. I'm going to lie here all day.'

And he did. He lay there all day in that puddle. The puddle had almost dried out by the end of it. But he wasn't going anywhere. Ollie and Ken loved each other and trusted each other and went to extremes not to let one another down. Everybody loved Ken. He was always open to ideas. If he got stuck on how to shoot a thing he'd always ask, well, what do you think? And if he liked it, he'd try it. He was filming with giant cameras, no Steadicams and nothing like those little tiny GoPros they use today. And when you watch the camera movement, it's pure genius. I learned so much from him. I loved him and I trusted him with my life, even though he often seemed hell-bent on killing me.

Everything was quite easy until Tommy regained his senses.

Visually, it became a harder story to tell; it just got boring. It was the same problem we had with *Lifehouse*. How do you film a feeling? Ken was the only director who could have got away with it. His camerawork was just extraordinary. He was happy to take risks, but he was happiest when his family of actors took bigger risks. He always said to me, 'I want you to do this and you will be safe.' And I always believed him.

In July, we went up to Keswick in the Lake District to shoot the climbing sequence in 'See Me, Feel Me'. I'm not good with heights. It would have been a good time to bring in the stuntman, but there was no stuntman.

'I want you to climb down that rock face, wait for me to say action, and then climb up again. And, don't worry, you will be safe,' says Ken.

I got down there, barefoot and topless, trying not to think about the 2,000-foot drop beneath me, and I waited. And waited. And I'm thinking, 'Come on, Ken, come on, Ken.'

Eventually, this voice comes down, 'We'll be about five minutes, we're waiting for the light.' The sky was pitch-black with angry clouds. That's the Lake District in late July. I waited on that ledge for 25 of the slowest minutes of my life, getting colder and colder and colder.

Finally, the sun came out, Ken shouted, 'Turn over, speed, action!' and I shot up that mountain like a spooked goat. I still remembered the lyrics, though. Watching it back now, you can hardly tell I wasn't enjoying myself. What an actor.

'Let's try it one more time ...'

Those were always the words you didn't want to hear but you always heard them. Keith really struggled with the repetition. He just didn't have any discipline. To edit a film you need to do everything over and over again. Once you've done a long shot, you need to do close-ups. It's got to all sync-up otherwise you can't cut it together. And Keith just couldn't remember what he had done from one shot to the next.

It didn't help that he and Oliver Reed were as thick as two intoxicated thieves. They didn't stay with us in our cheap motel during the main shoot. They stayed at the Grand. I only remember that because there was a fountain full of goldfish in the foyer and Keith used to take great delight in pretending to grab one of them, eat it and then spit out their remains. Of course it was only pieces of thinly sliced carrot – at least I think it was – but it still made all the old blue-rinsed ladies scream.

I don't know if it was a good idea that the two of them became such good friends. Keith was the only person who ever drank Ollie under the table. They had a bet one evening – who could put away the most brandy. After the second bottle each, Ollie passed out where he was sitting.

Keith looked at him and said, 'You're no fun at all.'

Halfway through the shoot, we almost lost Uncles Frank and Ernie. Keith and Ollie commandeered a fishing boat one night after another drinking competition and set off across the Solent. Something happened – it was impossible to work out exactly what – and they ended up a couple of miles off the Hampshire coast minus the boat, trying to swim home. Keith, as you know from the one and only time he tried his hand at surfing in Hawaii, was not a first-class swimmer. I remember them coming back, just as we were having an early breakfast. Keith always made light of things, no matter how dark they were. This time was different. It must have been a very close call.

We all survived that summer and, by early autumn, the epic shoot was almost over. The only thing left to shoot was the hang-gliding section. I had assumed we did it at the end in case I was wiped out. They'd have the film with a particularly poignant glider scene and they'd sell more cinema tickets if the main actor died for his art. I only found out afterwards that it was because they couldn't get the insurance.

'Don't worry,' said Ken. 'You'll be perfectly safe.'

Had I ever been hang-gliding before? Of course I hadn't. It's not something you do growing up in Shepherd's Bush. But on a cold, blustery October day, I found myself halfway up the Marlborough Downs, taking a quick lesson from the instructor.

Step one: 30 yards up the hill. 'Okay, push the bar forward to go up and pull it back to go down,' said the bloke. 'And you must wear a helmet for safety. Put this on.' Quite what good a well-aged Post Office telegram delivery boy's motorbike helmet would do from 500 feet up was baffling. His last piece of advice?

'Whatever you do, don't stall. You'll come down like a stone. You're always better off going too fast rather than too slow.' That was all right by me. I've always gone too fast. I ran down the hill, pushed out the A-frame like he'd said, and I was up and away, five, maybe six whole feet off the ground. I flew for a good 50 yards before landing, with a bump, flat on my arse.

Step two: another 20 yards up the hill. 'We'll just have another go before we try it from the top.' So off I ran again, pushed out the A-frame, felt the thing lift off the ground and it just kept going. Up, up, up. I'd caught a thermal and I was 200 feet up before I could react.

Don't stall, don't stall. That was all I could think. And, eventually, I got it back down again, at speed, into a very large gorse bush.

'An excellent landing,' said the instructor. 'Let's try it from the top of the hill.' So now I was fully trained.

And action: so now I was right at the top of the hill in my Tommy uniform. Jeans, no top, no shoes, no helmet. There were a few other guys up there with their gliders and they just looked at me, mouths open. What an idiot. I didn't mind. It was an adventure. I looked down the hill, I looked up at the clouds, took a deep breath and went for it. As soon as the thing caught the air, I started singing. And cut. I made a perfect landing in a field at the bottom of the hill. The field was full of thistles but I didn't care. I'd survived. Job done.

And, of course, there was Ken, all smiles.

'Let's try it one more time.'

. . .

When Ken asked me to play Franz Liszt in his next film *Liszt-omania*, I thought he was kidding. When I realised he wasn't, I said yes immediately. That was the only time I ever put myself before The Who. It wasn't just because I wanted to continue working with Ken. He was bringing things out of me that helped with my singing. It was also because I wanted to learn about acting. I wanted another string to my bow. It wouldn't hurt to do a bit of acting on the side. *Tommy* had been half a masterclass but I still knew next to nothing about the craft. I needed more experience. I needed to learn the ropes. For the next few years, I took any acting job, no matter how small. I did lots of stuff with the Film Foundation. And who can forget that I was the second house guest to die during a botched tracheotomy in Richard Marquand's 1978 horror film *The Legacy*.

But in 1975 I was still a complete acting novice. I just liked the idea of having a second career, not because I dreamed of ditching the microphone and becoming a movie star, but because I never knew when the microphone might ditch me.

Bands blew up all the time. The fact that we were still together had surprised everyone, including all of us. The way Pete talked about us in the music press or onstage between songs, it always felt like we had a month or two left, tops. And if we were going to split up, it was too late to go back to the sheet-metal factory. I'd been in a band since I was a teenager. I'd hit 30, which is old in rock years. I needed something to fall back on. Besides, working on a film was so much easier than slogging your body around the world singing. Yes, you had to get up early and I've never been good at that. But as long as you could find somewhere out of Ken's sight lines, you could always sleep between takes. It was the first cushy job I'd ever had.

I said at the time that *Lisztomania* would either be a huge flop or a huge success and, in the end, it wasn't the latter. It was certainly Ken at his most out there. The script was only 57 pages long – the rest of it was somewhere deep inside Ken's terrifying head – and the dialogue was dreadful. I could see what Ken wanted visually but I felt like I let him down. Knowing what I know now, I would have changed every single word of it and made the character work. But back then I didn't even know how to deliver a line of dialogue. I think I got better at it over the years through practice. But even now, if you write something that I have to read, I can't do it. I have to speak it from the heart or nowhere. I found singing much more natural. Life isn't a play, it's an opera. My singing comes from the heart. Speaking other people's words comes from the brain.

So yes, my second film with Ken Russell wasn't a great success. The Liszt Society wrote to film critics before they even saw it, warning that the story contained scenes of 'rape, blood-sucking, exorcism and castration'.

'The Liszt Society didn't know the half of it,' wrote *The Sunday Times* film critic. 'The film is impudent, vulgar, near pornographic. And I like it.' Most other critics didn't, but I thought parts of it, some of the vignettes, were absolutely phenomenal. The scene with Fiona Lewis in the Swiss chalet is extraordinary. And I came away with two things of which I could be tremendously proud. I'd procured both more invaluable acting experience, and an eight-foot penis.

The giant pink Styrofoam phallus that came home with me at the end of the shoot had been used as a prop in one of the fantasy scenes. It had looked a little forlorn in the store cupboard in Shepperton but not as forlorn as the end of the second penis, which had been guillotined off in one of the more disturbing fantasy scenes. I decided I had a better use for them at home.

Tommy had become a really big film and movie stardom was creating a whole new set of privacy issues with my nosy next-door neighbour. He was constantly opposing anything I wanted to do on my 35 acres of land. Even though the hedge along our boundary was ten feet high, I would frequently catch him peeping through. So I thought I'd give him something to look at.

One wonderful evening, I erected the erection in the centre of the circular drive in the front garden. Very early the next morning, there was a loud knock on the front door. I opened it to find a burly police sergeant and his colleague desperately attempting to keep their faces straight.

'I've come with a complaint about the erection, sir,' he said, as seriously as possible.

'Oh, you mean the prick,' I replied.

The officer nearly bit his tongue off.

'Who's complained?' I asked.

'We're not allowed to say.'

'But why would anyone complain, officer? No one can see it.'

'You do have a point,' smiled the sergeant. Off they walked across the drive to give the phallus a closer inspection before getting back into their car and driving off. I think every police car in the whole of Sussex must have driven up my drive over the next four days. I've never seen so many smiling policemen and women. On the fifth day, there was another loud knock. I was greeted by the sight of the chief of Sussex police. He had an expression that suggested a very bad toothache and he didn't beat around the bush.

'Mr Daltrey, do you think you could remove your erection from the front lawn?'

'But no one can see it, unless they're trespassing or they're a peeping Tom.'

'Technically, you are correct,' he replied, 'but your neighbour is making my life a misery. Could you remove it to keep the peace?'

He should have marched next door to make the correct arrest but, by this time, I'd had my fun and I felt rather sorry for him. So I removed my eight-foot penis and replaced it with the guillotined three-footer instead.

· · ·

Tommy premiered in March 1975 and, while Tina Turner, Elton John, Ann-Margret, The Stones, The Beatles, Dean Martin, Pete, Keith and John attended the various extravagant launch parties across America, I was still finishing *Lisztomania*.

Heather was at Pembury Hospital, awaiting the arrival of our second daughter, Willow. I wasn't there as much as I would have liked for Willow's first year. We found a nanny. She came via John Paul Jones, a Led Zeppelin nanny, and she was more Mary Poppins than Mary Poppins. But in those short periods when I was home, it was idyllic. I could look out across the Sussex hills and feel the calmness come back. If I hadn't had that – the family, the quiet, the place where none of the rest of my life had any impact – it would have been much harder. Because that year was hard. The attention the film directed my way was huge – a different level from anything I'd had in The Who. I remember I was in some shopping mall in Texas, promoting my second solo album *Ride a Rock Horse*. It was just a signing but there were thousands and thousands of people there. It was a mob and they were there for *Tommy*. Forty-odd years later, I can make some dry observation about life imitating art. At the time, it was scary, very scary. The hysteria was daunting and I couldn't handle it. I lost my way a bit.

As soon as *Tommy* was released, Hollywood came calling. I was nominated for a Golden Globe. Most Promising Newcomer, don't you know. I didn't win – Brad Dourif (Billy Bibbit in *One Flew Over the Cuckoo's Nest*) was obviously a more promising newcomer that year. Ann-Margret won best actress and Pete got an Oscar nomination for his score.

And, suddenly, I was on the American chat shows, and I wasn't ready. I couldn't cope with that level of scrutiny and the interrogation. I'd been doing interviews for years, but this was more personal and more intense. On a very basic level, my accent hadn't adapted at all for an American audience. I couldn't understand them. They couldn't understand me. Culturally as well as literally. There's an art to American entertainers. The way they talk to an audience – it's a whole different class of comfort and ease. I just let the old nerves creep back and with them came the s-s-s-stutter.

It should have been a fairy-tale time. Boy from Shepherd's Bush makes it to Tinseltown. Particularly given the fact that it was a pretty grim time to be living in Britain. This was 1975 – the height of socialist Britain. Harold Wilson was prime minister again, top earners were paying 98 per cent tax and all the bands were going into exile (we were one of the very few that stayed). The whole country was grinding to a halt. If I was going to bugger off to Hollywood, now would have been a good time to do it. But I quickly realised that it was all phoney. It was a fairy tale. Behind all those sparkling smiles and gushing compliments, there was a complete lack of sincerity.

As you climb the greasy pole, people think you move in these exalted circles. Was I friends with whichever actor or whichever musician? First of all, if anyone ever asked if I knew someone, my first instinct was to deny it. That's just an old habit from my days on the street in west London. No, guv'nor. Never seen him before in my life, just in case I'd be putting them in a frame.

Second of all, I didn't know everyone in my world. I'd met them because it was a small world, but did I *know* them? We rose up performing with The Beatles, The Stones, The Kinks. But I was never really friends with any of them. We passed like ships in the night. They did their gig, we did ours. If we happened to be on the same bill, it didn't make much of a difference. Robert Plant became a proper friend and so, later, did Eddie Vedder of Pearl Jam. Just a few people in the business but it's not big numbers. The band was my immediate family and, beyond that, I had my friends, my proper mates. To get to really know someone takes time and we never had time. And I never enjoyed hanging out at posh events, air-kissing celebrities. I was always nervous. Still am. At any gathering, I don't do it easy. I always end up in a corner, smashed up against a wall.

I find small talk very difficult. Maybe it's just collateral damage from years of being pushed and pulled at by people I've never met and never wanted to meet. These days, I love a dinner party. Six people maximum. Any more than that, and I can't hear. My hearing has got so bad, that's the limit. And if there are only six people, you get through the small talk pretty quick. Anyway, Hollywood was and still is the extreme version of all that meaningless hobnobbing, and I was a fish out of water.

The same people who assume you spend all your time partying with the rich and famous also ask if you've changed. The answer is that you haven't. Despite the ridiculous whirlwind you're living in, despite the dramatic change in circumstance, from skiffling teens to one of the biggest rock bands in the world, you don't change. It's all the same, only bigger. But people around you change, and I think that's what causes the insecurity. Every person you meet, you think, are they what they seem? Are they being straight with me? It's the same in any walk of life but when you're famous it's like you're putting a magnifying glass on everything. Small things become enormous. People think you're different and you're not. How some of these celebrities today are going to manage when they get older I have no idea, because some haven't even got a core talent to fall back on. After their 15 minutes, there is only darkness. Or *I'm a Celebrity*.

Under the magnifying glass, all the accompanying noise and light that came with film stardom was too much. So I came back from the Land of Eternal Sunshine to the Land of Eternal Taxation, took a deep and grateful breath of Sussex air and returned to the relative sanity of life in a rock band.

FIFTEEN

BY NUMBERS

P ete had been struggling with the same realisation about fame when he composed 'How Many Friends'. He said he wrote that song 'stoned out of my brain in my living room, crying my eyes out, detached from my own work and from the whole project. I felt empty.' Which is not how a soon-to-be-Oscar-nominated rock star is supposed to feel. We recorded that track and the rest of *The Who by Numbers* album in Shepperton in the spring of 1975, right in the midst of all the craziness. *NME* described it as 'Pete Townshend's suicide note'. He was giving long interviews full of self-loathing and loathing in general. He said our audience was rubbish and that we were rubbish on the last tour.

He's always told us how he feels via the medium of media. Why didn't we ever talk face-to-face? Why didn't he just pick up the phone? I don't know why. I really didn't understand it. But I suppose we weren't like that.

I'm a deeply private person – why else do you think it's taken so long to write this autobiography – so having my voice criticised by him in the full glare of the newspapers really hurt. I'd like to think we'd talk now. I think we'd pick up the phone. We have talked, face-to-face, man-to-man, at critical stages in our lives. I went to see him when he was stuck on heroin and, to his credit, he checked into rehab. He obviously listened. In that sense, we were very, very close. In difficult times, we are there for each other. We are friends. Not in the sense that we'd call each other up and go out for a meal. Social niceties are not our forte. But we have a bond. It's hard to describe but I think that's the point.

A lot of people are too frightened to talk to him – he lives on a different plane to the rest of us and it's not linear. Sometimes, with no warning, for no reason, he can cut you to the quick. He can come across very mean, and, as I've said, even spiteful, but that's not what he's like deep down. He's not the sort of person you want to hurt. I never wanted to hurt him, not even when I knocked him out. But I've never been frightened to talk to him and tell him how it is (although I do steer clear when I read the warning signs).

Pete, on the other hand, could only communicate his musical struggles through the press. He never came to us when he was in trouble. He never shared his problems. Maybe we could have kicked things around. We could have helped. Things do get solved in the studio, but we never, ever got into that position. He just told journalists in order to tell us how bad we were.

I'd been at the same gigs he was complaining about. I'd listened to John and Keith one night at the Rainbow Theatre, desperately trying to keep up with Pete. He got drunker and drunker and wilder and wilder until he became musically incoherent. And then, a week later, I think he'd taken a shot of heroin or something. He was off in different keys, on some wild trip, without warning or signal. It was a nightmare. And then, months later, we read that it's us. It was John and Keith that were crap, not Pete.

How could he turn around and tell them, via *NME*, that they were crap? They weren't crap. They were brilliant. They were dancing on pinheads.

There were three of us onstage working our bollocks off. The Who wasn't crap that night. Pete was crap that night. Well, he was never crap but he was drunk. Or off in the clouds. Take the responsibility. He could have admitted he was drunk, that he was under pressure. But he blamed us, and I stood up for the band. Of course, the music press loved the bickering. Rock stars wrestling. It sells papers. But I was genuinely pissed off.

On the management side, our relationship with Kit and Chris had deteriorated to the point that we were suing them, and they were suing us.

We'd come full horrific circle from that first meeting, full of optimism and promise, in the Railway Tavern in 1964 to two enemies on opposite sides of the boardroom table, flanked by lip-licking lawyers. Our foundations were crumbling and if we had unravelled completely that summer, imploding on our own success, no one would have been surprised. That was what happened with bands far less volatile than ours.

But then, by October, we were starting out on tour again. Pete had spent the summer with his family in America, baring his soul to Murshida Ivy Duce, the confidante of Indian spiritual master, Meher Baba. The command that came down from Ivy Duce, was 'to keep playing guitar in The Who until further notice'. Frankly, I couldn't have agreed more. I only felt negative about playing with The Who in one period in our entire half-century working together and that was still four years away.

Pete kept saying we were a nostalgia act. He said he hated touring. I've already said it was different for him. I couldn't sit on my arse and live off royalties. I had a young family and two kids elsewhere to support. But that wasn't the only reason I wanted to keep going. You have to tour. If you don't tour, you're dead. You're gone. All those people predicting our imminent demise would have been proved right if we'd stopped. I've only seen a few bands go away for a decade and when they come back, they've still got it. They pick up right where they left off. But more often than not, they don't come back. Or, if they do, their fire has gone out. Luckily, or as a result of divine intervention, Pete overcame his many objections to our continued existence and so we set off on the road once again with our new, brilliant, morose album.

In some ways, *The Who By Numbers* is my favourite album. It was our seventh studio album and I remember we didn't have a clue what we were doing.

Pete just chucked a load of songs at me, I chose the ones I liked and he was surprised by my selection. For me, songs like 'Imagine a Man', 'How Many Friends' and 'However Much I

Booze' expose our vulnerabilities and the album is wonderful for that. It's about inability in the bigger sense. I saw the lyrics and I thought, this has to be sung. If this can grab the ear of anyone of our age through this period of our lives, it will speak to them. And that's all I cared about.

We began with eleven dates in Britain and, after a rusty start, everything just came together. It felt like everyone wanted to be there. After the Netherlands, Germany and Austria, we arrived in the States at the end of November to play across the South. The venues were getting so big that we needed more sound and light. John Wolff, our production manager, was like a kid in a particularly outlandish sweetshop. He was experimenting with lasers and holograms, all pioneering stuff, and by the end of 1975 our crew were moving unprecedented amounts of kit from gig to gig. We had three argon lasers – one at the back of the stage and two on either side – and they were so powerful they had to be rigged up to the nearest fire hydrant to keep them cool. It was worth it, though. People had never seen anything like it back then. It blew their minds. It was genius lighting.

We didn't know it then, but this was us at the very height of our powers. When we picked up again in the early spring, Keith was in trouble. A couple of years after Kim had left him, he'd moved to California. He was out of reach. We had never been that close – we were friends, but we never ever mixed socially, it just wasn't part of our deal. That began to change when we were filming *Tommy* and then, when we were trying to get him home, we became much closer.

I went over there once to talk to him and it was a shock. It was like a flashback to the teenage Keith's bedroom wall in Wembley. It had all become real but the reality wasn't like the teenager's dream. He had bought the beach house next door to Steve McQueen in the Colony, the most expensive part of Malibu. Annette, his new Swedish girlfriend, looked exactly like Kim, the spitting image of a Californian surf chick. I arrived thinking, this is going to be great, but when I walked into the lounge with its huge picture window looking out on the Pacific sunsets, it was obvious that all was not well. The room was empty apart from two sofas and a giant Persian rug. On the rug were a dozen piles of dog shit. And the two of them hadn't noticed. Or they didn't care.

The dream of living next to his screen idol hadn't worked out for Keith either. The first sign was that the border between the two properties was lined with trees. Not hedges but full-size tropical rainforest trees.

McQueen had craned in these giant tubs with giant palms to try to keep Keith out. The relationship could have worked a lot better. They had central things in common. Both of them were from working-class backgrounds, both of them were under the spotlight, both of them were struggling with fame. They could have helped one another. But when Keith first went over to introduce himself, he upset McQueen's 16-year-old son and, when the resident guard dog bit him, he bit it back.

The result was a reckoning with McQueen at the Malibu district attorney's office, a chance to start again, but Keith chose to wear his Rommel uniform to the meeting and it didn't go well. He then installed spotlights shining on McQueen's beach-front in the hope of spotting Ali McGraw, McQueen's wife, in the nude. Hence the palm trees.

I went to talk to him because anyone could see he was out of control in California. He had no money and any money he could get his hands on, he was spending. When we refused to give him any more cash, he borrowed ten thousand dollars from our agent, Frank Barsalona. A week later, he came back and asked for more. Frank, quite understandably shocked, pointed out that no one, not even Keith Moon, should struggle to last a week on ten thousand dollars. Keith explained, quite understandably, too, that he had had to hire a plane to fly a banner reading 'Happy Birthday Ringo'.

On 9 March 1976, we were two songs into the show at the Boston Garden and Keith collapsed. The official explanation was that he had flu. The real reason was the usual one. Brandy and barbiturates, culminating in a rush to Massachusetts General. This time, there was no Scot Halpin from Muscatine, Iowa, to save the night. We hadn't got far enough into the gig to get away with it. We just walked off. The crowd was disappointed and the band was fed up with him. The next night, we were staying in New York. Keith was at the Navarro. I was at the Plaza with Heather. Word came through that he'd cut his foot badly in his suite. I remember saying to Heather, 'He's trying to destroy himself.' And I decided, in the middle of the night, to go along and see him.

Keith was propped up in bed looking very sorry for himself. The walls of the suite were decorated with what appeared to be large strokes of black paint. This was the aftermath of Keith's accident. He'd sliced through an artery in his leg and sprayed the walls with deep arterial blood. He'd been lucky to survive. Cool Hand Bill Curbishley had found him and managed to get a tourniquet on the wound before Keith bled out. Judging by the abstract art arching across the walls of the room, the ambulance had arrived in the nick of time.

'Sorry, Rog,' was all Keith could say now.

'Don't worry about that,' I said. 'But you've got to tell me what's going on. Why the self-destruct button? Is it Kim?'

Of course it was Kim. It was obvious. Every girl he was with, he dressed up like Kim. He even used to hire hookers and make them dress up like her, too. He always carried a blonde wig around with him to complete the effect. When I asked the question to which I already knew the answer, he started to nod and then he burst into tears.

'I'll never get her back,' he said. For a long while, there was silence, broken only by the sound of Keith sobbing. I didn't know what to say. I just stayed there at the bottom of the bed.

'Yeah,' I said eventually, 'she might not come back but if you love her and if you showed her that, then she'd always be there. That's how it is with your one true love. It might not be how it was but you don't have to lose everything.'

He just looked blankly back at me and we returned to silence. So I asked him, 'Is it Neil as well?'

And he burst into tears again. 'I'm a murderer,' he said. 'I'm a murderer.'

'No you're not, Keith. It was circumstances. It could have happened to anyone.'

I told him he did what he thought was the best he could at the time. I told him he had to let this stuff go. He had to get help. A few moments later he sat up and, as was always his way, he gave me a hug. I should have been hugging him.

When I left his suite some time later, he seemed a little more chipper. He was happy, or he was making a pretence of being happy. And we never talked about any of that stuff again. For the next 18 months, the rest of Keith's life, he would call me up. I don't think anyone else was answering the phone to him. He'd call at four in the morning when I was at home and the kids were in bed, and we always knew it was Keith. Heather was particularly good with him in that dark period and we did what we could. Of course, for the last four decades, I've spent a lot of time wishing I'd done more.

He did come back to London, though. He abandoned his tarnished dream in California, left Steve McQueen in peace and, borrowing more cash from Pete, rented a suitably grand pad on Curzon Street, Mayfair.

That was stage one. Stage two was getting him fit. He couldn't get through our gruelling set if he wasn't fit. I nagged him and nagged him and then one day he turned up at the studio in jodhpurs and a riding jacket.

He'd signed up for riding classes along Rotten Row in Hyde Park. For the exercise. His bum must have been pretty sore that night but it was a good sign. At least he was trying. Unfortunately, when we started work on our eighth studio album, *Who*

Are You, in the autumn of 1977, it was obvious that his physicality and his prowess on the drums had suffered badly from the last five years of abuse. He just had it or he didn't. And in those last months of his life, his natural talent was deserting him. And without that, he was stuck in a downward spiral.

In my time off, I was going the other way. Where Keith had hookers and drugs, I was obsessing with more mundane things. The house absorbed all my excess energy. I started with the lake below the house. When we arrived, you wouldn't call it a lake. Through years of neglect, it was not much more than a muddy puddle. I enlisted the help of Herbert, the son of the publican who ran our local, the Kicking Donkey. His favourite pastime was playing with giant bulldozers. He had the toys and I had the playground, and together we spent weeks and happy weeks digging out the silt and raising the dam until, finally, I had a proper lake. There is very little that's more satisfying than digging a bloody great hole and then watching it fill with water, watching the contours of the land shape a new lake, covering up the muddy mess we'd made and replacing it with something beautiful. And it's incredible how quickly they become inhabited with all kinds of wildlife. That's probably why I ended up with four interconnected lakes on the far side of the farm. Once you start ...

Given that I had all these lakes, I could invite all my old mates from the factory to come fishing almost every weekend I wasn't touring. They would sit there by the water, shooting the breeze, and they'd tell me it was criminal, Rog, to keep all this to yourself. What about the likes of us living in tower blocks, eh,

Rog? The likes of us would love to come to a place like this and fish. And, of course, they were right. So I opened it up to the public. In the early eighties, fly fishing for trout was the up-and-coming sport for the working man, and it gave me the chance to meet lots of people who were more interested in fish than rock star Roger. And I'm proud of what I've done to that land. If it had been left to fall fallow, the whole valley would have been lost. It takes a huge amount of work to keep the countryside looking and working the way it should. It means a great deal to me that I've looked after my bit of it. It's a cliché but I'm just the tenant. I'm keeping it in trust for future generations. Hopefully, I've left it in good shape.

It took me ten years to decorate Holmshurst. With the help of another very good, very loyal, very long-suffering friend, we scrubbed every inch of the wood with paint stripper. At some point in the Victorian period, its owners had decided to stain all the beams black and it took seven summers to get them back to their original honey colour. We were there in rubber gloves and boiler suits, sweating our bollocks off. I loved almost every minute of it. It was a straightforward, repetitive job, the opposite of anything to do with The Who. When I wasn't scrubbing, I was digging, and when I wasn't digging, I was making things.

Or restoring things. For several years, for example, I collected old gypsy caravans and Victorian hand-driven roundabouts. I'd become great friends with John Carter, formerly of the Slade School of Fine Art, latterly a towering, bearded hulk of a man who liked to accumulate vintage cars, bikes, slot machines and fairground rides. He even managed to get hold of a set of steam-driven gallopers (you could never call them carousels in front of John ... too American).

John was a bit strapped for cash back then. It was the mid-seventies. Most people were. So I'd buy some of the kit and have the joy of restoring them myself. Trouble was, as soon as they were finished, they just became objects to look at (and fill up the sheds). In the end, I sold two to a museum and the rest to John ... for a fair price, of course. And in 1977, he and his wife Anna set off with their wonderful Carters Steam Fair. It's still in the family and still chugging and belching around Britain today.

At some point in the 1970s, between the lakes and the caravans and the music, I built the kids a dolls' house. It took three months – one side is Rosie's, all clean and well kept, the other side is Willow's, the scuzzy neighbour. It's still in Rosie's bedroom today. And I look at it with the same affection with which I look at one of our albums. I made it out of plywood with a saw, no plan and a bit of brain power. It's pure satisfaction. And I think that's the key. I need to work. And I honestly believe that's part of the reason why I'm still here today. Pete, who has an incredible work ethic, survived by creating things in his head and on tape. I survived by doing things with my hands. If I didn't have a project during our down times, what else would I have done with my time?

Chance bad luck also kept me on the straight and narrow. In 1975, round about the time I was fielding calls from Hollywood, welcoming our second daughter into the world, launching my second solo album and wrapping *Lisztomania*, I dropped a large stone ball on my toe. It's one of the hazards of buying a rather grand home. There are lots of plinths and columns and some of them have large stone balls on top. I was trying to move one and I lost my grip. Two years later, I started to get gout in the toe the stone ball had flattened. The cure was twofold. I gave up booze and I gave up wheat. By my mid-thirties, I was the exact opposite of the hedonistic rocker. It wasn't because I had an obsession with longevity. It was because if I didn't stay healthy, I couldn't sing.

My vocal cords defined my lifestyle and that's why I'm still kicking around today. I'm kicking carefully, mind you. That toe still plays up.

SIXTEEN

THE END,
A BEGINNING
AND ANOTHER
END

On Thursday 7 September 1978, Jackie Curbishley, Bill's wife, called Pete and Pete called me. 'He's gone and done it,' said Pete.

'Who's done what?'

'Moon.'

Keith Moon died in his sleep sometime after breakfast, the morning after he and Annette briefly attended a party in Covent Garden hosted by Paul McCartney to mark the start of Buddy Holly Week. We hadn't toured all year because he had been in no fit state to keep up. It had been hard enough recording *Who Are You* at Ramport. 'Music Must Change', the fifth track on the album, almost didn't make it because Keith struggled with the six-eight time. He was never a musical conformist anyway, but this was different. After four takes and countless apologies, he leapt up from behind his drums and shouted, 'I'm the best Keith Moon-type drummer in the world!'

And he was, right until the end. He died after overdosing on 32 chlormethiazole tablets, sedatives prescribed to help with alcohol withdrawal. He had been talking about sorting himself out. He'd moved back to London. He'd gone horse-riding. He still wanted to be in the band. But it was a losing battle.

His death was something we'd been expecting for five years, maybe longer. It could have happened on any day during that time. But when the inevitable news came through, it was still a big hit. It's weird, when you've been expecting something for that long, it's actually more shocking than if he'd just gone unexpectedly. We'd got used to expecting it to the point where it was never going to happen. It left me, and I'm sure it left Pete and John, totally traumatised.

The next day, we put out a statement saying that we were more determined than ever to carry on, and that we wanted the spirit of the group to which Keith contributed so much to go on. We were in a daze, of course, but those weren't just platitudes. We meant it. I was determined that the band should survive because of the music. And, of course, there was self-interest as well. It was my profession and my life.

Later, Pete would say that Keith's death stopped The Who from petering out. That it gave us another few years. To look at it very objectively, it did give us freedom. We could never replace Keith but now he was gone, we had an opportunity. We had always been a foursome. A square. A four-walled room. Now, one of the walls was gone and the room was open to infinity. We had infinite options. We were open to a world of infinite possibilities. And then, somehow and suddenly, we closed up the room again.

In January 1979, Pete invited Kenney Jones to become our drummer. We all liked Kenney very much. He'd been a friend for years and he's a great bloke. During the tours we did with him, I got on with him better than the rest of the band. He was also a great drummer. But he was completely the wrong drummer for us. He was right for the Faces.

That's not meant to sound disparaging. At the time, people thought I was saying Kenney was a crap drummer. I have never ever said Kenney was a crap drummer. He was a crap drummer for The Who, just as Keith would have been for the Faces. He was wrong, very wrong, for us. They had their style and we had ours. They were a tight band, Chas and Dave with Rod Stewart, a jolly old singsong down the pub, and they needed a metronomic drummer like Kenney. The Who was completely different. We were nose-to-the-grindstone, workhorse rock. If you'd put Keith in the Faces, he would have clattered over everything else.

Still, the decision was made and Kenney was brought in. We signed him in for a quarter share of the band, which was just stupid. Pete wanted it that way so Pete had it that way and I gave in for the quiet life. On 2 May 1979, after a lot of rehearsal at Shepperton, we arrived at the Rainbow Theatre, Finsbury Park, to open our first tour with Kenney, not Keith.

At first, it wasn't bad. In fact, it was good to be playing again. It was a huge relief. A therapy. None of us found it easy to move on. Keith's absence was palpable. All those wild years together, night after night, were lost and so it was emotional. It felt like we were doing ten miles of a marathon each night, but we put our heads down and we dug into the music. We were silent between songs, but the music was as solid as anything. And Kenney, to his immense credit, was brilliant. He played to the energy levels demanded by The Who. A lot of the stuff we were playing on that tour was from the new album and that made it easier. It worked and we were gelling. It was only when we went back to the old stuff that it felt hollow.

We toured across Britain, France and Germany and the gigs got bigger and bigger. We did Wembley Stadium, we did the 65,000-capacity Zeppelinfeld stadium in Nuremberg, we did five sold-out nights at Madison Square Garden. Everywhere we went, the demand far outstripped capacity. Promoters were allocating tickets by lottery and all the venues were bursting at the seams. And then, in December, we arrived at the Riverfront Coliseum in Cincinnati.

It was a good show – a fabulous show – which made it even more painful to hear what had happened when we came offstage. It was an ice-cold night and it was festival seating – first come, first served. The promoter decided to open three of the 11 doors to the venue, so everyone made a dash for it, desperate to get out of the cold and into the front rows. It must have been like pouring a quart into a half-pint pot. Eleven fans died in the crush at the entrance. Thanks to Bill, the organisers made the sensible decision to let the show go on to prevent further panic, which stopped people clambering over the dead and injured. That meant we did the whole gig without any knowledge of the tragedy. Imagine how it feels to walk offstage, euphoric, buzzing, full of the joys of life, only to discover that people have died in their attempt to see you play.

I don't even remember if I had a reaction. It was immediately so public with people poking microphones at you asking, 'How d'you feel?' What stupid questions journalists ask before anyone has had time to process anything. How do you think I felt? Wonderful? It was horrible and I was just shocked. Numb. Sleep was entirely elusive that night and then, the very next day, we had to travel to Buffalo, New York, for the next show. It was a hard night. There was no communication with each other or the audience. But we played with pure venom arising from the grief we were all feeling.

We could have stopped, I suppose, but that was never even discussed. With Keith's death and now this, this worse thing, this meaningless thing, we could have just packed up the kit for good and gone home. But I honestly thought stopping would not have done anything for the situation at all. And it would almost certainly have made the suffering worse, for me at any rate. So maybe it was a selfish thing, I don't know. Or maybe to put your head into music, to immerse yourself in performance, was the only therapy to get out of it. Certainly, it helped. We got the tour done and we did play well. Those ten remaining shows after Cincinnati were among the most intense of my life. Musically, it was a great tour. Emotionally, it was a nightmare.

We stay in touch with the friends of the people who died, but I can't bring them back. I wish I could, I just wish I could. Have I ever felt responsible? Can I be responsible for what happened in Cincinnati? Of course I can't. I don't feel guilty. I feel sad, incredibly sad for the people who lost family. It was extremely hard to get through.

The hardest bit was coming home just before Christmas and seeing all my friends and family. To be reintroduced to normality after what had happened. It was like being hit by a cricket bat. It had made the headlines back in the UK but no one knew what it was like to be there. There was no one to talk to, to share the load. I went for long walks around my farm and I talked to myself. I'm agnostic, bordering on atheist. The whole God thing seems to me to have caused most of humanity's problems. But in that bleak winter, it would have been nice to have had someone else to have talked to, to pretend there was some divine plan and that what happened in Cincinnati was a part of it.

• • •

When we set off again in 1980, it was more obvious that things weren't right. Kenney watered down the energy of the band. He was pulling The Who back into a straight-paced, Small Faces pub-style performance, and I was finding it impossible to phrase the lyrics. We were playing all the songs, but we were doing them like a pub band playing covers. Nothing knitted together. The Who had gone and our songs, Pete's magical songs, were now just songs. I seriously considered buying Kenney a pair of brushes for 'My Generation' – it was lacking so much energy. And it's hard enough getting through a three-hour set night after night when things are working. You rely on the adrenaline and the energy of the music to get you through. When it's gone, it's debilitating.

So I sat Kenney down and said, sorry, chum, I can't go on with you playing drums. He didn't say much. Who can blame him? It must have been hard not to take it personally. But it really wasn't personal. You can't be anything but ruthless to get a band to succeed. You can't be mediocre. A band can either be terrible or brilliant. There is no middle ground. So you have to make tough decisions. I'd done it with Harry Wilson, my best friend, when we'd replaced him with Doug Sandom. I wanted to do it with Kenney.

So we had a meeting, a summit, a reckoning in Bill Curbishley's house in Chigwell. Pete and Kenney were sitting on one sofa; John and I were facing them and Bill was in the middle, mediating. There wasn't any aggression on my part. I loved Kenney, but he was wrong for us. I knew it. I know Pete knew it. I knew Pete was kicking himself, but he couldn't do the bad guy bit. So I just said what I needed to say. If you've got the wrong wheel on a car and you're weaving all over the place, you have to change it. So, an ultimatum. It's me or Kenney.

Kenney said nothing. Bill said nothing. John was quiet, too. But Pete didn't hesitate. Not for a second. He just said it was no choice at all. Kenney would stay. I should have left there and then. I hated the fact that Pete made it personal. Why would he choose Kenney over me? Well, you'll have to read Pete's book, but I did expect a bit more support. So Kenney stayed and, though I came to regret it, so did I. And we set off on another intense touring schedule.

Pete's refusal to make a tough decision consigned the band to a long, slow death. I also think it was the trigger for Pete to get heavily into heroin. He had all kinds of issues – his marriage, Cincinnati, the pressure, always, to write material – but it was when the wheels started to come off our band that he really went to pieces.

I got a call, I can't remember from whom, asking me to go and see him. I was down in Sussex but there were all these reports of Pete out and about in the clubs of London, off his face. I had to go and see him. In spite of everything, I was the only one he might listen to. In those days, it was very hard to open Pete up. It's different now. We're much more honest with each other. Back then, the walls could come up very quickly.

But I did go and see him. I swallowed my pride and I went up to his Eel Pie Studio in Twickenham and there he was, nodding out, surrounded by drugs paraphernalia. I sat there and I started talking. I didn't know if he could hear me. For the first half an hour or so, he definitely wasn't there. But I carried on for three or four hours. I told him nothing was worth this. He was too bright for it to end like this. He'd been against this junk for most of his life. Why change now? I was trying to get him to talk, to engage, but he wouldn't talk. He didn't answer any of my questions, so I just carried on and on at him. I left late in the afternoon with no idea if anything had gone in. The next day, he checked himself into rehab.

When he came out, we made our tenth album, *It's Hard*. And, Christ, it really was. Pete was tearing his hair out trying to come up with new songs. He got there in the end, but even at the time I didn't think the songs stood up to our earlier work. Everything felt wrong. If you listen to the record, every drum break was a straight roll down. Again and again and again. Dosh dosh dosh d-d-d-d-dosh. It drove me mad.

It all crystallised for me in September 1982. I was on my way to do the launch of the record's accompanying tour. Another 42 shows. Another three-month haul across North America. I was doing the launch on my own, as usual. Pete wanted nothing to do with promotion. He didn't want to do interviews or photo shoots. Nothing. So I was on my own in the car, trying to build up the enthusiasm, and I just made the decision. That was it. This would be our last tour.

I made the announcement at the press launch and I knew it was the right decision. It solved all our problems. Pete would have no more pressure on him. The drummer problem wouldn't exist any more. It took the band completely by surprise, but I knew that if we had just carried on it might have killed him.

So that was our farewell tour and we ground through it. And, even then, it still wasn't the bitter end of it. We were stuck with two-thirds of a three-record deal to fulfil.

About six months after we came off the road, Pete came down to Holmshurst. He'd been trying to write the next album and he was there to tell me he couldn't. He was finished. This really was the end.

'I can't write any more,' he said. 'I can't go on.'

And I think he was shocked when I just said, 'Fine'.

It was difficult because I'd already spent the advance and so had John, but it didn't matter. We found a way through and I was fully supportive of Pete's decision. He needed space to breathe. He needed to recover. So that was it. Apart from Live Aid in 1985 – which silver-tongued Bob talked me into – we were done. For almost a decade, that was it for The Who.

SEVENTEEN

LIFE AFTER

I wasn't happy to break up. It was just fate. But there was nothing to worry about it. If we didn't get back together, well, so be it. And if we did, we'd only do it if we found the right drummer. I knew that Pete wouldn't throw it all away. He's a very clever man. He's always been aware. We recognised his talent. And although there were times he couldn't admit it, he did recognise his own luck in finding us. He knew he'd somehow managed to find three other musicians who could present his talent. That number had dropped from three to two, but I never thought for a minute that it really was the end.

In the meantime, I had to pay the bills. So the eighties became about acting, solo albums and fish farming.

In 1980, I played McVicar, an armed bank robber and escaped convict in the film of the same name. That was different from all my other acting jobs. I wanted to do it because so many of my friends had been blaggers. They walked about like it was a really cool thing, just like the gangs do today. It's the thing to aspire to when you're on a slummy street or a rough estate. Crime seems like an easy way out.

I knew it wasn't. Eventually, it always caught up with them. Ask Bill Curbishley. Ask George Davis. He was put away for 20 years for an armed robbery at the London Electricity Board in 1974. The only trouble was he didn't do it. His wife Rose put together a great campaign to get him released and I was very happy to help with it. I went onstage wearing a 'George Davis Is Innocent' T-shirt and I celebrated when he got released. And then, about a year later, he got caught at the wheel of a getaway vehicle outside a bank and that was it. He spent the next seven years banged up.

I was glad he got off the one he didn't do and I was glad he got put away for the one he did do. And that's how it is. It's not glamorous. He lost his freedom. He lost his lovely wife. All these guys were mugs and, eventually, they found that out. John McVicar was particularly honest about it. He wrote the least glamorous account of his criminal life. He showed that being a robber was an easy way to make a living until it wasn't. I wanted to show that on film. I just thought anything you can do to deter people on the street from getting into that stuff in the first place has got to be good.

I don't think we glamorised him at all in that movie. It was just his story. And, as it turned out, there was a happy ending. His life turned around once he came out of prison. He became a very successful writer and he's never been in trouble since.

The process of making that film was an immersive experience. After several weeks, I found it difficult to stop being

McVicar. I was strutting around the place, giving off the gangster swagger. I'm not sure what Heather thought about it all. But I learned a lot. I did most of the prison scenes with Adam Faith, who was playing McVicar's cellmate Wally 'Angel Face' Probyn, and he was brilliant. He helped me learn to relax and let myself go. If you feel like you're acting, you're failing. If you feel you're doing nothing, it's working. It's strange. The lines are the least important thing of all.

You can tell I still haven't got the hang of it when I played Macheath in the BBC's 1983 adaptation of *The Beggar's Opera*. I didn't quite know how to deliver the dialogue, how to make use of the words. And I was scaling it wrong. I was scaling it like a film. In film, micro-movements are very noticeable, but it's not like that on the small screen and I was still learning.

I wasn't going to give up, though. It wasn't just because I needed to pay the bills. I still wanted to stick two fingers up at that bloody English teacher. I'd never got the part in the play at school. I was never going to amount to anything. All that stuff.

I think I got to give the two-fingered salute when I auditioned for *The Comedy of Errors* just after I'd finished *The Beggar's Opera*. This was Shakespeare. This was my chance. They told me which bits we were going to read for the audition so I spent ages learning my lines by heart because I'm a very bad reader. And off I went, prepared. When I arrived, James Cellan Jones, this renowned director, was sitting there poker-faced and I just launched into it. Quite early on, maybe three or four lines in, he started laughing and after that it just got worse and worse. By the time I got to the end, he was pissing himself. I just assumed I'd cocked it up.

To make matters worse, he then asked me to read another part. I hadn't learned it and I just couldn't do it. It was a mess. But at the end, he said, 'Right, then, do you think you can play both parts?' I could not believe it. I was shocked. You could have knocked me down with half a feather. I was cast as Dromio of Ephesus and Dromio of Syracuse.

And I loved it. Here I was, working with a Shakespeare text, understanding it, getting the jokes. No one was talking down to me. I was involved and it was an extraordinary experience. It was only at the end, when the two Dromios were put side by side in the edit, that you could see how involved I'd become. The Dromio whose master treats him with the most respect was a good two inches taller than the other one. Subconsciously, I'd shrunk to play the less fortunate twin.

• • •

I don't think the Kray twins approached me because they admired my hilarious portrayal of the Dromio twins in *The Comedy of Errors*. I suspect *McVicar* was more up their street. Whatever the reason, I got a call one day from Big Joey Pyle asking if I wanted to buy the rights to make the Kray film. I really got to like Joey. He was a respected villain. Honourable.

The police had been after him for years. He was tried unsuccessfully for the murder of a nightclub bouncer in the 1960s. They got him in the end in 1992 for 'masterminding a massive drugs ring' but I still went to visit him in Belmarsh. I used to enjoy visiting him and cheering him up. We never talked about the villainy. I understood what side of the water he was on and I didn't want to know.

Joey wasn't high-profile in the public's eye, but he was a mediator between the big crime families. He was the one who sat with them and sorted out the grudges. Imagine that for a day job. He was good at it, though. When he died in 2007, members of the Kray and the Richardson families went to the funeral. Mediating between me and the Krays must have been a relative piece of cake.

I thought it would be great to make a definitive film about the twins. Like it or not, they're a part of the social history of modern Britain. You'll always have people like them on the streets. You take them away and someone else takes over. That's how it was and that's how it will always be. But they had something extra. They had image and they knew how to use it. With the help of David Bailey's photograph, they made gangsters glamorous. The sixties were all about image. Look at Twiggy. Look at us. Look at the Krays.

I didn't like them and I didn't like what they stood for, but when you met them, you recognised that they were extraordinary. If Ronnie hadn't been mad, they would have had it made. They had the clubs and the casinos. They were earning a fortune. But Ronnie was a paranoid schizophrenic with an identical twin brother. I didn't want to make a film about the violence. I wanted to make a film about those particular cogs in those particular brains.

I'd never met the Krays before but I had had dealings with them. In 1965, I had a lovely Austin Westminster. Plush leather seats. Three-litre engine. I liked that car. I was driving it across Salisbury Plain – that long straight road which, in the sixties, you'd only ever do flat-out – and as I flew over the top of the hill I noticed a tractor turning right and another car waiting behind it, blocking the whole road. There was nothing I could do but brace, curse my youthful exuberance and hope for the best. By the time I'd clambered out of my crumpled, beloved Austin, it looked as if I'd run over a group of wheelchair users. In the wreckage, there were all these metal frames and buckled wheels. It took a while to work out the car I'd rear-ended had bikes on the back. What a mess. I drove more sensibly after that.

It also got me a big bill. The car had cost £1,200. The repairs were £400. I didn't have £400 and I couldn't find it. The banks wouldn't lend it. Management obviously never had it. So I had no transport, which meant I couldn't get to gigs. I hired a car for a couple of weeks but that was eating up more money than we were earning. Eventually, one of our roadies said, 'I know someone who will lend you that money.'

'Great, who is it?' I said.

'Don't worry about who it is. You can have the money for three months at ten per cent. There's only one thing. If you value your legs, make sure you pay it back on time.'

I took that as a piece of bravado, but the next day he handed me the cheque for £400. It was signed Charlie Kray.

I paid it back on time and I just thought, what a great bunch of guys. They stood up for me. They saved the day. And that was it until Big Joey called me up in the eighties.

When I first went to see Ronnie in Broadmoor, he was sitting at this round table. I sit next to Joey and Ronnie comes round and shakes my hand.

'Hello, Roger, nice to see you.' He's almost whispering. 'How's your mum? Would she like a box of chocolates?'

He sits down right next to me, he shuffles over and puts his knee right against my thigh and pushes really hard. What do you do with your leg when Ronnie Kray has his knee stuck in your thigh? I tell you what. Nothing. That leg didn't move for two hours. He was challenging me. It was all about front. How much bottle have you got?

Me and my thigh survived the meeting and in the days following, Don Boyd, my partner in the project, and I did the deal. A proper contract. Ronnie signed away all his rights in front of two Broadmoor doctors. What none of us realised, Ronnie included, is that the Krays had been living off those film rights for years. They sold them, the deal went south, they sold them again. But our deal was cast-iron. They couldn't do anything without my agreement.

Ronnie didn't like that. I didn't like that Ronnie didn't like that. We were never going to stop him doing what he wanted to do. But even then, it was difficult. He wanted Ray Winstone to play him, but I didn't want to make that type of film. I wanted Hywel Bennett to do it. He had the right voice. He could portray homosexuality without being overtly camp. That was the thing with Ronnie. He was very particular about what he was. He was not gay, he was homosexual.

I had it all within my grasp – I had even found an exact twin to Hywel in an actor called Gerry Sundquist – but in the end I just couldn't deal with Ronnie. I saw him beginning to turn. He got very angry. When I went to see him again, the old knee went in even harder. He used to talk more and more quietly. And then Ronnie had a flaming row with Don. He told him, 'You're either going to make my film or it's going to be all over.' Don came back from the confrontation looking very worried. He said there was someone else looking out from behind the eyes. And he was really scared.

After that, this other production team popped up and I was glad to let them have it. I just didn't want it in my life any more. It felt too dangerous. They went on to make that film with the Kemps. They weren't bad in it, but it glorified the violence and it missed the intrigue, the Bob Boothby connection, all those spies. That's why the Krays got 30 years. They didn't get it for bumping off two villains. Two people tried in the same dock at the same time for two murders in different places on different dates? It seemed like an establishment conviction. I'm not sticking up for the Krays, but they were much more than just growlers and I think it's a shame that story still hasn't been told properly. It could have been the English *Godfather*.

• • •

With no work since 1982, John Entwistle started to run out of money by the end of the eighties. For that matter, so did I. It's expensive living the life of a rock star when you're not earning rock star money. I hadn't thought about The Who for a long time. After a lot of persuading from Sir Bob, I'd put aside my feelings about Kenney and we'd done Live Aid, but then we'd returned to our separate lives. In the end, financial necessity drove us back.

We re-formed in 1989 with Simon Phillips on the drums and set off on our first stadium tour in seven long years. It was a big production – there were people on brass, there were backing singers, a percussionist and keyboards. Pete spent most of the tour playing acoustic guitar. He got someone else in to play the electric. He even thought about playing in a glass box to protect his hearing. I wish I could have got someone else to sing my bits. I would be very happy, standing there, doing the odd harmony. But that's what Pete wanted and I just gave in. On the up-side, Simon Phillips was a huge improvement rhythm-wise. It was better than our last final tour, but it wasn't good enough to make us rush into another one.

For the first time in my life I had nothing much planned work-wise. Instead, I had the joy of spending more time with Heather and the kids. I had always done bits and pieces of the daily chores. I've never been afraid of putting out the bins and doing the washing-up, and I always enjoyed sharing the school run which, when you live in the countryside, is unavoidable because public transport is virtually non-existent.

It was on one school run back in 1992 that something that had been out of my life for 20-odd years came roaring back. Football! I had picked up my son Jamie and a couple of his mates from school and noticed that Jamie was wearing a red and white scarf.

'What's that you're wearing around your neck?' I asked.

'It's my team's scarf,' came the reply.

Oh shit. I hope he's not a Man United fan, I thought.

'What team's that then?'

'Arsenal, Dad.'

What a relief …

'When are you going to take me to see them, Dad?'

When your ten-year-old son asks you that question every day for a few weeks, there can only be one answer.

I had been a Queens Park Rangers supporter until the early seventies when the violence that was common back then got really bad. One day, I just walked away. I hadn't even watched a game for 20 years. Fortunately for me, Robert Rosenberg, Bill's right-hand man in the management office, was a lifelong Arsenal fan. So I gave in and took Jamie to Highbury to see them play. The atmosphere was fantastic – friendly and funny with wonderfully loud singing. I was hooked on the game again, and this feeling hadn't been passed from father to son, but from son to father. I became an Arsenal fan and Robert became a really great friend.

EIGHTEEN

THE RE-FORMATION

Years passed. Projects came and went. I continued to pursue my little acting career and, when the phone rang, I answered it. In July 1991, I was lucky enough to receive a call from Paddy Moloney from The Chieftains. Would I sing a guest spot with them at the London Palladium?

I said yes. I always say yes to a challenge. It's one of the few rules I stick to. It was a challenge because there would be no rehearsal, which is always nerve-racking. I'd just have to walk onstage and fit in with what is, as I've said, almost certainly one of the quietest acoustic bands in the world.

I'd learned the words to 'Raglan Road' and within three minutes of hello they were playing the introduction and we were off. For the first time in my life onstage with a band, the first time in thousands of gigs, I could hear myself sing. I've told you I don't like hearing my own voice, but it does make life easier when you're performing. The song went so smoothly. Clockwork. So I suggested we try 'Behind Blue Eyes', my favourite Who song.

289

'Let's give it a go' came the reply and it was wonderful to hear a song I'd performed so many times done in such a different way. A few weeks later, I went back for more, recording a live album with The Chieftains and the talented American folk singer Nanci Griffith at the Grand Opera House in Belfast. It was billed as an Irish Evening and this time there were to be rehearsals, but about half an hour into the first session someone came onto the stage and calmly informed us that they'd received a credible bomb threat. Would we mind leaving the building?

So we all trudged out into the car park at the back of the opera house. A few minutes later, the same someone suggested we might like to move a bit further away. We ended up in the doorway at the back of another building and I'll never forget the sight that greeted us. It was a full bingo hall in all its afternoon glory. Row after row of chain-smoking blue-rinse ladies running up to six bingo cards each, a study of concentration and anticipation. The smoke was so thick you could hardly see the other side of the room. It would take more than a bomb scare for them to give up on their numbers. They weren't going anywhere.

It was going to take three hours to check our building was safe but the show must go on so we decamped to a room above a pub round the corner and finished the rehearsal. That night, the show did go on and it was a great success. I went home the next day, thinking about the beautiful atmosphere rather than our disrupted afternoon. In fact, I didn't give the bomb threat a second thought until, a few months later, the IRA set off a 1,200-pound car bomb on Glengall Street and blew that beautiful opera house to bits. Miraculously, no one was injured. Whether it stopped the bingo is another question.

• • •

On 1 March 1994, I turned 50. It was an eventful day, not because the half-century felt like it had passed so quickly, but because of a letter. I was out on the farm – we were building something, I can't remember what – and I came in for lunch. Heather always opens the post and she just handed me this letter. 'Here's another present,' she said. 'Happy birthday.'

It was from a Jewish girl called Kim. She had enclosed photographs of herself and her son and, immediately, I could see the resemblance. She had the Daltrey look. I could see my mum in her and I could see my sister. It was obvious she was my daughter.

I just sat there feeling two overwhelming and contradictory emotions. First of all, there was joy. Here was this beautiful person, all grown up and happy. Kim's adoptive father was a renowned orthodontist at Guy's Hospital and he'd given her a wonderful education. It had all turned out okay for her. But there was also a real pang of sadness. It can't have been easy growing up with the knowledge that your dad wasn't around and your mum had given you up. And it must have been awful for her mother, too.

Looking back, I could have done things differently. I could have behaved more responsibly. Just like I could have done with Jackie. But as I already said, I was young, I was arrogant and I was ignorant. And, yes, I admit it, I was enjoying myself. Besides, I never knew Kim's mother was pregnant. I don't even remember meeting her. I remember the mothers of my Scottish daughter, my Swedish son and my daughter who lived in Yorkshire.

But this one, I never had a clue. And I still don't regret the act and I can't regret the consequences. To do that now would be to regret my daughter. What I can do is deal with it.

I called Kim that day. Not long after, we met at a little Italian restaurant in St John's Wood and we both felt an immediate connection. She had first tried to find out who her birth parents were when she was 18 but the social worker had told her the birth certificate was water-damaged. When she tried again, at the age of 27, it turned out that had been rubbish and she got the answer. This man is your father. She describes it as 'quite a shock' and I don't blame her. She looked at some photographs of me and watched a couple of my films, and then she knew it was true.

'Hand on heart,' she admits now, 'I wasn't a big Who fan, but I'd seen *Tommy* and then I found out Tommy was my dad. It was a strange moment.' She waited two months and then she wrote that letter. I'm so glad she did.

A few days after I met my 27-year-old daughter Kim for the very first time, I took her back to meet Heather and the rest of the family. I'm sure it wasn't easy for Kim and I know it can't have been easy for Heather either. But she welcomed Kim and it all worked out well. With all my surprise children, it's worked out. We're very good friends and I love them all, but I'll be completely honest, I don't feel the same way about them as I do about the children I had with Heather. I missed their childhood; they have other parents, so it's a different kind of bond.

It is nice, though. I see all my children as often as possible. I go on little tours every year. All of this could have gone another way. It might not have worked out so well for my children or for me. Each one of them has, at one time or another, thanked me for giving them life. And I'm grateful for that. I am a lucky bugger.

Not everything in my life was going quite so smoothly. Over the last year or two, my singing career had taken a downturn. The arrival of rap and hip hop meant that rock music had more or less disappeared from the radio. It was all Eminem and Ice Cube. I released my eighth solo album, *Rocks in The Head* at the end of 1992 and it had sunk more or less without trace. I thought it was a good album, but it was almost impossible to get it any airtime. Back then, radio was the only way to get exposure for a record so it was doomed from the start.

Music moves on – it has to – but unless I was going to start rapping, which, don't worry, I wasn't, I was stuck in the doldrums. I had become disillusioned with my management. Bill had decided to live in Spain with his beautiful Argentinian wife and their two young children and although this was great for him, it left me feeling isolated and unrepresented. I was about to turn 50. That didn't bother me. It was just another day. But it still felt like it was time for a change.

So I decided two things. First, I would mark my 50th with a gig. I'd take a rock band and a full orchestra, and we'd play Carnegie Hall in New York. Daltrey Sings Townshend. This was something I'd wanted to do with Pete's music for quite some time. Explore a whole new way of presenting it. Why not?

Second, I'd leave Bill on his sun lounger in Spain and move to what appeared to be a more proactively creative manager. Richard Flanzer had come recommended from various people in New York. He was coming up in the business and he was, they said, a mover and shaker. If anything needed moving and shaking, it was my career.

Putting the orchestral component together was straightforward. I decided to use a student orchestra from the Juilliard School. They were young, talented, hungry musicians, all the essential ingredients to bring Pete's music to life. Michael Kamen, the prolific film composer, would arrange the score and conduct. I also recruited a fabulous collection of guest artists, including Eddie Vedder, Sinead O'Connor, Lou Reed, Alice Cooper, the Spin Doctors and, once again, The Chieftains (finally, as mentioned earlier, my Machiavellian plan to put Mr Entwistle on the same stage as my quiet Irish friends would be realised).

Predictably, the rock band component wasn't quite so straightforward. Flanzer had already started moving and shaking, and he'd managed to get a DVD deal to cover the costs of production. The one caveat in the DVD contract was that Pete had to appear in the show. The one caveat Pete had was that I would then agree to use the musicians he planned to tour with solo after Carnegie Hall. So I agreed, he agreed and my birthday concert was all set.

After two weeks of rehearsal, everything sounded fantastic. All the guests had been a dream to rehearse with except one. Pete was the fly in the ointment. I don't know why. One day, his dog was ill. The next, he didn't want to play with an orchestra. The next, he didn't want to play at all. I only needed him to play one song to fulfil the contract and pay the rapidly escalating production costs. But two days before the show, I still wasn't sure if he'd show up.

In the end, he did show up and of course he was brilliant. But my stomach was churning like a cement mixer. We performed the show on 23 February 1994, and again the following night, but it didn't go well. I didn't realise at the time but Kamen, our esteemed man with the baton, was on the Colombian marching powder. A conductor on coke means one thing: everything was speedy. The band also played twice as loud as they had in the rehearsals. Double the speed, double the volume. It was such a shame. In rehearsal, the orchestra and the band had been in synergy, two sounds working in harmony, revealing the light and shade of Pete's music. Now they were working against one other. Above the ensuing cacophony, I couldn't hear myself clearly and I oversang. The reviews of the show were not good and they were right. I didn't sing well. I couldn't.

All the same, it wasn't long before Flanzer was on the phone telling me about some amazing offers he was getting to put my orchestral show on around the US. The promoters didn't care about the reviews. They were more interested in the news that the *Daltrey Sings Townshend* special had broken the Carnegie Hall's two-day box office record. It was the fastest sell-out in the venue's 103-year history. Promoters only care about the bottom line and here, clearly, was an opportunity to make some money. I was tired of the doldrums, too, so I agreed to do a summer tour.

In the big cities like Detroit, Las Vegas and Los Angeles, the orchestras were world class and the shows were well received. In the smaller towns, the musicians were a little more ragged and the music was less tight but, overall, I thought, still okay. The problem was that the up-and-coming Mr Flanzer hadn't got to the lesson about the economics of touring. He had only booked three shows a week. We needed to do five or six to meet the budget for the very expensive band and the overheads. What he had mastered was the ability to run up expenses on my behalf. At the end of the tour, I was down a million bucks or so and up one legal dispute with Flanzer over the show's copyright. My experiment with new management had ended. The Flanzer affair made me see how good Bill was, even from that deckchair in Spain. Lucky for me, he was happy to have me back.

It might well have been a wasted summer except for one seemingly small discovery which would end up becoming a much more significant factor in the decades to come. At the outset of the tour, I had been compelled to make adjustments to the rock band due to the expense. One of the adjustments was a new drummer. Fifteen years after Keith's death and we still hadn't found anyone who came close to replacing him. So I auditioned seven or eight and the last one was Zak Starkey. It was like finding a diamond in a barrel of sawdust. Here was someone who could provide the mad rhythmic computations we'd lost when Moon died.

You could say Zak had it in his blood. He was Ringo's son and Keith's godson. In fact, Keith had taken Zak under his wing when he was a young teenager. What a wing to be taken under.

He'd done some solo work for John and, in 1985, I'd used him for one of the drum solos in *Under a Raging Moon*. I'd kept my eye and ear out for him ever since. The trouble was, he had a bit of a reputation as a loose cannon. He had that in his blood, too, and it was a concern because I don't think I could have survived another Moon. Still, you go with the music and, after some straight talking and a gentleman's agreement, I gave Zak the job. He was with us that summer and at least that part of it felt right.

• • •

It was May 1996 when I got a call from Pete asking if I'd do a one-off special for the Prince's Trust in Hyde Park the following month. I asked him straight out if this meant he finally wanted to get The Who back together. His response was a bit cagey. He never quite said yes but he didn't say no either. He just explained that he'd written a stage version of *Quadrophenia* that would have an onstage narrator as the main protagonist, Jimmy, and various singers playing the other characters.

'Who am I supposed to be?' I asked. 'Jimmy's brain?'

'Something like that,' he said.

'How do I play a brain?'

I fought for adjustments on the staging and a big edit on all the dialogue, but by the time we reached the soundcheck on the day before the show, the whole project felt like an overblown ego trip. Ade Edmondson was cast as Ace Face. Gary Glitter was the Godfather. Then there was Stephen Fry as the hotel manager, Trevor McDonald as the newsreader and Phil Daniels narrating. There was a full brass section, backing singers, percussion, the works. When it came to the decision of who would be in the band, I insisted that Zak took the drums, and, thank Christ, Pete accepted him. We still had to carry another guitarist to play lead because Pete was still struggling with his hearing and would only play acoustic.

Given our cast of thousands, this particular soundcheck was critical. A soundcheck is not a rehearsal. It's an opportunity for the artists to make sure they can hear what's going on. But Glitter never understood that. While the band was playing his opening song and I was walking around the stage listening, he decided it was showtime and started swinging his microphone stand around his head. Then, everything went black.

The next thing I heard was a voice asking if I knew my name. There was no face or body attached to the voice and it kept repeating the same question. 'What's your name? What's your name? What's your name?' Eventually, I got fed up with this persistent voice and answered.

'Well, I'm not fucking Mick Jagger, am I?'

I had been unconscious for about 15 minutes. One of the tripod feet of the mic stand had hit me square in the left eye socket. Someone was holding a cold compress over my eye and blood was pouring out of my nose. It was dark red, almost black.

Heather saw the whole thing from out front and, as they moved me slowly back to the dressing room, she was trying to get someone to call an ambulance. An hour later, it still hadn't arrived. By now, I was sitting up, feeling pretty shaky. When I tried to blow my nose, it felt like my eye was coming free from the socket.

'Fuck this,' said Bill Curbishley, grabbing his car keys. 'We're going.' It's the fastest I've ever been across London in rush hour.

The doctors had good news and bad news. The eye was okay but the socket was fractured. I had a brain scan at nine on the morning of the show and they confirmed there was no internal bleeding so I left the hospital with a bag of painkillers and a gig to perform. To solve the problem of the eyeball trying to escape its socket – a sight that would have upset the front few rows – I procured a patch stuffed with cotton wool. Pete's brother Paul painted a bullseye on it – and in the end, the audience thought it was all part of the act.

I did that show rattling like a maraca, whacked out on a cocktail of painkillers, and when I got back to the dressing room I found a typewritten note from Pete. 'You have performed in Pete Townshend's *Quadrophenia*,' it read. I didn't have time to let that sink in. I had to meet royalty. At least Prince Charles asked me how my eye was.

Within days, the promoters were on the phone again and Bill was asking if I would do Pete Townshend's *Quadrophenia* at Madison Square Garden. Once again, I asked where The Who came into the picture. Bill just said it was The Who that would sell the tickets and that I'd make some money. After two years of patchy acting work, I agreed. In 1974, we played a four-night stand at the Garden. In 1979, we did five. On 16 July 1996, we started a run of six shows in seven nights.

Promoters from all over America were offering tours, but this time I said I'd only do it if some changes were made. This whole Jimmy's brain business was a struggle and the endless narration between the songs just killed the energy. It felt like a racing car in the hands of a learner driver. Every time we got going, it stalled. It needed sorting out. Pete agreed to some of the changes. He agreed to have the live narration recorded, which saved money and made it more likely that the people at the back of the gig could hear what was going on. He also agreed to cut it down and, to my surprise, he even let me do the rewrite.

After about two weeks trying to sell tickets to Pete Townshend's *Quadrophenia*, the name changed, too. It became The Who's *Quadrophenia* and in the end it was a sell-out. We played 25 shows across North America that autumn and set off on our first European tour since 1975 the following spring. The economics were still all wrong. We made a few quid from the US shows but, even with the changes, we came back from Europe with the princely sum of £16,000. It was only when the tour had finished that the whole expedition made sense. That note in the dressing room after Hyde Park was Pete's way of creating a Grand Right. It was hard not to conclude that me and the rest of the band had been used, but it was still progress. And even if I still hadn't done *Quadrophenia* the way I thought it could be done, even though I'd have to wait another 16 years for that, it was the start of a proper renaissance. Pete began to play more lead guitar and, gradually, it felt like we were back. So many bands never recover from a long break, but I always knew we would. Our return wasn't going to be straightforward, but nothing ever is with The Who.

• • •

In the end, the band got back on the road again because of a con man and a large bag of cash. We didn't know he was a con man at the time. All we knew was that an agent had called the office to say that Michael Fenne, the CEO of dot-com company Pixelon, wanted us to play a show in Vegas in October 1999. He was a huge Who fan. He'd be honoured. And he'd pay us two million quid.

The deal came with one big string attached. One of us would have to go to Cannes to publicise Pixelon at some tech event. And, of course, the one of us would have to be me. So off I flew with Harvey Goldsmith and a whole file of information to present convincingly. You'll be astonished to hear that I am not an IT expert. I know very little about computers or the internet. I know nothing at all about how they actually work. But what the hell? I'm an actor. I can learn lines.

My talk at the conference lasted about 25 minutes. I explained how Pixelon's software would enable users to stream films via the internet. Of course, these days, with fibre optics, that's just normal. But in 1999, you still had to 'dial-up' to get on the internet. The idea of downloading anything more than a couple of short emails was revolutionary. Or so it said in my briefing notes.

I think I sounded like I knew what I was talking about. No one booed. But then came a surprise Q and A. That would have been the time to fake a stroke, but I'd spent the last few hours listening to all the sales people jabbering on and, frankly, they all sounded like they were winging it, too. This was the height of the dot-com bubble. It was a time when you could sell anything to do with technology, no matter how ridiculous, as long as you sounded convincing.

Somewhere in the briefing notes, there was a section on 'band widths'. Anything to do with bands – even the width of them – I could spiel. So I blagged it and I got away with it. There was even a round of applause (maybe they were just being polite). And then we all flew to Vegas to earn a fast buck.

A few weeks after the Vegas job, the truth came out. The whole thing had been a hoax. There was no such technology. Worse, Fenne was not Fenne. He was David Kim Stanley, a convicted con artist and fugitive who'd been on the run since 1996. He'd raised more than $28 million for his venture and spent $16 million of it on the free launch party. It wasn't just us. The lineup included Tony Bennett, the Brian Setzer Orchestra, Dixie Chicks, Natalie Cole and KISS. And we all got paid. It seems Stanley just wanted to throw the biggest ever free party for rock fans and his own mates. The strangest thing of all was that Stanley, aka Fenne, the world's biggest Who fan, never showed his face at our gig. Maybe he was wearing a disguise. Maybe he wasn't the world's biggest Who fan after all.

Still, that gig and the two we agreed to do on the back of it for Neil Young's Bridge School Benefit in California brought us back together again. It was the first time since 1983 that we'd played as a five-piece. We had Zak on drums and John 'Rabbit' Bundrick on keyboards. And we were playing the hits. For the first time since 1966, we were opening with 'Anyway Anyhow Anywhere'. We did 'Pinball Wizard', 'Baba O'Riley', 'Won't Get Fooled Again', 'The Kids Are Alright' and 'My Generation'. We were another step closer to where we'd been however many decades earlier.

• • •

Towards the end of 1999, I had a call from Bobby Pridden. 'Cyd,' he said (he's called me that ever since I found him and the roadies broken down 60 miles from a gig in Newcastle in 1969 and flagged down a Cyd Transport flatbed truck to take the gear the rest of the way). 'John's in trouble again.'

John was the Ox onstage, stoic and unemotional. Off-stage, he was extravagant. Even a two-million-dollar gig in Vegas wouldn't keep him going for long. He lived like Elvis and it never seemed to bother him that he didn't have the income of Elvis.

His Graceland was Quarwood, a 55-room Victorian gothic pile in 42 acres of deepest Gloucestershire. It was approached, as an estate agent might say, by a long driveway and an entrance with stone lions on plinths. The first thing to note is that there were two cottages on the property a little way from the main house, and his mother Queenie lived in one with his stepfather, Gordon, whom John had hated ever since he'd moved in with Queenie. Right outside the kitchen back window was a fenced-off chicken run. Of all the possible places to keep chickens in those 42 acres of land, it seemed like a strange place to settle on.

'A bit smelly and noisy to have outside your mum's window, eh, John?' I asked him one visit. 'Why don't you move the chickens somewhere they won't bother anyone?'

'They love it there and Gordon hates chickens,' he replied with a smile. As I said, John had a spiteful side. He loved getting revenge.

The second thing was Quarwood itself. In the grand hallway you were greeted by a regiment of suits of armour. From the wrought-iron cantilevered staircase, John had hung a life-size

Quasimodo from a rope. If you survived the entrance, you'd end up in this grand kitchen–dining room which he'd made from five rooms knocked through. The walls were lined with bespoke walnut dressers and on every shelf and picture rail he'd hung these really tacky limited-edition plates depicting scenes from the American Revolution, Jane Austen novels and the reign of Queen Victoria. He must have had about five thousand plates in his collection. You needed a drink after getting through all that and, fortunately, he had a large bar area filled with the stuffed marlin and swordfish he'd caught whenever he was doing his Hemingway impression. He'd even gone to the trouble of putting one of those battery-powered moving hands in the mouth of a shark. He kept skeletons in some of the bedrooms in case anyone was feeling too relaxed as they turned in for the night. It was like the Hammer House of Horror crossed with the foyer of a Vegas casino.

The suits of armour were reproductions from Harrods. The plates were from Harrods. In fact, almost all the stuff was from Harrods, a shop I've been determined to stay out of for my entire life. I'd like to have it on my gravestone. *'Here lies Roger Daltrey. Died and never set foot in Harrods.'* John felt differently. He liked everyone in the village to see the Harrods van coming through the gates. Even when the money ran out, even when his old employers at the Inland Revenue came calling with a very large bill indeed, he didn't stop shopping there. It was one of several bad habits he'd picked up playing the extravagant rock star.

He was an alcoholic and he had a good nose for hoovering up whatever was left of the party. And, by the end of the nineties, it had all caught up with him. So I went to see Pete at his home in Richmond and asked him to help out. We should get the band together. Properly.

Pete wasn't sure. He was an addict himself. He knew the risks. If we helped John out, we risked becoming his enablers. Maybe tough love would work better. In this case, I was convinced it wouldn't. John would never change. But after talking for two hours, Pete still wasn't sure so I left him to chew over it.

The chewing worked. He came back and said he wanted to do a huge tour. Thirty dates. Forty. Bigger than anything we'd done for a long time. I was happy not only because I needed the cash and John needed the cash, but because this is what I do. All the other stuff, all the other variations on performing, never matched up to the unadulterated joy of being in The Who.

So off we went into a whole new millennium on a proper 'Hello – we're back' tour. I don't think we actually called it that but that was what it was. We started in Tinley Park, Illinois, and four months and 37 gigs later we ended up at the Albert Hall in November for two charity shows for Teenage Cancer Trust. This was a charity both Pete and I had been patrons of since its inception in 1990. We were back like I always thought we would be, ever since I decided to call it quits in 1983. After all the experimenting, it turned out that the original format – a rock band playing rock music – worked. Who would have guessed?

NINETEEN

BROTHERS

I n the days immediately after the Twin Towers came down on 11 September 2001, the Robin Hood Foundation called to say they were putting on a show at Madison Square Garden for all the first responders and their families. This time, there was no protracted discussion. Of course we'd be there. There was no question.

'Great,' they said. 'We'll send a jet.'

'Send me a United Airlines ticket,' I replied. Because fuck them. I'm not giving an inch. I'll be there and I'll fly with an airline the terrorists attacked.

The dilemma was what to play. The overriding emotion at the time was total shell shock. How can you possibly come up with a set list for that?

For once, Pete had the straightforward solution. He just said let's do what we do. Let's play rock. And he was right. It was the only way to do it. So we went out and we played 'Who

Are You', 'Baba O'Riley', 'Behind Blue Eyes' and 'Won't Get Fooled Again'.

We've been lucky enough to play a lot of special venues. We've headlined all the great festivals and walked out on all the biggest stages. In 2010, we played the half-time show at Super Bowl XLIV to a television audience of 100 million. In 2012, billions watched us close the London Olympics. I've always said you treat each event, no matter how momentous, as just another gig. But that night at Madison Square Garden was different. It was special.

We played to a whole sea of uniforms – mostly fire department but thousands of cops and paramedics as well. They'd got in with tickets and, if they didn't have tickets, the uniform was the ticket (as well as a free pass at the bar). The place was packed, the beer was flowing and it was raw grief and raw defiance in one extraordinarily intense burst of emotion. And it was hard to get through, hard not to let that emotion completely overwhelm you because, in between all the firemen at the front, they had some of the children of the guys who hadn't made it out. They were wearing their dads' helmets.

Off the back of that night we decided we would tour again in 2002. It just felt like the right thing to do for the band. We played a few gigs in England at the start of the year and I remember feeling optimistic about another big American road trip. We'd wasted so many years doing nothing. Why waste any more? The world had changed. It had become darker. It needed music to heal itself. I needed to get back on the road.

After rehearsing in London, we flew to California at the end of June, ready for our first gig in Vegas. The day before the gig, I was in Los Angeles having lunch with my daughters in this tiny little Korean restaurant in the Valley. I couldn't have been happier. I had my family with me. I had the band. But then the phone rang and it was Pete asking where I was. I told him and then he wanted to know if I was sitting down. I asked what's up and he just said it.

'John's just died.'

'Oh.'

John had heart problems and in those last years it was beginning to show. He had a pallor to him, the pallor you have if you're still starting the day with a brandy for breakfast. But even the obvious visual signs that all was not well didn't make him slow down. He was unconditional about how he wanted to live his life, and fuck you if you didn't like it.

So he would have liked the way he went. He'd gone to bed the night before with a nice lady and whatever magic powders he had to hand, and he'd never woken up. He died of a heart attack in Room 658 of the Hard Rock Hotel and Casino, Las Vegas. If they'd put a glass case round his bed with him still in it, he would have been delighted. He would have thought, this is exactly where I deserve to be. Rock and roll.

His timing was terrible, though. Checking out one day before a huge tour, he had left us well and truly in the shit. There was no time to grieve. No time to think about what, if anything, we could have done differently. I went over and saw Pete and I knew we had to be a bit clever. We didn't know what had happened, but we were pretty sure they'd find drugs in him. And we were looking at 27 shows across the US and Canada. Of course we were insured but the insurance would have been null and void if we'd cancelled. That's pretty high up the list of exclusions. No payout if Class As are involved.

Far too soon, Pete and I had to have the conversation. We'd survived Keith. Could we survive this? We'd have to! Once again, it wouldn't be the same but the music was good enough. We could do it together. The two of us. We just had to knuckle down and get through these shows. All 27 of them. We had no option. You have to understand what it's like the day before you start a tour. You're in the red. You've paid for the rehearsals, the insurance, the rentals, the crew, everything, and you're in the hole to the tune of a few million quid. You're as indebted as you ever want to be. You pay off the debt through the tour. The weight lifts. The overwhelming sense of impending financial calamity fades away and only in the last few shows of 30 or 40 do you finally make it into the black. If you're lucky. That's the economics of a tour. It's all on us – the three of us. Or now just two. So we had to carry on. We moved the two opening shows to the end of the tour, but only three days later we would walk out onstage and we'd perform.

The same day we found out John was gone, we managed to get hold of Pino Palladino. It wasn't like trying to find a replacement for Keith. By now, the die was fixed. John had changed the way the bass was played. He'd established his own neoclassical art form. He'd brought the bass guitar into the limelight. Pino was a master. He could channel John and channel the Who vibe.

We had three days to rehearse and on 1 July 2002 we walked out onstage at the Hollywood Bowl.

It was emotional. It took a lot out of us. That sense that you have no choice but to perform, that you have to find the energy, is hard. We were upset. We'd lost John. It took everything just to walk onto the stage. Each performance teetered on the brink of the abyss and Pete and I had to fight each night to keep it all in check. And, of course, we ground through those dates; we drove though with the intensity of a band fighting the darkness. The audiences felt it. They felt the intensity and the anger and the emotion, and it was a good tour. It might even have been our best tour. Despite everything, we were back on top, playing to 20–30,000 people a night. When I focused on that, it felt great.

Then, suddenly, at the beginning of October, I was home and I had time to breathe. That's when it hit me. Once the crisis was over and I was back in Sussex, looking out across the hills, thinking about what had just happened, that's when I struggled. John had checked out like the rock star he was. For everyone else, he was a story. For me, it was real. It hadn't been real for four months and now it was. No one around me could understand that. They hadn't been there. They didn't know what it had been like. On more positive days, I could take solace in the fact that at least we were okay. Me and Pete and the music. That was enough. And then, a few weeks later, we lost that, too.

· · ·

On 13 January 2003 I opened the newspaper to discover that Pete had been arrested for accessing child pornography. He'd given his credit card details for access to a site that turned out to be part of an FBI sting.

The first thing I did was to call up his brothers. I knew what the news was doing to me and Heather so I called Paul and Simon, who had become like a brother to me. I asked if they were okay and of course they weren't. It was a complete nightmare.

I didn't call Pete for three days and then I saw a photograph of him getting out of the back of a police car. He didn't have the standard-issue blanket over his head. He wasn't trying to hide. In fact, he was looking directly at the cameras. I knew that look. When he has something difficult to say, he looks down, but here he was, fronting up. Right then, I knew that he hadn't done anything. He was innocent.

I called him and asked what the hell he was doing. And then I tested him. Couldn't he have said someone else got hold of his credit card? And he said, 'No, you don't understand. I did it. I put my credit card details in. I wanted to find out where the money went.'

I told him he was a stupid, arrogant twat but I knew he was telling the truth. He'd been on at the government for several years. He was furious that his young son could access pornography so easily. And the response was always the same. There's nothing we can do. One site closes down, another one pops up. So he concocted this plan to follow the money. He thought he could prove that the credit card companies were taking money from child pornographers. I didn't know enough about computers to know if it was a good plan. All I know is that it was a horrendous time. Pete was hanged, drawn and quartered in the press. They didn't know his history. They don't know how much work he does for charities supporting abused people. They don't know how much of his life was tied up in the abuse he endured as a kid. It's in *Tommy*, but everyone drew their own conclusions.

The investigation took months. Pete had about 30 computers and they went through every one of them with a fine-tooth comb. And for that entire period it was as if a huge dumper truck of shit had been poured over everything. All our lives, including our families. Everything we'd done. Everything we'd achieved.

And in the middle of this we had John's family asking for their share of the profit from the tour. There was also the issue of the ownership of the band name. It would have been impossible for us to go on into any kind of future having to pay John's estate to use The Who, the name we'd always called ourselves.

It was left to me to meet with John's mum Queenie and his only son Christopher to sort out the mess. We met on neutral ground at my old mate Nobby the Fibreglass Kid's house in Chiswick, but it didn't make it any easier to sit opposite them and tell them there wasn't going to be any money from the tour. If anything, the estate should have been thankful to Pete and myself for fulfilling the contract. If we hadn't, they would have had the pants sued off them from all sides.

When it came to the name, I quietly pointed out that unless Pete and I had full ownership it would bring the curtain down on any future for the band.

I also gave them my word that if they gave it to us for a small fee I would do everything in my power to make sure we'd work our way back to the top. This meant the royalties from the back catalogue would keep coming and provide a heathy income for them in the future.

Thankfully, they seemed to understand their position and that under the deal I offered them they had more to gain by keeping The Who going.

This was the darkest time in the history of the band and I became very depressed by it all. By the time the week of Teenage Cancer Trust shows at the Albert Hall arrived, I was cracking up. I had no headline act until, at the last minute, I called Eric Clapton.

'What do you need, Rog? ... Okay, I'll be there.'

'Thank you so much, Eric. You're a good man.'

When you have depression, you go outside and it can be a midsummer's day with the bluest sky, but it's as if you can't find the dimmer switch to turn up the light. And it's like that for days and days and days. The worst thing is that you go and see the doctor, the doctor diagnoses you and then gives you pills. That's always the answer. I took those pills for a few days and I walked around like a zombie. It clearly wasn't helping. It just made things worse. And I just thought, sod this. These are going to turn me into a pudding.

So I chucked them out and threw myself into projects instead. I did things I would never have done in my life, anything to escape Britain. I filmed the Extreme History series for the History Channel across the US. I did *My Fair Lady* at the Hollywood Bowl with John Lithgow. I played a crazy rock star mash-up of David Bowie and Alice Cooper in the comedy series *Rude Awakening* with Lynn Redgrave. All these things helped take my mind off the chaos at home, but they didn't help with the depression. They just postponed it. Every time I went back, the darkness returned.

In the end, I took a friend's advice and contacted the hypnotist and self-help guru Paul McKenna. Paul has made a very lucrative career from making big claims. He can make you thin. He can make you quit smoking. He can make you confident. But could he make my lights go back on? I had no idea, but I'm not sceptical about these things. I've used a lot of alternative medicines and therapies in my life and I reckon the Western world could learn a thing or two from Eastern medicine. Throwing drugs at the problem is not always the answer. So I went along to see him and he listened as I explained my situation.

He got to the heart of it very quickly. We hadn't been able to grieve after John's death. We had just pushed on through that intense tour and then, only weeks after we'd got home, before we could process it all, Pete was arrested and all our lives got turned upside down. In the face of a sustained crisis, your brain stops coping. According to Paul, it shuts down to protect your heart.

There were times when my brain was telling me I couldn't go on. The depression was just too intense. I could see no way of getting out of it. I became more and more miserable. So I'm not exaggerating when I say Paul McKenna saved me. He got me through that terrible year and I still use his tapes before I go onstage. You know who your friends are when you're down. Paul was there for me. So was Eric, Noel Gallagher, Paul Weller and Kelly Jones. So was Richard Desmond, the newspaper proprietor, who did everything he could to keep the charity money coming in when the chips were down.

This is a memoir, not *This Is Your Life*, but I'm still going to use it to say thank you to all those people. The music business can be cut-throat. It can chew you up and spit you out, but those friends kept me going and they kept Teenage Cancer Trust going. Every March, I have to fill six or seven nights in a row at the Albert Hall. I have to find musicians and comedians who are willing to drop everything and come and play for nothing. That's hard when you're struggling anyway. It relies on goodwill and I'll be forever grateful to all the guys who stepped up when I asked for help.

Pete had to wait a long time to find his way out of his darkness. In May 2003, the charge that he'd downloaded photographs was dropped. They hadn't found a single picture. He hadn't been on the website. He hadn't viewed any images. I'm sure if he had they would have done him. As he put it years later, when he finally felt able to talk to the press about it, 'A forensic investigator found that I hadn't entered the website, but nonetheless, by the time the charges came to be presented to me, I was exhausted.' He had admitted that he'd provided his credit card details right from the start and that was enough to break the law so he took that part of it on the chin.

And in the end, we did what we always did. We got back onstage. We were due to headline the Isle of Wight Festival in

June 2004 and, although I wasn't nervous, it was obviously a big deal for Pete. He had changed. He'd become more humble and much more approachable. Even though he was innocent, he'd been shocked into it by the humiliation. And he needed to be out there and face the world. Which he did.

The crowd that night were amazing. It was wonderful to get back out there and realise the nightmare was over, that our audience was still with us, that the music would go on for another few rounds at least. It's easy to get things out of perspective when you're caught up in the eye of a tabloid storm. It feels like the whole world is caving in but, for everyone else, it's just a page in a newspaper that is quickly turned and then used to wrap your fish and chips. That night, no one jeered or whistled. It was our first festival gig since Pete's arrest, our first in Britain since John had died and our first time back at the Isle of Wight since 1970. And it felt great.

Pete's way of saying thanks came in the form of a song on *Endless Wire*. He handed me the demo tape for 'You Stand By Me' and said, 'I wrote this for you.'

When I'm in trouble
You stand by me
When I see double
You stand by me
You take my side
Against those who lied
You take my side
Gimme back my pride.

It meant a lot for him to write that and say that. Of course, he later went on to say that he'd written it for Rachel, his girlfriend, now wife, and that was fine, too. She'd been there for him and she was very good for him. For us, it was simple. Brothers can squabble. They can fight. They can fall out. We'd done plenty of that over the years. But when the shit really hits the fan, you realise that your brother is your strongest ally. I always knew that and I think Pete has come to realise it, too. Come what may, I would stand up for him.

And I had to do that again sooner than either of us would have wanted. It was 2006 and we were about to release the new album and set off on the new tour. The idea of doing promotion was tricky at the best of times, but after the last few years Pete could hardly be blamed for wanting to avoid the journalists altogether. We agreed to do one interview on Howard Stern's radio show. We agreed because he promised not to bring up Pete's arrest. He gave us his word.

Of course, Howard hadn't even finished introducing us before he brought it up. Pete stormed out. I ran after him and said, 'Come on, Pete, you have to come back. You have to stand up for yourself. The Old Bill says you're innocent. Say that.' But he couldn't do it. He was in bits. He was all over the place. So I went back in there and I laid into Howard. I gave him an earful. I'm really glad I fought for Pete. And in 2012, Howard publicly apologised to me and Pete for being such a dickhead.

Thank you, Howard. Apology accepted – we can all be dickheads. It's just that some of us can be dickheads more often than others.

TWENTY

I HOPED
I'D DIE

We kicked off the *Endless Wire* tour on the Leeds Refectory stage in June 2006. The university had decided to put up a blue plaque commemorating our 1970 *Live at Leeds* gig – the one where I oversang – and Andy Kershaw, a former Leeds Uni social secretary, had asked Bill if we'd pop up and unveil it. And, while we were there, do a gig. You can laugh about the plaque – we've been around so long, we are now a historical monument – but I felt quite proud. It's good to have a legacy and it's good to think we made our mark. The gig itself was too loud and, because they were filming it, too bright, but you can't have everything, right?

We set off happily on another elongated tour across Britain, Ireland, Germany, Switzerland, Monaco, France, Switzerland again for some reason, Austria, Spain, Canada, 30 US cities, back around Europe, back across the States again and then, at the end of 2007, a one-off gig at Ellis Park, Johannesburg. From start to finish, it was a 13-month journey (with a few weeks off here and there) and, apart from the one disastrous night in Tampa, Florida, which I mentioned way back in Chapter One, it all went without a hitch.

Looking back on it now, it's telling that we ended each night on that tour with 'Tea & Theatre', a simple little song from the *Endless Wire* album. For me, it summed up exactly how we felt. Where the two of us were in ourselves and where we were with our audience.

A thousand songs
Still smoulder now,
We play them as one,
We're older now,
All of us sad,
All of us free,
Before we walk from this stage…

That was it, exactly. It's reflective, almost melancholy. We had been through a traumatic few years, but our music was still there … smouldering. We were beginning to rebuild. These days, we're in a better place. We go out on 'Pinball Wizard', 'See Me, Feel Me', 'Baba O'Riley' and 'Won't Get Fooled Again'. We finish with a bang. But, back then, it just felt right to close the show on a more intimate note.

And despite the minimal promotion, we broke even. Yes, this was a tour on which we didn't lose money. It was also the first time we streamed the gigs on the internet. How cutting edge of us, even though, with hindsight, that was probably the beginning of the end for a financially viable music industry. The internet could have been a chance to make music, particularly new music, more accessible, but with it came the music-sharing sites, the biggest thieves in history. All the internet has done for most musicians is rob them of their income. I don't mind if you give away all of our music for free, as long as my bills are paid. But it doesn't work like that. It might one day, but not yet. The way it is today, it's very hard for anyone starting out in the business. We thought we had a hard time back in the sixties but at least we got paid … sometimes.

Anyway, the tour was great. So great, we came back for more the next year and toured across America again. In 2007, we had got that blue plaque in Leeds. In 2008, we got the Kennedy Center Honor, traditionally awarded for 'a lifetime of contributions to American culture through the performing arts'. We were the first rock band to make the grade and we were British. But that was okay. It felt like the completion of a circle. We'd grown up in post-war austerity. Our inspiration had come from American bands, from rhythm and blues. Our rebellion came from black America's rebellion. Now, we were in the White House, hanging out with the establishment. We were dignitaries. VIPs. Us. To be recognised in America was special. We could have stopped there and been pretty pleased with ourselves, but we just kept playing.

• • •

I do get asked, quite often, what a particular gig was like. What was it like at Woodstock? Wembley? The Railway Hotel in 1965?

And, as I've said earlier, I usually find it quite hard to answer. If the crowd stretches to the back of the pub wall or all the way over the horizon, it really doesn't make much difference to me. I don't treat things differently even if the view is different. But the half-time spot at the Super Bowl in February 2010 does stick in the memory. You have a couple of minutes to create a stage on the midfield. You then have 12 minutes to blow the bloody doors off. You then have another minute or two to get the hell off. It's completely crazy. Any other gig, the crew have a day or two to set up, to sound-check, to make sure everything's plugged in the right place. At the Super Bowl, if one lead is in the wrong socket, you're screwed in front of 74,000 football fans in the stadium and another 100 million on their sofas. (They record a safety track just in case – to this day, I don't know if you got the live version or the safety because I've never listened to it.)

So, of course, it's rehearsed to within an inch of its life. When they invited us, I quite liked the idea of Miami in February. Nice to get a bit of sun. Of course, it was the coldest winter they'd had in years. All week, it was bloody cold and raining. We rehearsed and rehearsed and rehearsed in a giant hangar with the hundreds of volunteer crew until they had got the assembly of the jigsaw circular stage down to a fine art.

The day itself began glamorously enough with a police escort to the Sun Life Stadium. And then we were dumped in a dressing room smelling of New Orleans Saints' jockstraps to wait out the first half.

Five minutes before you're due on, you're waiting in the tunnel. The players rush off, the volunteers rush on and this is the moment when I try to slow everything down. John McVicar told me that before he went in to rob a bank, he'd be sitting in the car telling himself, over and over, get a grip, get a grip. Because otherwise you'd lose your bottle. I wasn't going to rob a bank but walking out onto the Super Bowl stage also gets the pulse racing. I wasn't nervous. It's just a process. You slow it all down. People don't realise – or I hope they don't realise – just how much communication goes on, particularly at the start of a set. Between you and the other members of the band and with the sound guy, the in-ear monitor guy – it's an intense time. Even in a normal show, there are 60 people working to bring that night off. If you've slowed yourself down, it helps to make all the minute adjustments to get it right.

At no point did I think, 'Shit, there are millions of people watching this.' There is no time for reflection. I sang the whole thing and then I was off, the stage was dismantled and the Saints won the game.

• • •

The *Quadrophenia* tour in 2012/13 almost didn't happen. Which would have meant our 50th anniversary tour wouldn't have happened. Which would have meant it was all over before we really got back to the joy of being in a band that's firing on all cylinders. The last five years have been a complete pleasure. The band has been great. Home life has been great. I've had time to spend with my grandchildren – more time, perhaps, than I got to spend with my own daughters. But it could have been different.

In 2011, I sang *Tommy* at the Albert Hall with my band. As I've said, each year, I have to organise six or seven gigs in one spring week for Teenage Cancer Trust. Each year, it's quite a challenge. Who is around? Who is on tour? Who can find a gap in their schedule to play at the Albert Hall? That year, after a lot of hustling, I was still one short so I decided to fill it myself. To my genuine surprise, it was a sell-out. I'm not being coy here. It wasn't The Who. It was me and my band. No Pete. No Zak. But people still came and we had a fantastic night.

Off the back of that, my little band went on tour and, for the first time in a long time, everything ran like clockwork. People turned up on time. People did what they said they were going to do. Lovely.

This was not how things were with The Who. Although we were enjoying the music again, the grind of touring was hard because people were effing about. If one person's late for a hotel transfer, then you're all waiting. And if that happens at every point of the day, you spend your whole bloody time waiting. And it's not that I'm an impatient man, but I hate lateness. I hate wasting time. If we arrange to meet at a certain time and you're half an hour late, then that's half an hour of my life I'm never going to get back. If you have a proper excuse – you got stuck in the lift, you fell down a mine shaft – then fine. But if you just couldn't be arsed to get out of bed, then not fine. I enjoy my life. I don't have a lot of it to spare. On tour, there's enough schlepping already without the extra hassle of standing around in hotel lobbies or departure lounges because one guy couldn't get his act together.

So when Pete said we were going to do *Quadrophenia* the way we'd always done it with a band that couldn't get out of bed on time, I just said no. We'd met to discuss it with Robert and Bill. Pete was adamant, I was adamant, and that was it. Another tour that wouldn't happen because neither of us would budge.

I remember going off from that meeting feeling quite happy. I honestly thought that would be it because it was different from all the other times we'd stopped. I was enjoying my solo projects. I didn't need to carry on. Why put myself through months and months of grief? And we'd done *Quadrophenia* in 1996 and I felt it wasn't as good as it could have been. Why just repeat that?

The very first time Pete started explaining all the many complex layers of *Quadrophenia* in 1972, I clung on to one fundamental idea. There were four guys in the band who represented four facets of the character. *Quadrophenia*. Simple. When a band is firing on all cylinders, that is how it feels. You're jamming, you don't know where it's going next but when you go, you go, instinctively, together, like a flock of starlings.

The 1996 version was not like that at all. There were no starlings. There was just a car that kept slipping back to first gear every time it tried to move into fifth. There was a lot of extra stuff that obscured the simple concept that had stuck in my brain all those years ago.

'If you trust me, I know we can do it in a different way.' That's what I said to Pete but he said no. We'll do it with the same personnel and the same format as before. And he walked out.

Three hours later, Bill called with surprising news. Pete says he'll do it your way. I had a free hand. Incredible.

Over the next few months, I worked with Rob Lee, a brilliant friend who did our website. He had brought in Colin Payne to edit the Tommy stage videos with a bunch of students from Middlesex University. On Quadrophenia, they stuck with my simple vision and the whole show developed around the four of us singing on film to our older selves onstage. Colin and Rob helped me get to the heart of what it had always been about. We ended up with a show that felt modern and relevant. That's always been Pete's skill: to write music that never ages. But sometimes he needs help telling the story in a way that everyone else can understand.

We opened in Sunrise, Miami, on 1 November 2012 and the show went down an absolute storm. Before, in the instrumental, we'd just had footage of waves hitting rocks. Now, we had all this archive footage spanning the last 50 years of social and cultural upheaval, cut in with us performing over the decades. I thought it was a pretty mind-blowing sequence. The audience did, too. They stood up in that section and went crazy. And, most importantly, Pete got it. He got that we'd found our way back to that very first idea. Over nine months, we played to more than half a million people across the US and Europe. The classicist Mary Beard came to the last show on that tour at Wembley in July 2013 and found me afterwards to talk about that montage. She said we'd encapsulated the late 20th-century period perfectly. An A+ from a proper academic. That really made me happy.

. . .

In 2015, I celebrated The Who's 50th anniversary by contracting viral meningitis. Thirty dates on the North American leg of

The Who Hits 50! tour were postponed. Instead of walking out onstage, I was lying in a hospital bed absolutely convinced I was going to die. I was phoning people to say goodbye.

This was the end and that was a shame because, after all the struggles, we had finally hit a golden period. We were enjoying ourselves and each other.

Looking back, it's possible that things started to go wrong long before that dreadful summer. In December 2014, I did a gig in Cardiff when I should have cancelled. I had a bad cold but the crowd was already in the hall so I went on and wrecked my voice. I had to put so much strain on it to get through, it did something to the nerves in my neck. We moved the next two concerts at the O2 in London to March and the doctors said I couldn't sing for two months. By February, I was starting to sing again but I couldn't get higher than a Johnny Cash top note. Sports Phil, a man who used to massage Kobe beef, was doing what he could to loosen things up but, as the concerts approached, it still wasn't right. Phil is the strongest masseur on the planet. He has fists and fingers of steel. That's what it takes to get my old gnarly wreck of a body onstage these days. But even he was struggling.

So he recommended Jan-Jan, a doctor in Holland, who I immediately decided to fly over to London for the first O2 show. You'll do anything to get things right. Jan-Jan arrived in my dressing room three hours before the show. Like most Dutch people, he was more than six feet tall, he looked fit and healthy and he had a confident smile. Unlike most Dutch people, he never went anywhere without a bag full of hammers and chisels.

'Where's the problem?' he asked, and I pointed at my neck.

He told me to take off my shirt and sit facing away from him on his portable table with my back to him. For the next few minutes, he did what felt like an engineer's drawing on my back with a marker pen. So far, so relaxing.

Then he said, 'Are you ready?' And off he went. It sounded like a blacksmith was running late on the day's orders. Chink, chink, crunch. Chink, chink, crunch. I could feel and hear the bones moving. I've been hammered before but never like this. Jan-Jan knew what he was doing, though. He got me through those shows and, by the summer, I was starting to sing well again.

• • •

On 30 June 2015, we played at the Zenith in Paris. We'd just headlined Hyde Park and Glastonbury and, for the first time that year, I felt like I was back. That night in Paris felt fabulous but it was hotter than a witch's tit. It must have been 40 degrees outside but inside the Zenith there were 6,000 people. That's 6,000 one-bar electric heaters. The gig was great, really fluid, but when I came offstage I was completely drained.

I remember Liam Gallagher came backstage to say hello afterwards. I love Liam. He's one of the last few bastions of old-school rock. He'd be the last one in the trenches with you, always, and he'd carry you out. That night, in that boiling heat, he was still wearing his parka. Ridiculous – but it was great to see him.

It was the small hours by the time I got back to the hotel and had a lovely bath. Because we get to stay in posh hotels these days, the bathrooms are always full-on marble affairs. When I stepped out of the bath, the floor was like an ice rink and I was over, out cold. There are times when I miss those crappy motels we used to stay in. Peeling, mouldy linoleum might not be as aesthetically pleasing as marble but it's a lot less slippery.

I couldn't speak for a few minutes and a doc was summoned. He said everything was okay, so I popped a couple of aspirins and went to bed thinking nothing more of it. A spot of concussion never killed anyone.

The next day, the whole band and crew took the train from Paris to Amsterdam. It was one of those wonderful high-speed European trains we always hear so much about but the air-con had packed up. So, another four hours in 40-degree heat. We all just sat there in our underpants, sweating our bollocks off as the northern French countryside flew by.

One gig and two days later I was home, about to head off to rehearse in Acton for a gig I was doing with my band at Chris Evans' CarFest. And I had to cancel. I'd come down with a sort of flu. I don't know if the bang on the head had anything to do with it – today, I suspect it might have triggered the whole thing – but over the next few days it got worse and worse. I was taken to hospital and tested for everything. Aids, TB, leukaemia. I had four lumbar punctures and two brain scans, each of which rendered me completely deaf for a couple of days, which was very unsettling.

Through all of this, I was going a bit nuts. I had blackouts, memory loss, hallucinations. I had a hard time working out where I was and what was going on. At one point, I just got up and left the hospital to attend a dental appointment. After that, they stationed a nurse by the door, but I still managed to escape. I couldn't tell you why I was trying to get out. It makes no sense looking back at it now. But I turned up at Holmshurst one morning and point-blank refused to return to London.

After three days hiding out, Heather put her foot down. I wasn't getting better, I wasn't making much sense and I was in a lot of pain. So back I went for more prodding and poking. At the height of it, before they worked out what it was and got me on the right drugs, the agony was unbearable. I was in tears. Nothing could hurt this much.

And then, at the point where I could hardly bear it, the pain just went away. It was sudden and stunning, like sunshine after a storm in New Orleans or White Lake, New York. I reached a point of absolute peace and tranquillity, a floating sensation that felt incredible, not just because the pain was gone but also because there was contentment.

For some reason, I was turned around, looking at my life as though I were someone else. First, my time in the Boys' Brigade. Then the skiffle band which provided solace from the horrors of school. Our debut as the Detours in Shepherd's Bush. Reggie on bass. Harry on drums. Me on guitar. Then The Who. I thought about Woodstock and that moment when I knew we'd finally cracked America. The feeling of hard-won success, traced all the way to getting a CBE in 2005. How much that meant to me, not because it changed anything but because it was the final recognition that my headmaster was wrong when he told me I'd never do anything with my life.

We're all unique. We all have our own unique lives. But seeing my life like that, I just felt overwhelmingly lucky. In the middle of this strange out-of-body experience, I said to myself, 'Would you ever imagine the things you've done?' And then all I could think about was my family. I wouldn't leave any of them in trouble. There was no debt. Heather would be okay. The kids were all set. I could see that I'd done enough. I lay there feeling at peace. It wasn't a religious experience. There was no light at the end of a tunnel. No voice from on high. Maybe I'm going downstairs. But the sense of calm was wonderful. It was spiritual. It's my belief that when you die, it's not the end. It's just the transferring of energy from this body to somewhere or something else in the universe. Today, as I write this, I have no fear of death. If and when I start going, I don't want to be resuscitated. When my time comes, that's it, and I'm fine with that.

Of course, my time hadn't come that summer. Here I am, three years later, and we're still going. We did all those dates we had to postpone. We did more dates the following year. And more this year. It felt great. I have a little joke I tell interviewers. The Who was exciting in the old days because you didn't know what would happen. Now, we're exciting because you don't know if we'll get to the end of the show. It's a joke that comes with an element of truth but the last couple of years have been good. I've felt good. Maybe it's because I'm not trying so hard. Maybe it's because, finally, I'm beginning to relax.

I still have to be careful. It took a long time for the pain to go away and the meningitis can come back. I have to avoid doing too much. But I love what I do and I can still do it. I'm on our last tour. I just don't know how long the last tour will be. When we launched it back in 2015, I said it was the beginning of the long goodbye. I guess now we're somewhere in the middle. It will go on for as long as we can do it. I am resigned to the fact that one day, possibly quite soon, I'll open my mouth and it won't be there. And that will be the day I say, 'Sorry, guys, this is over.'

What I hate about touring is the movement. A lifetime of planes, trains, automobiles and hotels and you become allergic to movement. We now tour in the very height of luxury. Posh hotels, private jets, gold taps and marble, bloody marble. It's a million miles from how we did it when we started. Between Gordon, my wonderful wheeler-dealer assistant, and Rex, our ruthless tour manager, we've fine-tuned life on the road to make it as smooth as possible. It's like a military operation. There is no hotel check-in. We just go straight to the room. There is no check-in at the airport either. And you should see the speed with which we go through security and passport control. It's all organised to the last detail to avoid losing time, compared with five decades of flight delays, traffic jams and overbooked hotels. Not to mention however many weeks or months or years of dressing-room incarceration because the gig's running late. Not to mention Keith Moon's own special way of unravelling our plans. Yes, I think I've done my share.

What I love about touring is the bits between all the movement. Onstage, performing Pete's music the way it's supposed to be performed. And that's what we're doing now and that's why we're happy now. The band is having fun, we can laugh at ourselves. We still have plans. We still have things to do.

You don't retire from this business. This business retires you. You can play notes and you can sing notes but what you can't do is cheat on the intention of the music. And I think that's why we're still successful. We still don't cheat. The chemistry between me and Pete is still special. We were given that gift and now The Who is the two of us. He tells me I'm a 'fucking romantic' but I know what I see with my own eyes. Empathy, that's the root of it all. If I can empathise with where he was when he was writing it, I'm at the root of the song. And most of those songs were written from a place of pain, as well as spirit. I struggled at first to find that place and you can hear the struggle. But then I inhabited it. I didn't have to become Pete. I just had to find my own vulnerability. I had to tear down all my own defences, the defences I'd put up to survive. And I'm lucky. Everything happened in a way to make that possible. The raw nerves. The fights. The constant criticism. The personal battles. The relationship with Heather that survived it all. My God, I'm glad she stuck with me and we've reached the value-added part of our relationship. People split up too easily these days. You've got to work at it because it only gets better.

All those elements, that exact, strange combination, made me what I needed to be. It could have gone a million other ways but it went the way it did. I could have been telling a completely different story or no story at all. When I sing the songs, it's a balance of vulnerability and strength. When I'm onstage, the walls are down and I sing to you.

In the end when you come to think of it, when we're all gone and dust, the music will live on. And I hope people will say about us that we held it to the end. And that will do for me. I've been lucky. I've had a lucky life. Thank you very much, Mr Kibblewhite. And I really mean it.

ACKNOWLEDGEMENTS

My thanks and acknowledgments go to the people who have helped me with the writing of this book.

To my wife Heather who has been the not so silent partner. She has advised, encouraged and given perspective to me throughout my life.

To Bill Curbishley, Robert Rosenberg and Jools Broom at Trinifold Management and to Calixte Stamp and Keith Altham for their help and support.

To Jane Howard, Nigel Hinton, Matt Kent and Jack Lyons for checking all the drafts.

To Richard Evans for checking the drafts and for invaluable help on the artwork and design.

To Chris Rule for photo layout.

And, of course, a huge thank you to Matt Rudd.

To Jonny Geller at Curtis Brown and the teams at Blink Publishing and Henry Holt & Co.

And, it goes without saying, thanks to Pete, John and Keith... without whom this would have been a much shorter story.

INDEX

(the initials HD represent Heather Daltrey; JD = Jacqueline Daltrey;
RD = Roger Daltrey; JE = John Entwistle; KJ = Kenney Jones;
KL = Kit Lambert; KM = Keith Moon; PT = Pete Townshend)

and KL's mannerisms 100
marriage of 131, 155
and McLagan 173
nervousness of 166, 220
RD seizes stash of 103–4
and riding classes 257
and smashed instruments, *see* Who:
 and smashed instruments
stage collapses of 220–1, 255
stage position of, as drummer 91
and Super Glue, piranhas and snake
 149–50
surfing by 130–1
syncopations of 74
and Tara House 172
tooth injury to 129
US arrest of 129
working-class nature of 48
Moon (née Kerrigan), Kim 131, 155,
 172–4
 KM left by 173, 253, 256
Moon, Mandy 172, 173–4
Murray 122
'Music Must Change' 265
My Fair Lady 316–17
'My Generation' 116, 131, 144, 270,
 302
 recording of 111–13
 release of 113

'Naked Eye' 221
Nevison, Ron 214
New Action 98
New Orleans Jazz Festival 168
New York Times 185
Newman, Thunderclap 203
NME 249, 251
Nobby the Fibreglass Kid 134, 315

O'Connor, Sinead 294
Oldham, Andrew Loog 76
Oldham, Ted 205

Page, Jimmy 94, 95, 153
Palladino, Pino 188–9, 312
Parker, Charlie 96
Parmenter, Chris 97
Payne, Colin 330
Pete Townshend's *Quadrophenia* (*see also*
 Quadrophenia):
 on stage in UK 297–9
 on stage in US 299–300

Phillips, Simon (*see also* Who), Who
 joined by 285
'Pictures of Lily' 116–17
'Pinball Wizard' 161, 167, 168, 302, 324
Pixelon 301–2
Plant, Robert 244
Polygram 203
Presley, Elvis 22, 29, 45, 62
Pridden, Bobby 57, 147–8, 217–19,
 303
 and smoke bombs 39
Prince's Trust 297
Pyle, Joey 280–1, 283

Quadrophenia 186, 207, 212–13,
 230, 327, 329, 330 (*see also* Pete
 Townshend's *Quadrophenia*)
 original mixes on 214
 rehearsals for 215–16
 US–Canada tour of 219–25
Quads 115
Quatro, Patti 129

'Rael' 143–4
Under a Raging Moon 297
'Raglan Road' 289
Railway Tavern 78, 89, 251
Ramport Studios 213, 214
Redding, Noel 125
Redgrave, Lynn 317
Reed, Jimmy 70
Reed, Lou 294
Reed, Oliver 234, 236–7
Reeves, Dave 215
Reid, Terry 146
Richard, Cliff 54
Rickman, Jacqueline (Jackie), *see*
 Daltrey, Jacqueline
Ride a Rock Horse 243
Riverfront Coliseum, deaths at 268–70
Rocks in the Head 293
Rodgers, Paul 5
Rolling Stone 156
Rolling Stones 46, 70, 76, 77, 242, 244
Rosenberg, Robert 286
Rude Awakening 317
Russell, Ken 5, 230, 232–6 *passim*, 237,
 238–9, 240

Sandom, Doug:
 band joined by 56, 271
 band left by 73

ILLUSTRATION
ACKNOWLEDGEMENTS

All images in this book are courtesy of the author's private collection with the exception of the following:

My first mic swing at the Golf-Drouot Club. © HBK-Rancurel Photothèque. Photo by Jean-Louis Rancurel.
At the Goldhawk Social Club. © Wedgbury Archive. Photo by David Wedgbury.
The famous van that got stolen. © Roger Kasparian.
With former girlfriend Anna at Ivor Court. © Colin Jones/Topham/Topfoto.
With Emmaretta Marks. © Granger/REX/Shutterstock.
At the Rolling Stones Rock and Roll Circus, 1968. © Alec Byrne/Uber Archives/ Eyevine.
Live in Copenhagen, 1970. Photo by Jan Persson/Redferns/Getty Images.
Isle of Wight, 1970 (black and white). © David Goodale.
With Pete and Kit at IBC Recording Studios. © Chris Morphet/Redferns/Getty Images.
Arriving by jet in Finland, 1966. © Motocinema, Inc.
At the "My Generation" shoot. © Wedgbury Archive. Photo by David Wedgbury.
Chris's Viking boat. © Calixte Stamp.
Outside the Goldhawk Club, 1977. © Robert Ellis.
With Bill Curbishley, 1975. © Terry O'Neill/Trinifold Archive.
In the chamois shirt. © Waring Abbott/Getty Images.
With Heather outside Elder Cottage, 1969. Photo courtesy of Barrie Wentzell.
Heather "likes me," 1989. Photo by Tony Monte.
Flying low while filming Tommy. © Alamy Stock Photo.
With Ken on the set of Tommy. © Mondadori Portfolio via Getty Images.
Tommy. © Rbt Stigwood Prods/Hemdale/Kobal/REX/Shutterstock.
Me playing Franz Liszt in Lisztomania. © Michel Ochs Archives / Getty Images.
Me and Keith with Peter Sellers in the stage version of Tommy. © Michael Putland/ Getty Images.
The Comedy of Errors. Photo courtesy of the BBC.
McVicar. © Everett Collection Inc./Alamy Stock Photo.
With Arsene Wenger. © The Arsenal Football Club plc.
With Bruce Springsteen. © Michael Putland.
Boys' night out, 1985. © Alan Davidson/REX/Shutterstock.
Quadrophenia *rehearsal.* © Ethan Russell.
With Keith Richards and Mick Jagger. © KMazur/WireImage/Getty Images.
Kennedy Center Honors. Photo courtesy of the Office of George W. Bush.
At the Royal Albert Hall for TCT, 2005. © Camera Press/Rota.
Neil Young Bridge School Benefit, 1999. © John "Nunu" Zomot.
Daltrey, Ride a Rock Horse, *and* Under a Raging Moon *album covers.* Photography and cover designs by Graham Hughes.
Madison Square Garden, 1974. Waring Abbott/Getty Images.
Recording with Pete. © Colin Jones/Topfoto.
Quadrophenia *in Hyde Park.* © Stefan Rousseau/PA Archive/PA Images.
Two old geezers, 2005. Photo by Rob Monk.
Closing out the 2012 Olympics. © Jeff J. Mitchell/Getty Images.